WIND
OF THE
SPIRIT

G. de PURUCKER

 THEOSOPHICAL UNIVERSITY PRESS

WIND
OF THE
SPIRIT

Second and Revised Edition
with Glossary and Index

PASADENA, CALIFORNIA

THEOSOPHICAL UNIVERSITY PRESS
POST OFFICE BIN C
PASADENA, CALIFORNIA 91109
1984

First Edition published in 1944
Second and Revised Edition copyright © 1984
by Theosophical University Press

The paper in this book meets the standards for permanence
and durability of the Council on Library Resources.

Library of Congress Catalog Card Number 84-50118
Hardcover ISBN 0-911500-67-7
Softcover ISBN 0-911500-68-5

Manufactured in the United States of America

Contents

vi   *Wind of the Spirit*

Foreword

"THE WIND OF THE SPIRIT that is blowing over the world, tumultuous, cold and biting as it seems to our sensitive lives, is nevertheless the *wind of the spirit*" — this is the theme of an address given by Gottfried de Purucker in 1940 and used as the title and opening chapter of the present book. He urges us to penetrate appearances and discern the eternal beyond the temporal, for behind and within the current turmoil there is "power, spiritual power."

In the near-half century since these words were spoken the winds of destiny have been blowing hard, at times with gale force. Certainly not a nation or race, not a single human being, not Mother Earth herself with her families of lives, has been untouched by karmic change. Yet out of the pain and disruption a new worldview and a new and grander vision of humanity's role in the cosmic drama are coming into focus. Despite the prevailing self-seeking in subtle and gross forms, the practice of altruism is on the rise as the counter-impulse toward spirit gains momentum.

During his leadership of the Theosophical Society (1929–1942) Dr. de Purucker lectured constantly on the manifold aspects of theosophy, both in Europe and in the United States, and these addresses form the basis of his larger works. *Wind of the Spirit* is different. In this seemingly random collection of remarks made spontaneously at public and private gatherings and drawn from letters and notes to students, we rediscover how immensely practical theosophy is. Of course there is teaching aplenty — it could scarcely be otherwise, so profound was his knowledge of the world's spiritual and literary heritage; but it is de Purucker's lucid and direct response to human need that constitutes the book's appeal: always compassionate of human frailty yet ever challenging the nobility within each of us to shine forth. Understandably, when *Wind of the Spirit* first came out in 1944, within two years of the author's death, it was an instant favorite.

In the present edition the eight formal lectures included in the first edition are omitted as the subject matter is amply treated elsewhere by the author. Outside of this, only minor editing of the text has been done so as to preserve the vitality of the spoken word; and, as an aid to the reader, an index and glossary of philosophical terms, prepared by Ingrid Van Mater, have been added.

Wind of the Spirit concludes with the talk given by Dr. de Purucker a week before he died: "Aham Asmi Parabrahma" — I am Parabrahma, the Boundless. This was the alpha and omega of his teaching mission: to remind us again and again that at the core of every human being, indeed of every atom in the cosmos, is a living divinity. "Think if every man and woman on earth were thoroughly convinced of the utter reality of this cosmic truth! Never again would the hand of man be raised against man. Always it would be the extended hands of succor and brotherhood. For I am my brother — in our inmost *we are one*."

GRACE F. KNOCHE

June 21, 1984
Pasadena, California

WIND
OF THE
SPIRIT

Wind of the Spirit

THERE IS ONE THING I learned when I was a boy, and I learned it well, and it has been one of my best friends ever since. It is that I can learn from everything, and that if I allow a single day to pass without increasing my store of wisdom, without enlarging and enriching my inner life, by however small an increment, that day is a lost day in my life. Too many of us are asleep; we sleep and dream. We dream dreams, and all too often these dreams are evil dreams, for they are the upsurgings of the lower, personal, easily self-satisfied ego of ours. But others of us dream visions of incomparable beauty — and I mean not merely physical beauty, but beauty of any kind: spiritual beauty, intellectual beauty, ay, even beauty of wondrous nature around us. And every such new envisioning of a marvel awakens us by just so much. Oh, how we sleep, and are forgetful of what we are and of the richness around us which is ours for the taking, ours if we *will* take it! For there is naught that stands in the way of taking except oneself. There are none so blind as they who refuse to see; none so deaf as they who refuse to hear; and, on the other hand, none so wise as they who meet every new experience in life's wondrous adventure with the feeling: there is an angel behind this for me. I must discover him; learn what that angelic messenger is trying to tell me. Every experience is such.

I think one of the grandest things that theosophy does for us is to unveil our eyes, unstop our ears, so that seeing, we see somewhat more, and hearing we hear somewhat more; until finally we begin to hear what the silence tells us — the voice of the silence, which is the greatest and the richest and the most wisdom-pregnant voice to us. Theosophy were but a farce, were but as tinsel if it did not awaken us out of ourselves and make us more than we were. That is its one purpose; and that is the whole purpose of our study of it: to become ever more enlightened, a little bigger, a little more receptive.

Just here we see the difference between the beast and the man. The beast sees and knows not, recognizes not; the man sees and understands somewhat; and the master sees and hears, and the message enters in in its fullness; and the god, the producer of that which we see and hear — all the gods have to receive their light from still sublimer worlds, planes, spheres of universal life.

So now facing what is taking place in the world today we must recognize it as no chance event, no haphazard or fortuitous occurrence, not the blind blows of fate, but the working out of the events which are coming. We must recognize that behind these events there is power, spiritual power, spiritual force. It will all work out to an already predestined and sublime ending. For despite the agony and the sadness that we in our blindness feel, there is the wind of the spirit sweeping over the earth, rearranging, remaking, reshaping. And the agonies and sorrows that come, come from ourselves, blind humans that we are who will not enter into nature's majestic processes, helping her, but instead oppose her, and in opposing her suffer.

One may say: "Alas, we know not how to act in consonance with nature's laws!" But the statement is not true. It is a lie, for men have been taught since immemorial time that right is right, just is just, wrong is wrong. How then may we choose between the right and the wrong? Just here enters in a difficulty; not that it exists in itself, but we create it. It is not right to employ violence and force — there is the first law: "Thou shalt not kill." Violate this law, and you set yourself in opposition to nature's processes. Even in ordinary affairs man's genius recognizes this, and it is imbodied in our systems of jurisprudence today, an advance truly; for no longer is it considered

logical for the avenger, the one wronged, to seek out his enemy
and engage in mortal combat. We are advancing, for the time
was when to refuse to recognize what was then called one's
honor would have subjected a man to shameful ostracism. Our
ideas have enlarged. Is there a man or woman in the world
today who would dare to tell me that the only way to settle
disputes is by violence, when, mayhap, victory will perch upon
the banners of the one who is less right than the other?

The way to settle disputes is by reason, by refusing to accept
anything less grand than that. For he who takes up the sword,
as the avatāra Jesus put it, by the sword will he perish. Perhaps
not immediately, but in the long run. Disputes are righteously
and in justice composed on the basis of reason and right, not
on the basis of the heavy hand of violence.

We ask why we suffer. We ask why these things have fallen
upon us. In our ignorance of our own higher selves, and in our
lack of a perfect confidence in the eternal laws of cosmic life,
we assume, we take to ourselves, the duties of the avenger.
What man knows enough to judge any other man unto the
scaffold? So well are these principles recognized that there is
not a civilized society today that recommends them. They all
want justice; they all want to use reason. Why don't they use
it? And using it, why don't they abide by it? Face facts if you
want to know the reason of the suffering and agony, the terror
and appalling privations that are upon us. It is no extracosmic
God, or intracosmic God, who has put these horrible things
upon us, his blind children. *It is we ourselves.*

I am not preaching a doctrine of illogical pacifism, in the
sense of submitting to anything without struggle; for society
must protect itself. But let it protect itself by means which
laws, national and international, have already established, and
to which the greatest and supposedly most civilized nations on
earth have years ago pledged their honor and their allegiance.
But when the test comes: "Oh, no; this is a matter of national

honor. We will attend to this ourselves!" Then when the heavy blows fall, when happiness and honor have fled, when want and misery stalk through our streets, we cry unto high heaven and say: "What have I done that these things should fall upon me?" Were there no means of securing, of establishing right, it would be a different matter. But there are the means, recognized and accepted means, to which the so-called statesmen of our world have pledged their allegiance in solemn compact.

The wind of the spirit that is blowing over the world, tumultuous, cold and biting as it seems to our sensitive lives, is nevertheless the *wind of the spirit*, and it will blow away the fogs and illusions; and men once more at last can see peace, heavenly peace, and prosperity, and self-respect.

It is well to remember that while our hearts may ache — and the man is inhuman whose heart today does not ache over what our brothers in humanity are everywhere enduring — behind the suffering there is learning; behind and beyond the present events there is a dawn. Let us as individuals, not merely as theosophists, do our part in helping to bring the new day, when violence will be seen for the folly that it is, and the reign of justice and reason and fellow feeling will be with us and around us. If not, we shall have a recurrence, and worse, of what now we are passing through, and after that another recurrence still worse than the former, and so on to the remains of our civilization, until our civilized society will vanish in flame and blood.

Those of you who may be alive to see the handwriting on the wall had better awaken.

MENE MENE TEKEL UPHARSIN!
Weighed, Weighed, Wanting — the Persians!

The tragedy of society is that it has lost its trust in an abiding spiritual power in this world of ours, and reason has lost its seat. This entire universe of ours is but an appearance, an outer shell, a physical body, manifesting the tremendous forces at work on the other side of the veil of nature; and no man, no demigod, or god, can offend or oppose these powers with impunity. Law rules this world and sooner or later the gods will descend from their azure seats. Let us see that they come to us as envoys of happiness and peace, rather than with the flaming swords avenging overthrown innocence.

You will tell me: "You are preaching after the event." But this is not true, for worse will come unless we heed. These things have been told to mankind from immemorial time. The man who said, "God and I are a majority against the whole world" was no flamboyant egoist — if we understand his meaning.

I have felt impelled to speak of the wind of the spirit blowing over the earth. It will extinguish all false lights; the true and the holy will but burn the brighter and will remain. Yet judge not. Things do not happen in a day. Perhaps it may be fifty years before we know at least something of the inner meaning of what is now coming upon us: of good, of ill; of high, of low; of pathos or of bathos. But this that I have called the wind of the spirit is clairvoyant in the heavenly sense. It is the spirit of Earth, if you wish, and its works are utter true. All that is grand and unselfish will live. What is false and selfish, this wind will not merely pass by, but mayhap overthrow. Put your whole trust in the divine power behind nature and live in accordance therewith, and nature will look upon you as working with her and therefore as her master and will make obeisance. Those of you who have ears to hear, hear!

The Heritage of Man Is Man Himself

THE HERITAGE OF MAN is man himself. Each man is the builder of himself, and the destroyer maybe. Each man is his own regenerator and savior, and each man undoes the work upon himself which mayhap for aeons in the past he had been building. This statement may sound recondite, difficult to understand, a dark saying; and yet I wonder that anyone could or might doubt so self-evident a truth. Is it not clear enough that what a man is, he is; and that what he is, is the result of his former lives, the resultant of his thoughts and his feelings, the resultant of his previous willings and thinking and feeling? We make ourselves, we fashion our own characters.

This is one of the commonplaces of human experience. But just think what it means to grasp it in fullness. We make our lives shapely from day to day and year to year and from life to life; or we make them very ugly; and no one is to blame on the one hand, and no one is to be praised on the other hand, except the man himself. Think how just this is. We have nobody, naught outside ourselves, to blame if we have made ourselves unshapely and ugly and full of sorrow and pain; and there is none to be praised when our lives become shapely and beautiful in symmetry through our own efforts, save we ourselves. A man by thinking may change his character, which means changing his soul, which means changing his destiny, which means changing everything that he is or becomes in the present and in the future. Why blame the blameless gods for our own faults, for molding us in the patterns that we ourselves have shaped? It is the old idea of passing the buck — slang, but how expressive! — throwing the blame on someone else. This is the surest way to go down instead of going up; for the recognition of truth and of justice and the cognizance of responsibility in a man, by a man of himself, are the first steps to climbing the path higher; and what hope there is in this. Think of the mistakes we have made in the past, the wrongs that we have wrought on others and on ourselves. Only half the story is told when we say that we have made ourselves and that we are responsible for ourselves. The other half of the story is what we have done upon others: how we have helped to shape their lives in beauty, or to misshape their lives in ugliness.

This recognition of man's responsibility not only to himself, but to others, is the lost keynote of modern civilization which seems to be infatuated with the idea that things will run themselves, and that all that men have to do is to get what they can from the surrounding atmosphere. I think that is a hellish doctrine, and can but produce its harvest of misery. Let a man realize that he is a man and that what he sows he shall reap, and that what he is reaping he himself has sown, and see how the face of the world will be changed. Each man will become enormously observant not only of his acts which are the proofs of his thoughts and his feelings, firstly upon himself, but perhaps more important, of the impact he makes upon others. I think it is the lack of this feeling of individual responsibility and also mass responsibility in the world today which is the cause of the many, many horrors which are growing worse instead of better. It fosters the belief that violence can right a wrong. It never can. Violence never has perished by adding violence unto it. No problem ever has been solved after that manner. It is against the laws of being, against the laws of things as they are.

What is a man's heritage? I say again, it is man himself. I am myself because I made me in other lives. And how ashamed I am of myself at times that I have not made me wiser and better and higher and nobler in every way; and how I bless the whispering intimations of divinity within my heart that I can say I am not worse than I am! You see, this is the first realization of my responsibility to all — and the all includes me. And here is a wonder-thought: when a man does right, no matter at what cost to himself, he strengthens himself and he strengthens all others. It is a work of wonderful magic. And when a man does evil, is it not obvious that he weakens himself? First there is the weakening of his will, then the soiling of his thoughts, and then the lessening of the strength of his genuine inner feelings. The very contact with such a man, provided he follow the downward path long enough, causes the self to be soiled. Even as one rotten apple, they say, will ruin a whole barrelful of sound fruit, so will an evil character adversely and evilly affect not only himself, but all unfortunates who may be near him.

We can save ourselves from this very easily, because there are few things so revealing as evil. It has naught to stand upon except illusion. Leave it alone and it will vanish like a mist. Do not strengthen it by pouring more evil into the illusion from your own energy. If it has naught to stand upon, no source of vital activity within itself, it falls, it goes to pieces. How different is good, which is health-giving and strengthening and cleansing. Such simple truths, and so profound! I suppose the most simple things are the most beautiful and the most profound.

So this doctrine of the heritage of a man which is himself is simply the doctrine of another chance for the man whose life has been spoiled by himself. No other man can spoil you unless you yourself cooperate in the spoiling. None other can make you evil unless you conjoin in the suggestion or in the doing. Blame not the other for your fall. It is yourself who fall, and you will never fall, you would never have fallen, unless you had preferred that which brought about the fall. Such simple truths, and yet they comprise a code of divine conduct for us men on this earth. A child may understand these things because they are so clear, they are so obvious.

The doctrine of another chance! Think of the man — any one of us — who has made a mess of his life and wonders why ill fortune and misfortune and unhappiness and misery and other terrible things come upon him, until sometimes in the agony of self-reproach he cries, "Lord, deliver me from this hell." It is the old weak appeal to something where no help lies, for help is within. The divinity lies in your breast, the source of all strength and grandeur; and the more you appeal to it the more you exercise it, the more you strengthen your own self, advance in truth and wisdom, rise above all the planes of weakness and sorrow and pain brought about by evildoing.

So you have made yourself; and in your next life you will be just what you are now making yourself to be. You will be your own heritage. You are now writing, as it were, your last will and testament for yourself. When a man realizes this wonderful fact, he no longer blames others, no longer sits in judgment upon his brothers. He no longer says: I am holier than thou — an attitude which is the sure mark of the weak and of the poor in spiritual life.

There is a wonderful French proverb which runs thus: *Tout comprendre c'est tout pardonner:* "To understand everything is to forgive all." To understand all the hid causes, the results, the past destiny, the present strength, the temptation, the virtue, whatever it may be — to understand all this is to have divine knowledge, and it means to forgive. It is a wonderful proverb and must have been uttered first, I venture to say, by some human being who had a touch of illumination. I know myself by my own experience that when I have been hurt, or am hurt and think I am unjustly treated, I say to myself, even when it seems to me that the wrongdoing unto myself is obvious: If I could read the heart of my brother who has wronged me, read back into the distant past and see what mayhap I did to him to wrong him, perhaps I would realize that he now is as unconscious of the wrong he does me as I was then of the wrong I did to him. I shall not increase the treasury of virtue and happiness and peace in this world by taking up the gauge of battle and injecting more fury and hatred into a hatred-ridden world. But I can do my part in strengthening myself, do my part in getting some illumination from above-within, from the god within me, by doing what I myself have taught: *practicing what I preach*. Peace and happiness come from this, and the sense of increased self-respect and the growth of pity.

Do you know, I sometimes think that pity or compassion is one of the most celestial visitors to the temple of the human heart. The old sages used to say that none but the gods really pay men exact justice, or what they think is justice and flatter themselves that they are right. The gods hear all, see all, feel all, understand all, and are filled with pity. Think, if any one of us human beings were weighed in the strictest scales of karmic justice untempered by pity and wisdom, what chance do you think any one of us would have to escape condemnation? Does any one of you think that you are so spotless in virtue and holy strength that the scales would not fall against you? If so, you are very, very happy — or very, very blind! I think that if such spotless purity of past karma were yours, you would not be here as a man on this earth working out your own heritage — yourself.

True it is that in the future all the human race are going to be gods, and there is no reason on earth why we should not begin in the present instant of time to grow towards godhood. You win all, you gain all; you lose naught. From driven slave of past karma you become the orderer in time of your own destiny, for you are your own heritage. What a doctrine of comfort! What light it bestows!

Where Are the Sages and Seers?

THE GREAT SAGES AND SEERS, the masters of wisdom and compassion, belong to no race, and especially to no creed. They are the children of the spirit, awakened men, whose familiar thought is truth itself; and hence their sympathies are universal. They need no frontiers of race, of caste, of creed, of color. They are truth-seekers, truth-teachers, and the Theosophical Society was founded by them to promulgate the truth, the cosmic wisdom, the cosmic philosophy, that existed before the foundations of the mighty mountains were laid, ay, even before the sons of morning began to sing, to chant their hymns celestial. For truth has no age. It never was born, it never has not been. It is timeless because universal. Its appeal is to the hearts and minds of all men. It matters not a whit from what part of the world a beautiful truth may be drawn; and hence whenever any human has so attuned the seven-stringed lyre of Apollo — which is his heart or his seven principles — to whisper and ring like an aeolian harp when the winds of heaven blow upon it, then, for the time being and as long as he can hold this plane of consciousness, he is one of the sages and seers, whether his fellowmen recognize him or not; and this means you and me and all men, at least any one of us who may have attained thus much.

And mark you the promise in this statement: that precisely because we are children of Infinitude, not merely sons of the gods but the very offspring of the celestial spaces, there is that within us which is attuned with them, and which therefore is timeless, which therefore is infinite, which therefore is eternal.

How true the old statement in the New Testament is, which you so often hear me quote because so lost sight of by Christians in these days! I link two such statements together: "Know ye not that ye are gods and that the spirit of the eternal liveth within you?"

Where are the sages and seers? Where they have always been. The question at first blush may strike one as being foolish, but I suppose it arises in the desire to explain to people why the masters do not take the human race in hand, and oblige it, force it, to be decent. But what good would that do? How may you convince men by compulsion that this, that, or some other thing is true? Isn't it obvious that men believe only what their own hearts teach them; and that no matter what they hear or are taught, if there is not an answering response in the human heart, and an instant answer in the human intellect, there is no acceptance, but a worse than steel wall raised?

Truth is eternal. Truth is always with us, and the devotees of truth are always with us and always have been and always will be; and it is we in our folly and ignorance and blindness who refuse to accept them. Open your hearts and open your minds, and the light will come pouring in. There is the promise of all the sages the human race has ever given birth to. The teachers are always ready when the pupil is ready. If we see no evidence of masters in the world today, it is partly because we are too stupid, partly because we have forgotten the god-wisdom in the world, and partly because we won't hearken.

Yes, the truth has been laid down by the titan intellects of the human race; and if men do not accept it, whose fault is it? Not that of the teachers. If I prefer strife and wretchedness and crime and horror, why shall I say to the deaf heavens: "Where art thou, O God?" Of all the agonies of stupidity, we see here just one more evidence of man's attempt at self-justification of his own folly and ignorance. You might as well say, where are the laws of nature? What has become of them? Why don't they take the human race in hand? A nice spirit! Even ordinary human parents know better than that. Ordinarily a father or mother would not attempt to interfere with the growth of a child by force. It never worked and never will. You cannot cause a leopard to change its spots, and no amount of starving or chastisement or vengeful so-called punishment will ever make a leopard anything but a leopard — until that leopard has evolved.

Do you want truth? You can have it whenever you want it. The world is full of it. The great teachings of the ages are full of it. What prevents our seeing it? Is there any man so blind as he who won't look? Is there any man so stupidly deaf as he who refuses to hear? These are some of the simple truths known to every child; yet we prefer hypocrisy and cant and self-justification to righting the wrongs we ourselves wreak on others, and then raise a clamor to the immortal gods for help when we ourselves begin to suffer from our folly. Yes, we choose hypocrisy; and how many of us can say before the tribunal divine within our own hearts: "I am not a hypocrite. I am pure. I thank God that I am not as other men!" Now honestly, hasn't that ever occurred to your hearts and minds? And don't you see that that is the first shackle you yourself have placed on your limbs as a pilgrim: self-justification and self-righteousness? Don't you see that by so doing you blind your own eyes?

How true it is that truth is not popular, that truth is not welcome, that people do not like it. Why? Because it means change. It means an evolution of feeling and thinking. It means a revolution of the moral instincts to become alive and vigorous again. To become acquainted with, to have firsthand individual knowledge of, the great teachers, the first step is to become as far as we may and can, alike unto them. There is no other way. The heart must be consecrated to truth at any cost. Are you strong enough? If you are, you are ready for chelaship, for discipleship; and you will be a disciple before this life is ended — perhaps before tomorrow sees the setting of our daystar.

The masters, the great sages and seers are ready for you always. There is no barrier to them whatsoever except yourself, absolutely none; and if you don't attain chelaship in this life or in the next or in the following one, blame none but yourself. How can you become a disciple or a chela before you are ready for it, before you have become it? How can you see the light before you have eyes with which to see it? How can you appreciate beauty or get a touch of beauty anywhere, until beauty already is taking birth within your soul, so that the beauty within you can sense beauty without? How can you recognize a great man until some grandeur at least is born within yourself to enable you to recognize grandeur? If you are paltry and small and mean, how can you recognize the opposites of these?

It is like the men who go through the world incognizant, blind and deaf to the divine beauty in their own fellow human beings. One of the easiest ways to find beauty, to find truth, and more quickly to come into instant magnetic sympathy with your fellow human beings is by becoming yourself sympathetic and seeing. If a man has no sympathy in his soul, how can he sense the sympathy in the souls of others? If he has no beauty in his heart, how can he see beauty anywhere, or as Shakespeare phrases it:

> The man that hath no music in himself,
> Nor is not mov'd with concord of sweet sounds,
> Is fit for treasons, stratagems, and spoils.

You will never see the master-self until you have become masterlike within yourself, because you won't recognize him. It would be impossible. You have not developed the vision inside, the faculties inside; but those faculties are there.

These sages and seers exist today; they take pupils, to use the ordinary phrase. Indeed more, they pass through the world searching, seeking, not so much like Diogenes for an honest man, but searching everywhere for good material, sensitive human souls, looking wherever they may see, however dim it may be, a touch of the buddhic splendor in a human heart; and when they see that, instantly their attention is attracted. They feel the impact instantly in their own hearts. They approach, they aid, they inspire; they do everything they can to foster the trembling flame of vision and of feeling. They foster it and feed it, until the flame finally burns strong, and the man is reborn, no longer born of the flesh, but reborn of the spirit, of the inspiration from within and from the teacher without.

Above and beyond and back of these sages and seers there is their own great Chief. What a marvelous figure of celestial wisdom and beauty, utterly dedicated to the spirit and to the world and all that is in it, irrespective of race, nation, creed, caste, color, or sex. This being is a god. Theosophists speak of it in reverence and awe as the Silent Watcher. He is the chief of the masters. He is one of us — brilliant guide, teacher, friend, brother, the source so far as men are concerned of all enlightenment and wisdom and beauty and love. In the deeper reaches of the theosophical teachings we may say with great reverence, yet with all truth, that back of all our labor however imperfectly we human beings may be doing, back of it as its origin and inspiration is this grand divinity.

What a hope! What a wonder to look forward to! I think that there are millions, hundreds of millions of men and women in this world today who are yearning, in reverence, in universal love, to advance upwards and onwards forever. Oh, that they might be collected all together into one band of impersonal workers! What a power in the world they would then be! No longer would problems vex man's intelligence, problems born of his selfishness. No longer would the human race be afflicted with poverty, misery, and with most of the dreadful, appalling wretchedness that now exists. I sometimes think that the most heart-touching, the most heart-rending story in the world amongst our fellow human beings is that story which is not heard, which is carried in the dumb agony of the silence. Oh, how human beings suffer so needlessly!

I know of no loftier title to give to the great teachers than this: Friends of mankind and of all that lives!

Shifting Our Center of Consciousness

WHAT AILS THE WORLD? Can its ills be cured by shifting politics, changing forms of government which change themselves with time, or by a change of mind and heart which actually will produce effectual results that every normal man today feels are needed — if for nothing else than to divert into harmless channels the psychic energy gathering for the crisis which all, clearly or vaguely, feel impending? But what about politics? Had we naught but politics to depend upon, I for one feel that the case would pass from being desperate to being hopeless. Fortunately there is a way out.

I have always felt that the theosophist, as an individual, should follow what politics he pleases; but I have likewise felt that ethics, individual and collective, are an incomparably more practical and interesting phase of human life. Political theories change and vary from century to century, or oftener; and what one age thinks is the proper way in which to conduct the affairs of the world is usually rejected in the next age. People usually fight like Kilkenny cats about politics, and fight as foolishly; but all agree upon the fundamental verities of morals or ethics — and the grand lessons taught by philosophy and the inspiration of religion — as contrasted with religions — are of unsurpassed importance in their sway over human thought and imagination. As a rule it is only when men have lost confidence in religious matters, or have come to look upon philosophy as a dry-as-dust system of empty speculation without practical value, that they turn to politics in order to find what seems to them an interesting and sometimes, alas, a lucrative pursuit and outlet for latent energy.

As regards the sometimes mooted question of the individual

ownership of money and property, I myself, as a follower and student of the ancient and traditional path of discipleship, believe that no permanent, no enduring, no genuine happiness, can be found merely in the ownership of material things at any time. In other words, I might even be said to believe in and to accept the old statement found in the New Testament, summarized somewhat as follows: "Except ye leave father and mother, wife or child, and property, and follow me, ye cannot enter into the kingdom of the gods." Obviously, this stern mandate applies only so far as the individual is concerned who is desirous of becoming one with that sublime brotherhood of noble-hearted men whose whole life is devoted to the betterment of the human race as a whole; for if such individual disciple have family attachments or property attachments, he is thereby bound to them, and his energies and interests are more or less diffused and dissipated thereby.

This in no wise signifies that a man should neglect any smallest duty if he has already assumed it; nor should he leave father or mother, or wife or child, or even property, until he has made proper, equitable, and generous provision in all senses of the word for those depending upon him, and taken proper care for the administration of the property which every true man must realize he holds in trust for the happiness of others. Remember that a man's future destiny depends upon that which his heart most loves now. If his heart is set solely upon acquiring personal property for himself and for those associated with him, how indeed can he free himself from the bonds of personal ties, from the bonds which hold him fast in the worldly life? That of course is not politics; but it is ethics and religion and philosophy and true science, because when properly understood its meaning is this: *love* not these things; set not your heart upon them so that your heart thereby becomes enchained, bound, shackled. Use them, however, as you use all other good things of earth; but use them as a master of them, not as a slave to them.

Lest I be misunderstood, let me say here once for all, that I have absolutely no patience with, nor sympathy for, the actions of the man who abandons those who are dependent upon him merely for the sake of pursuing his own career, even if it be a spiritual career. A man cannot fulfill a greater duty if he willfully and cruelly neglects or ignores the smaller duty. A man who does at all times and in all places even his worldly duties is the man who is on the right path. Should it happen — and this is one of those rare, exceedingly rare cases — that he is called to follow the path of chelaship, of discipleship, he cannot make a proper beginning in following this path if he plays the part of a coward by ignoring the duties he has already assumed. These duties he must either first fulfill and then become free in an honorable and upright and kindly way and by mutual under-standing with those depending upon him, and after providing for them; or, if they are already provided for, then by mutual agreement that, after a time at least, he shall be free to follow the dictates of his soul. The theosophist above everything is not a nonsocial being; he recognizes his social obligations as keenly as anyone. He believes in marriage; he believes in being a good citizen, a good husband and father, son and brother, and in doing his duty by the state under whose protection he lives. This applies to all, irrespective of who they are.

The theosophist as a believer in and teacher of brotherhood and peace, which includes amelioration and betterment in human relations of all kinds, is de facto a believer in law and order and an upholder of established authority; and as a good citizen he therefore recognizes his duty to his country and obedi-ence to the laws under which he lives. He realizes that believing in brotherhood as a universal fact of being, he should therefore first exemplify it in his actions and conduct by becoming in himself a living example of order, good will, and willing acqui-escence in the laws of the country where he lives; the while always seeking in every lawful and proper way for an improvement in the social structure, for the changing of imperfect or bad laws into better ones; and in doing what good he can as an individual to his fellowmen.

What I am trying to say in these brief and rather aphoristic sentences is that as earnest men and women we should strive at all times to weaken the merely personal and selfish bonds which cramp the winging flight of our souls into higher regions. For such selfish desires and bonds cause, by conflict and friction both with ourselves and with others who hold the same views and who act similarly, the larger part of the human misery and moral degradation in the world.

It is not money per se that is the root of all evil; it is the selfish love of it. Money in the hands of a noble and wise and good man can be a most useful instrument for helping mankind. It is in the selfish love of these things for oneself alone, or for the sake of those immediately associated with one to the detriment of others not so closely associated, that lies the evil and the consequent wrongdoing. This is what Jesus the avatāra meant, and what the great sages and seers of all the ages have meant and have taught: tie not your heart unto the things of earth, but enter into the profound deeps of the spirit within you, and there you will find utter freedom and immense peace and ineffable happiness.

The wise man is he who lives in the world and uses the things of the world — never in a merely worldly way, but with wisdom and kindliness and due regard for the rights of others, yet with his heart free from all attachment to these worldly things, and free from all love thereof. This is the chela path, this is the path of the disciple — at least in the beginning of it. This is the reason I have answered the question which has been more than once asked of me: "G. de P., if someone gave to you ten million dollars, would you accept it? And if so, what would you do with this money?" My answer has been immediate: "Gladly would I accept it, and devote it all to works of usefulness and beneficence for mankind. For myself, not one penny; I am pledged to personal poverty. Yet I am no idiot; I know the power of a good instrument, and money and property can and should be instruments for good. It is not these things themselves that injure; it is our selfish reaction to their influence which is injurious — not only to ourselves but to others."

Consequently, though the Theosophical Society as a society shuns politics, yet every individual member thereof holds and practices such politics as he pleases. I think the world is approaching the time when it will realize that the only way in which men can "save themselves," to use an old-fashioned term, and "save the world," is by *being*, and not by preaching — whether it be preaching politics or philosophy or religion. Politics, at least such as we understand them today, will vanish away as an illusion, and I believe a pestiferous illusion, once men realize what riches lie in the human heart, the great secret mysteries that lie there: love and brotherhood, compassion and peace, the love of a man to be a man, and to grow, to improve himself, his mind and his morals, and his yearning to allow his instincts for right and justice towards all full play and activity. These are the great things that should come into the world, for the world's universal benefit. I believe that some day a great man will appear with an idea, or a series of ideas, of a spiritual and intellectual character, which will show the present tottering civilization the sure way to safety, human concord, and peace; and bring about, not a crash as some wrongly suppose, but a new superstructure of thought and ideals on a nobly strengthened social foundation. It is, after all, ideas that rule the world; and it is precisely because people misthink and wrongly suppose that money or property is a thing in itself of absolute value, and that politics is a thing in itself having intrinsic worth, that these feeble instruments and products of human endeavor have their grip on mankind and wield their sway over human hearts.

Men make politics, men make money, men make things, men make property, men make civilizations. It is *ideas* that rule the world, and it is likewise from men that come ideas. Let us then change our ideas, and follow ideas which are composite of good, ideas based on universal brotherhood, ideas of intrinsic moral beauty, of spiritual and intellectual grandeur, ideas which in time will bring about a confraternity not only of the peoples of the earth, but of all the smaller social units that go to make up a nation. Then, with these ideas permeating our consciousness, we shall not need to bother about petty politics and the rights or nonrights of private property, or what not. The world of humans will then run as easily and smoothly as a well-ordered mechanism; and we shall have happiness and peace all over our globe.

This is not the pipe dream of a vaguely visioning and idealistic dreamer. It is an actuality which can be put into practical operation simply by a reorienting of our thinking and of our feeling into new standards of human conduct; and in such a new world men will be judged not only by what they do or produce, but by what they think, because thoughts of brotherly and humane benevolence will be carried into constructive action. They will then not be judged by what they have or own. Property will not be the standard of righteousness nor of the proprieties, nor again of respectability.

We must shift our moral center of gravity to ethics where it rightly and truly belongs, and away from property where it has been falsely placed during the last few thousand years because of unfortunate contributing historical causes. It is easier far to make such shift of values to their natural, proper, and therefore legitimate sphere, than it is to continue being involved through centuries of the future in the horrible struggles of an international or internecine character with their bitter animosities and unforgetting hatreds, their dislocations of social and political life, and the consequent misery weighing so heavily upon us all.

There is not a single logical or reasonable argument to be urged against it — this shifting of our center of consciousness — except ignorance, prejudice, and dense human stupidity, due to the inertia brought about by moral somnolence and empty disbelief in our own powers to carve our destiny shapely.

It would seem to be undoubtedly true that unless there come upon the world a new outlook and a change of our habit, mental and psychical, of envisaging events through the distorted lenses of our present-day sense of values, our already badly shaken civilization runs a danger of sliding down into a welter of confusion, despair, and human misery, such as the annals of known history have not yet chronicled. The peoples of the earth gathered into nations must learn to look upon each other, and to treat each other, with decorum, high sense of honor, and instinct for mutual service, instead of continuing to follow courses of conduct based upon the very shaky foundations of opportunism, expediency, and convenience, that have so often governed and disgraced international relations in the past, thus presenting a picture of international morals probably far beneath even the standard held by the average man in the street. The case is by no means hopeless, however, for the remedy is simple indeed, practical and practicable, and lies merely in a shifting of our center of gravity of consciousness from politics and profit to morals and mutual service. The average intelligent businessman today has come to realize that a successful enterprise must be founded upon honesty and service; otherwise he is doomed to failure. There is no ostensible, no actual, reason why nations should follow courses which the average man would consider disgraceful in his own case. The whole secret lies in a change of outlook, in a change of vision; and then the apparent difficulties will be understood for what they are, illusions; and they will be gladly cast aside for the standards prevailing along the pathway of safety, progress, happiness, and peace.

I most emphatically do not wish to give the impression, when speaking of the loss in recent centuries of a sense of ethical values, which arose in a translation therefrom of our center of gravity of consciousness to property as the pivot around which our national and individual interest revolves, that the theosophist is in any wise blind to, unconscious of, or indifferent to, the really great and harrowing misery that exists in the world in individual cases because of a lack of proper resources or support. Very much to the contrary. But we point to such conditions as an illustration of the power which material possessions have gained over both human heart and mind; for the insane race for wealth and the desire for acquisition for the individual himself, even to the detriment of his fellows, has blinded him to one of the primal human duties: a brotherly regard for, consideration and, in needful cases, proper care of one's fellowmen less fortunately placed by karma — or destiny — than he himself is.

It is good to note that during recent times the whole tendency in the various countries of the world is towards doing everything possible, both through the state and by the individual, to ameliorate the condition of the needy, combined with the growing realization that essential values lie not in property but in human beneficence, and in that universal brotherhood which is inherent in any properly organized and enduring social structure.

Some of the noblest men who have ever lived have suffered all the pangs of personal humiliation as well as the great disadvantages of dire poverty, while it is a commonplace of history that great riches have often lain at the disposition of the unworthy or the incompetent. The world is rapidly moving towards a time — provided its course be not interrupted or broken by some catastrophe — when it will be recognized far more keenly than now it is that every human being has an inherent right, in the words of the American Constitution, to "life, liberty, and the pursuit of happiness," and that it is one of the noblest duties of an enlightened State not merely to provide equal opportunities for all, but actively to aid those who, from one cause or another, often greatly to their credit, are not accumulators of property. Such things as the need of old-age pensions, free education, and the providing of work for every willing hand, have become commonplaces of conversation, and rightly so.

Yet, admitting all this, and much more, and after stating that the tendency above alluded to is all to the good, I take occasion to point out that the root of all the world's troubles in the past has lain in the wrong centering of our human sense of permanent values — in property rather than inherently residing in human beings themselves. The natural and inevitable consequence has found its culmination in the present-day worldwide unrest, conflict, endless arguments, and a talk about rights ad nauseam, but we discover very little talk about the duty which a man owes to his fellowmen. Once our center of gravity of moral consciousness is taken from property as the pivot of civilization, and placed in man himself as the center of all greatest and primal values, then 99 percent of the world's constantly recurring paroxysms of agitation, perturbation, and violence will vanish; and human relations of whatever kind, international, national, social, or political, will automatically adjust themselves to and for the common good. Universal brotherhood — not as merely vague sentimentalism, but as a recognition of human solidarity based on nature's own laws — is, after all, the keynote of any true civilization, and without it no civilization can endure.

Altruism

HUMAN NATURE IS SO PRONE when hearing or reading about altruism to imagine that it is something foreign to us, lugged into human life as a most desirable thing to follow, but, after all, highly impractical — that it is not inherent in the characteristics of human beings to be altruistic naturally. In other words, they are all fascinated with the idea of isolated self-interest. Is not this supposition utterly unfounded in nature? For wherever we look, whatever we consider or study, we find that the individual working alone for himself is helpless. In all the great kingdoms of the universe, it is union of effort, cooperation in living combines, which is not only what nature herself is working to bring about and therefore which we find everywhere, but that anything that runs counter and contrary to this fundamental law of the universe — unity in action — produces disharmony, strife, and what in our own bodies we call disease. Health is that condition of bodily structure where all parts work to a common end in what we may call friendship, union.

Consider the stones: are they not combines, are they not unions of individuals composing, making, producing, a thing? No single atom of any of the chemical elements of which any stone is composed is the stone itself. How about the lovely flower? How about the bodies in which we live? How about a single man? Could he alone produce the great works that men have bent their genius to achieve? What is civilization but the combined efforts of human beings to produce great and noble effects in human life: increasing comfort, dispelling danger, bringing about the productions of genius from greater men which redound to our own comfort and use. Show me a single instance where pure self-interest has produced anything. If we consult nature in all her kingdoms, we find naught but unity of working brought about by multitudes of individuals cooperating to a common end. And what is that but altruism? Altruism is the word we give to this fact when we see its ethical significance, and this significance is in no wise, nor in any great way nor in any small, different from what we see in the world physical. Altruism means the one working for the all — nature's fundamental law in all her grand structures — and the all standing as the guard and shield and field of effort of the one. Think of the deep moral lesson, the deduction, to be drawn from this greatest of the universe's — not mysteries but verities; so common around us that usually we pass it by unseeing, with unseeing eye. Show me anything that can endure sole and alone for a single instant of time.

Two or more atoms uniting make a molecule; two or more molecules a larger production; and it is the countless multitudes of such unions which produce the universe. Any single entity essaying to follow the ignoble path of isolated self-interest sets its or his puny will against the force which keeps the stars in their courses, gives health to our bodies, brings about civilizations, and produces all the wonders that are around us.

There is a point of teaching in this connection which it is important to introduce into the world today, and that is hope. You know the old Greek story about a certain very curious and inquisitive person who opened a box and all the evils in the world fled out, and there remained therein only hope. I think this contains a great deal of truth which has a practical bearing on life's problems. As long as a man has hope he does not despair. Weak or strong, it matters not; if he has hope, something to look forward to, if his inner spirit, the spiritual being within him, teaches him something of hope, he not only will never despair, but he will become a builder, a constructor, a worker *with the universe*, because he will move forwards. And this is altruism.

We are all children of the universe, of its physical side and of its spiritual and divine side. This being so, there is in every human breast an undying font not only of inspiration, but likewise of growth, of hope, of wisdom, and of love. So that the world today, although apparently in a parlous condition, in a desperate state, still contains in it men and women enough to carry the evolutionary wave of progress over its present turmoil and strife; for the majority of mankind are essentially right in their instincts, especially the higher instincts.

Therefore, I do not see anything horribly hopeless about the world's condition today. I believe not only that there is ground for hope, but that the undying spark of spirituality, of wisdom, and love of altruism, always living in the human heart, will carry the human race not only out of its present series of impasses, of difficulties, but into brighter days, which will be brighter because wiser and gentler. It is not the crises, when things crash or seem to crash; it is not the horrific noise of the thunder or the crash of its bolt, which govern the great functions of life, human and cosmic; but those slow, to us, always quiet, unending silent processes which build: build when we wake, build when we sleep, build all the time; and even in the human race carry it through folly after folly after folly into the future.

There is the ground of our hope; and it seems to me that all good men and true should rally to the defense of these primal, simple verities which every human heart, adult or child, can understand. I believe it is about time that men and women began to look on the bright side of things, to see hope around us, to forget themselves and their petty worries, and to live in the Infinite and in the Eternal. It is easy, infinitely easier than making ourselves continuously sick with frets and worries. Within each one of us there is something divine to which we can cling, and which will carry us through.

Don't talk to me about altruism being something foreign or exotic, unusual, impractical, and therefore impracticable; for it is the only thing which perpetually lives, the only thing which endures for aye. When any single element or part in a human body begins to run on its own, we have disease. When any single element or part in any structural combine which helps to compose the world around us begins to run on its own, i.e., what we call self-interest, there we see degeneration and decay.

Deduction and question: which of the twain should we follow — the pathway of the cosmic intelligence bringing us health inner and outer, peace inner and outer, strength internal and external, and union inner and outer? Or the teaching of a tawdry and isolated self-interest which seeks its own to the prejudice of all?

Is it not high time that we gave the world a few of the simple inner teachings of the god-wisdom of the ancients? Will you show me one more sublime, more appealing to human intellect and to the dictates of human conscience, than that of altruism, which puts us in intimate union with the throbbing of the cosmic heart, and which idea, if we can pass it over into the minds of men, will more than justify all the work that the great masters of wisdom have been doing for mankind since time immemorial? Ethics above all!

Carving Your Destiny

You HAVE INFINITY before you, eternity. Face it. Thus teaches the god-wisdom: a doctrine of hope, rich with the promise of the future. No man need ever say it is too late — those terrible words, *too late*. No man need ever say that. Every instant of time is a new choice. As in the past he has made himself what now he is, so in the future he can carve his destiny and make himself to be precisely in accordance with the vision that he has of himself to become in the future. What a grand doctrine! Man is but a reproduction, a cyclical evolutionary reproduction of himself out of the past, in the present, marching into the future. There is your destiny.

After Death: You Are Yourself

I HOPE THAT THE TIME will come when we shall weigh more strongly than we have been doing on the teachings of what happens after death. The average man seems to be today not so much immoral as amoral, that is, seems to have largely lost the sense of moral responsibility. If men and women could realize what is going to happen to them after death, it would awaken a certain sense of needed behavior or conduct.

Let us try to restore to mankind the teaching of the ancient wisdom: as you live so will you be after you die. It is a simple teaching and it is so logical, it appeals. Some may resent it at first, they may not like it; but there is a thought there which on account of its logic, its justice, will finally throw forth sprouts of thought in the mind.

If you want to understand the kāma-loka and the devachan, just study yourself *now*, and you will know what you are going to get. Just that. You are going to get a continuation of precisely what now you are. If a man indulges in vice, what is going to happen to him? He reaps the consequences of his evildoing. He learns by it the lessons that come out of the suffering. If a man fills his mind with gross thoughts and evil dreams, he learns by it in the long run through suffering, for the effects and consequences on his mind and character will ensue. He suffers, he is in torture, he pays the penalty, he has poisoned his inner system and he won't have peace until the poison has worked itself out, until he has become what is called re-formed, re-shaped. Then he will have peace again; he will be able to sleep in peace again.

Study yourself in your daily consciousness; and also study what kind of dreams you have. Why are these two conjoined?

Because your dreams are from your own mind, and therefore are a part of your own consciousness. A man during his waking hours has evil dreams, evil thoughts; when he sleeps he has nightmares. He learns by them when he sleeps; he certainly is not going to have a heaven of dreams because he has filled his mind with horrid, hateful, mean, degrading thoughts. He has not built the substances of heaven.

There you have the answer; and the kāma-loka is simply a state of consciousness which the man's consciousness enters after death because he has made himself during his lifetime to have that kind of consciousness. It works itself out, and then he rises or sinks into whatever is his destiny: a weak devachan or no devachan at all, according to the individual. In other words, if he has made for himself a character which is X, he will have that character X, whatever it is, after death. He won't have character Y, or Z, or A, or B. Contrariwise, a man who during life has kept himself in hand, has controlled himself, has lived manly, experiences the same law precisely: the after-death state will be unconscious in the kāma-loka, or very nearly so, because he has no kāma-loka biases in himself; and probably there will be a blissful devachan.

Suppose a man has no marked character at all, is neither particularly good nor particularly bad. What kind of after-death states is he going to have? He will have a colorless kāma-loka, nothing particularly bad; and he will have a colorless devachan, nothing particularly beautiful or blissful. It will all be like a sort of vague, intangible dream. It doesn't amount to much, and consequently he won't amount to much after he dies.

Or take the case of a young man of evil ways who reforms, let us say, at about middle age, and spends the rest of his life in deeds of virtue, of self-improvement. What will be his fate in the worlds to come? As stated, the kāma-loka and the devachan are simply a continuation of what the man is when he dies. So consequently an evil young man becoming a good old man has practically no kāma-loka of an unpleasant kind at all. He will have to pay to the uttermost farthing for any evil he did as a youth — but in his future life; his evil deeds are thought-deposits there. But as he reformed at about middle age, and lived a clean decent life thereafter, his kāma-loka will be very slight because it will be simply a continuation of what he was when he died, and the devachan will be in accordance likewise.

One can be in the kāma-loka, as well as in the devachan, before death comes; indeed, it is possible to be in the avīchi-condition even while imbodied. And here is a very important deduction we should draw from this fact: if we have kāma-loka while imbodied men and women, we shall have it after death; and precisely according to the same law, because we have spiritual yearnings, dreams of a spiritual type or character while imbodied, we shall have the devachan after death. To repeat, the kāma-loka is a prolongation or a continuation, until it is worked out, of what you have been through in your life. If you set your thought and mind and heart on things which bring you pain, which make you suffer because you are selfish, and stiff-necked in pride and egoism, you will assuredly continue the same bending of your consciousness after death. It cannot be otherwise. It is simply you. Therefore, the devachan and the kāma-loka are prolongations or continuations of the same states of consciousness respectively that you have gone through on earth, with this difference: that being out of the body, which is at once a blind and a shield of protection, you are, as it were — thought, naked thought. And if your thought has been during life on things of horror, or if you have allowed your thought to bend in those directions while imbodied, you won't be washed free of stain merely because you have cast off the body. Your thought, which is yourself, will continue and you will have to pass through kāma-loka and exhaust that phase of thought. It will have to die out as a fire will burn itself out.

Similarly, indeed exactly: if in life you have had beautiful

thoughts, grand thoughts, sublime thoughts, you will assuredly
have the same in the devachan, but a thousandfold stronger
because no longer smothered by the body when you have cast
it off. So if you want to know what your destiny will be after
death, just study yourself now and take warning. There is
a very important and pertinent lesson that we can learn from
this fact, just in that. You can make your postmortem condition
what you will it to be now, before it is too late. Nothing in
the universe can prevent the bliss of devachan coming to you,
or rather your making it for yourself. Deduction: take yourself
in hand.

There you have the teaching of the kāma-loka. There you
have the teaching of the devachan. It is very simple. All the
intricate, abstract questions I think arise largely in failing to
understand the elementary principles of the teachings. When
you lie down you dream, or you are unconscious. When you
die you dream, or you are unconscious. You have, when you
lie down at night, evil dreams or good dreams, or you are unconscious. When you die you will have evil dreams or beautiful
dreams or you will be unconscious — all depending upon the
individual and the life he has led. So the kāma-loka and the
devachan, and indeed the avīchi, are not things that are going
suddenly to happen to you when you die; but because your
consciousness has been that way while imbodied, they, one or
the other, will continue after you die.

You see now the importance of ethics, and why all the great
sages and seers throughout time have tried to teach men to
spiritualize and refine their thoughts, to live in the heart-life,
to cast out the things which are wrong and evil. The devachan
is not waiting for you; the kāma-loka is not waiting for you — I
mean as absolute conditions now separate from you. If you
had them in life, you will have them after death. The man who
has had no thought of hatred or horror or detestation or venom
toward another, in other words whose heart and mind have

never been nests of evil, will have neither an avīchi in life nor after death, nor an unhappy kāma-loka in life or after death. He will have an exquisite devachan, and will come back refreshed and vigorous and strong and renewed to begin a new life and with everything in his favor.

After death you continue to be precisely what you are when you die. There is the whole thing. There is the secret of the kāma-loka and of the devachan and of all the intermediate states of the *bardo*, as the Tibetans call it. All the rest is detail, and that is why I keep emphasizing in my public lectures and in my writings that death is but a sleep. Death is a perfect sleep and sleep an imperfect death. It is literally so. When you sleep you are partly dead. When you die, you are absolutely asleep. If you grasp these simple ideas you will have the whole teaching on your thumbnail, a thumbnail picture.

Now another point: I have heard people say that they don't want to remain in devachan, it is a waste of time. This is a misunderstanding. You might as well say, I don't want to have sleep tonight, it is a waste of time. As a matter of fact, you need the rest, recuperation, assimilation of the experiences of the past life. You are strengthened by it, you grow by it. So that while the devachan is not a time for evolution it *is* a time for building, for recuperation, for assimilation, for inner digestion, for strengthening, and is just as much needed as a night's rest is for the body.

There will come a time in human evolution when even the devachan is no longer required, because the man has learned to live in the higher part of his being. Devachan, however beautiful, is an illusion. The time will come in the future when men will no longer have to sleep at night; they won't require it. They will have different kinds of bodies and thus learn to do without the devachan, and will reincarnate almost immediately in order to help mankind — which is the thing they love most of all — and all other beings. These men are what we call masters, in all their grades. But for us ordinary human beings the devachan is a necessary episode.

The devachan, however, while a beautiful experience of the consciousness, is an experience of the higher *personal* consciousness, the higher part of us human egos, the higher part of the personal man, its aroma, so to speak. In this fact lies the training bringing about the shortening of the devachan. If you learn to live outside of the personality and in the Eternal, while you are imbodied, if it becomes habitual with you, your devachan will be correspondingly shortened because you won't want it. You won't need it. The bent of your mind is not in selfish beatific satisfactions of the soul. That is what the devachan is, a fool's paradise. When compared with reality, it is an illusion. But just because men and women strain for those things and suffer to attain them, the devachan in nature's infinite pity becomes the time when they have it, the resting, relaxing time, the time of recuperation, digestion, assimilation. As we grow, as the ages pass, in future ages we won't long so desperately to have these beatific satisfactions of the soul. We shall find our happiness in impersonal attachments to things of beauty, things which belong to the higher spiritual man, and not to the hungry human soul.

This is where the training lies that all chelas are taught, that same truth, that and nothing more. Rise out of the personality so that you learn to use it as a willing, acquiescent instrument, and live in the spiritual part of you, which means impersonally; live universally so that you are not swayed by your own hunger for the things that please and help and rest you; but live in the spiritual, in the universal, and all these other things will be added unto you.

SERVANT
OR DISCIPLE

The Secret of Human Conflict

THE SECRET OF CONFLICT not only amongst men, but even in the universe, is in the existing degrees of ignorance, selfishness, and lack of altruism — the noblest emotion that can possibly enter the human heart. It is only in altruism, in thinking of others, in putting others before ourselves, that we forget ourselves, and in the forgetting lose the pains and sorrows and the little happinesses that we hug so close to us and call our selves.

Don't you see that the only pathway to wisdom and universal peace and utter happiness is putting the whole before the insignificant, the many before yourself; and therefore living in the universal life instead of living only in your own small compass of vital comprehension? There is the secret of it all; and it is precisely this secret that the modern world has forgotten. It has forgotten that in self-forgetfulness is greatness, peace, and happiness; that our lack of peace and our unhappinesses come from hugging our little pettinesses and worries close to us; for these anxieties and hatreds gnaw the very fiber of our inner being, and then we suffer, we are hurt, and we raise our eyes to divinity or to the gods and exclaim: "Why has this happened to me, to us? What have I done? What have we done?" Yet the merest cognizance of spiritual and natural law should tell us that everything that happens in the great and in the small — because the small is included in the great — happens according to divine law; and that misery and unhappiness and conflict and wretchedness and poverty and all the array of accompanying ills, arise out of human negligence to obey the cosmic law. It is as simple as that.

The great lost chord of modern civilization is forgetfulness of the fact in nature of universal brotherhood, which means not merely a sentimental or political brotherhood; it means that we are all of one common cosmic or spiritual origin, and that what affects one affects all, and therefore that the interests of the unit are insignificant as compared with the interests of the multitude. But forget not that the multitude is composed of units, so that you cannot be unjust or cruel or do wrong even to a single unit without offending the whole. These are simple laws that have been hammered into the consciousness of mankind from time out of mind, from an age preceding ours so far back in the remote past that what we now call the eternal mountains were not even yet dreamed of and were sleeping in the ooze of archaeozoic slime.

Now this lost chord, this forgotten truth, the forgetfulness of human brotherhood, can be expressed otherwise: the loss of the conviction that nature is fundamentally spiritual, and therefore is ruled by law, and therefore has compensation for meritorious conduct and retribution for unmeritorious; and that these twain, the compensation and the retribution, are as infallible as is that cosmic law itself, for they are but the expressions of it. When a man allows these wondrous and yet so simple thoughts to sink into his consciousness so that they become a part of the very fiber of his being and of his feeling, no longer will he willfully injure another. He cannot. It is no longer his character. He has drawn himself out of the mud, and seen the golden sunshine. He recognizes that fundamentally all is one, all beings are one, and that the unit is as important as the whole, and the whole is as important as the unit; and that the unit within the whole is infinitely more important than the unit, single, alone. By the units themselves thinking in this way, the cosmic rule of harmony is preserved unto infinity.

That is what we have lost: the conviction that we shall meet compensation or retribution for our thoughts and for our feelings; that good will infallibly come to us if we sow good and do and think and feel right, and sow seeds of justice and honor and probity and decency in our conduct towards all other men — *all* others, not merely "my" friends — *all*. For the cosmos is a unity and knows no divisions or human separations. This is what we have lost. This is where we fail. This is the secret of all human conflict.

Now mind you, this thought — because of the very complex character of modern civilization, and because of this fact only — raises a bewildering series of embarrassing questions. But any man with a heart in the right place, can solve such questions because he is illuminated by the god within him, if he will allow his heart to speak. Then his judgment is virtually infallible. And when I say the heart, I do not mean emotion; I mean the man's instinct of upright honor and inner moral and spiritual cleanliness. The fact is, we of the Occident have been cowards entirely too long, always wanting to put the fault on someone else. So we have erected a pure figment of our imagination, and we speak of it as Christ Jesus, and on his shoulders lay all our sins; and at the end we shall be washed white in the blood of the lamb if only we believe it. Aye, but how about those who have suffered under my evil doing? Because I am saved, does that help them? How about those whom I in my stupid, ignorant and evil past, perhaps have given the shove downwards instead of the brotherly helping upward lift? How about them? Don't you see that those ideas are the complete reversal of a cosmic philosophy? Don't you see that it is all wrong? That it is not so important what happens to the unit; the greater thing is what happens to all others, the endless, toiling, hoping, working, suffering multitudes. That is important, and every weakened unit knows it and feels it.

Now this inevitability of retribution or of lovely compensation is what we call the doctrine of consequences, the doctrine of karma: that what you sow you shall reap, either now or at a later date, and that there is no escape. We know it perfectly well in the ordinary things of life; it does not require any argument. If you put your hand in a flame or touch a live wire, the fire is not going to not burn you because you are stupid and ignorant, and the electricity will not refrain from perhaps killing you because you don't know the laws of electricity.

Fortunately there is another and beautiful side to this. Our most wondrous teacher, the greatest friend we have, is our sorrow. What is it that softens a man's heart so that he can understand the suffering of others and feel with others? Sympathy, feeling together. It is when we suffer ourselves that we grow. Nothing softens the heart like one's own suffering. Strange and beautiful paradox, it puts steel into our character likewise. It makes us stronger. The man who has never suffered is without feeling, is a very "in-volved" person indeed — he is "turned in" upon himself.

Who is the great man? The man who has never suffered? Or the one whose sufferings have given him strength, inner power, vision, who knows what suffering is, and because of his own recollection of it, never will bring suffering upon others? With him the heart has begun to awaken. Consciousness is once more aroused to these simple cosmic verities.

You see then how wonderfully the universe is constructed, so that although we are stupid and ignorant, and may lack the noblest feeling possible to human beings which is altruism, love, and feeling for others, yet by our very sufferings and stupidities and ignorance we learn the better way, and with each step in learning we grow, we grow greater. After a long period of this very slow and wholesome and painful evolutionary journey, we come to the point when we shall say to ourselves: no more of that; I have had enough. From now on I shall take myself in my own hands, and govern my life by self-directed evolution. Hereafter I shall choose my path. Naught shall sway my will to this side or that. There is the goal, and that goal is a cosmic one. No longer shall I be a slave

of fell circumstance.   From now on I rule my own pathway.
I choose my own destiny.   I have seen the Law.

It is a strange paradox that once the soul begins to awaken
and the eyes to open, because of the very complex and really I
think disastrous state of modern life, the man who is earnestly
trying to do his job, to do his duty in life, to live manly, uprightly,
meets a thousand times more difficulties than the man who just
goes along because, like the animals, he is too stupid to think.
But would you be a mere human animal, not thinking, not
reflecting, not having the godlike feeling of choosing your own
way in life?

It is, then, my conviction that human conflicts would end,
and fairly rapidly too, if all of us were to realize our individual
responsibility towards our fellowmen.   I think that just that
one rule would run through all the fabric of human life from
the highest to the lowest: our solidarity as units in a human
hierarchy, so that what affects one affects all, whether for good
or for ill.

I have often wondered how many think of these things in
the silent hours of night, or when they are puzzled and anxious
as to what course to follow, and are afraid to follow because the
multitude does not.   The multitude likes to follow what it thinks
is "enlightened selfishness."   I cannot conceive a more diabolic
or satanic notion than what is covered by that phrase.   It is a
deliberate obscuring of every noble intuition of the human soul.
Just ask yourselves: Do they do a thing because it is beautiful
and because it is right and just, and because it will bring happiness and security and peace to all?   No, these proponents of
enlightened selfishness say "If I do it, it ultimately will be good
for me and mine."   Now suppose people in different parts of
the world followed that gospel, what would you see?   What
you see today.   And it can all be stopped, all human conflict.
Mind you, I don't mean stopping differences of opinion, which
is one of the most beautiful things about us humans.   Differences

of opinion, if honestly and courteously and altruistically culti-
vated, lend spice and enchantment to life, lend charm and
beauty. The French have a wonderful proverb: *Du choc des idées
jaillit la lumière*, "From the shock of ideas springs forth light."
That is the principle of congresses and parliaments and unions
and reunions of men: to exchange ideas and to skim off the best.

So I don't refer to differences of ideas. These are natural.
I mean conflicts, hatreds, lack of respect for the other man, lack
of seeing in him something which is as wonderful as what he
can see in you. Have you ever tried just this simple rule,
looking into the eyes of some other man when you are talking
with him; not trying to force your idea into his head as we all
do; not trying to persuade him and make him believe as you
do; but just looking into the eyes of that man. Do you know,
you can see marvels, a world of hitherto unexpressed and unknown beauty there. That man's whole soul, if you just give
him a chance, is ready to come out and meet you. But of course
he may be just as much scared of you as you are scared of him,
and just as much afraid of being a man as you are afraid of
being a man.

I assure you that if men would trust each other and expect
decency from each other, they would get it. I have never known
it to fail. I will tell you frankly I have never been betrayed in
a trust I have given, because I have given my trust always
without stint and as an appeal. It works, and it is the principle
upon which modern business, the highest type, is based: mutual
trust, mutual confidence, mutual honor; and when a man does
not live up to these things, he very soon gets a rap.

Now, I have actually heard it said that it is good for the
human race to be in continuous conflict because it makes men
strong. Yes, I have heard of pugilists, but I have never known
any of them who have been especially famous for genius or for
setting the world on fire with their brains or for changing the
course of destiny or of history. Pachydermatous human beings,

thick-skinned human beings, have their value, but they are not exactly the type that we choose when we want a man to handle some very difficult, delicately balanced, and intricate negoti-ations. There we need a man not only of brains but a man of heart, because the man of brains who has no heart cannot under-stand the other man who may have just enough of a heart-touch to give him a very heavy advantage over the heartless man. The man without heart is only half-built in psychology; he is at an enormous disadvantage. The other man will put it all over him. Heart and brain working together make the complete man, be-cause there is the understanding of both the song of the heart and the philosophy of the mind.

Shall we continue these interminable conflicts? I think they will pass away. I think that beauty and respect are in the offing even now. The way to begin is with ourselves: I with myself, you with yourself.

The Divine Proportion

WHAT SYMPATHY IS TO LOVE, which is cosmic harmony, consciousness is to divine intelligence. In other words, love awakened or in action shows itself as what we humans call sympathy; intelligence awakened to action and self-cognizing being expresses itself as consciousness. This includes likewise self-consciousness which is but consciousness reflected back upon itself so that it "sees" or "feels" itself. Indeed everything in the universe, and consequently everything in man, who is but an offspring of the universe, is ultimately reducible in the last analysis to one: whether you call it the one cosmic ultimate or the cosmic principle, is a matter of words only; from this One — which is not monotheism in any sense — from this abstract unity there flow forth into activity what we call intelligence, consciousness, mind, sym-pathy, etc. Thus then what sympathy is to love, which is cosmic harmony ultimately, consciousness is to cosmic intelligence.

Civilization Built upon Thought

THOUGHT IS THE MOTIVE POWER of men. It governs even emotion and can control it, and although sometimes thought is evoked by feeling, I think that on the higher planes they are one. The world we live in is a world of thinkers and feelers; and if the world is bad, it is because our thoughts and feelings have made it so. If human conditions are inharmonious, even diabolic at times, when brute force takes the place of reason and justice, it is because our thoughts have made it so.

Ideas control actions. There you have the cause of the unrest in the world we live in, and its cure. If a man wants to reform himself, he does so by first of all changing his thought; he begins by feeling differently. It is the only lasting way, for it means a change of character. If you want to prevent a quarrel you have to begin your work before the quarrel threatens. If you try to interfere in a quarrel between two people, not only are you apt to hurt yourself, but you will have a quarrel of three. It is no way to stop a quarrel by going to the quarrelers and preaching. By so doing you have not touched them where they are susceptible, you have not changed them, you have not appealed to their thought or their feelings. You have been trying mere palliatives.

Make them see that they are acting a bit worse than the beasts are when they fight, because the beasts have not our reason and common sense. Make your appeal with ideas; awaken thoughts. Put into their minds a new sequence of thought and feeling. Then they will begin to realize that you cannot settle a quarrel by brute force, for that simply means that the chap who has got the worst of it is going to bide his time to see if he can best the other fellow by brute force. They will begin to see that you cannot stop wars by making wars to stop wars.

It has never worked and never will, because it is a wrong psychology, as well as foolish.

All civilization is built upon thought, and if you want to change a civilization, you must change accepted thought by giving a new thought. What is an invention? A thought. What is literature? What are philosophy, religion, science? Thought. What is the social structure under which we live? Thought. Every movement in the world today is built upon thought: social, political, philosophic, religious, and scientific. Nine out of ten of these movements began in the mind of one individual, and spread. You see in the pages of history the tremendous cataclysmic effects of thought. What is war? Not only the result of thought, but thought itself. Men fighting because of ideas, thoughts. To avoid another world war we must begin before the next one happens — begin by starting a new current of thought in the world.

These truths are so simple they pass us by and we do not take them in and digest them. It is ideas that shake the world. It is ideas that make the world. It is ideas that unmake men and the world of men. Consult the annals of history. Look at the amazing results that spring from movements which begin perhaps with a handful of earnest people. For years they may work and preach and labor apparently without result. Suddenly, for some remarkable reason, the idea catches and spreads like wildfire. At times ideas take hold of people in the most amazing way. What were the Crusades, when men left home and hearth and fireside and everything they held dear to go and fight the paynim, in a distant foreign and unknown land? These tens of thousands of men collected from all over Europe *for an idea*. Still more remarkable: what was this amazing and thought-arresting idea which even caught the thoughts and imaginations of little children? Have you not heard of the Children's Crusade? Out of Germany and what is now Belgium and Holland and France and Switzerland, down into the south of France and into Italy suddenly children began to arise — boys and girls from toddling ones up to those of thirteen or fourteen years — they took to the roads and went by the scores of thousands till the highways were black with their marching feet. Hundreds of miles they went, dying by thousands on the way, and horribly treated by human monsters who battened on them. Nobody knows how this thought arose. Suddenly the children in the various countries took it into their heads: "We will go fight, we will go save the Holy Sepulcher." Fancy children talking like that! They got it from their parents, of course; but look at the psychology — a psychology that swept every home, took one or more children from every fireside. The mothers and fathers could not stop them. They would steal out by night. They would go by byways and devious pathways to the great highways, those bands of helpless children going south, going south! All for an idea, a thought!

What was the idea of the wonderful tarantella which is best described by the historians of Spain and Italy — Italy particularly? Suddenly for no understandable reason, grown men and women got the idea that they must dance; and they began to dance, and danced on and on until they fell down unconscious, exhausted. They could not stop themselves from singing and dancing, singly and together, whole countrysides, whole districts of them — a psychology, a thought, an idea.

It is just such kind of insane psychology that rules the world of human thought today. Men and women have got the idea that it is impossible to prevent another great war. They really believe it. That is one of the reasons it will happen unless sanity resumes its sway over our minds. What makes and carries on any war? Thought. What stops any war? Thought: a changing of the thoughts of men; for by changing their thoughts you change their hearts, you change their lives and therefore their civilizations. If a war comes, it is because men and women have brought it about by their thinking. Their thinking arouses their feeling. Their feeling arouses their jealousy and fear. Evil thought will be followed by similar thought. You cannot extinguish fire by fire. You cannot stop war by war. This is as simple as ABC. These are thoughts which fly unnoticed over our heads because we are so accustomed to them, and yet they are the secret of all good and all evil. A man's life is changed sublimely by his thoughts; so too can he go to hell or the gallows by his thinking. It is thought which makes the gentleman or the boor. It is thought which makes the courageous man or the coward. It is thought which produces forgiveness or carries on hate.

It was because of these facts that the Theosophical Society was begun: to try to change the thoughts of men and women towards better and higher things; to arouse inspiring and benevolent ideas in the minds of individual men and women. Why don't theosophists all go out and take lunch baskets around to the starving, and go to the bedsides of the people who are smitten with disease, and dying? Many of us do it and have done it. But our main work in life is to try to *do away* with poverty, rather than tinkering with the needs of the poor; and this will gradually be accomplished by changing people's minds so that our civilization will be an enlightened one. That, among other noble objectives, is what we aspire towards. There is no other work which is farther reaching than that. It goes to the root of things, instead of only putting plaster and ointments on the surface of the festering wounds. And in a still higher field our work is to teach men and women what they as individuals have locked up within them: powers, capacities, faculties, which the average man or woman today does not suspect. Yet they are there. The titan intellects, the greatest men who have ever lived, have proved what the human mind is capable of; and every normal person has the same potencies within himself. It is a part of the work of the Theosophical Society to re-arouse belief in these things, so that human beings will yearn to cultivate themselves from within outwards, to awaken what is within, and to become greater and grander. What a world we shall live in then! It is thought that will do it, and the feeling which follows upon thought. Then indeed will the Christ, crucified in us every day we live, ascend from the crucifix, our own being, the body of each man, and enter into his brain and enlighten his life, and reform his conduct towards his fellows. Just that one thought alone, if you could get men and women to believe it and inwardly to know it, would bring about a universal "conversion" — a "turning around," a changing — of our minds and hearts to the living Christ within, the living Buddha!

The Injunction of Pythagoras

REMEMBER THE RULE laid down by Pythagoras. It has been quoted again and again, but it loses none of its beauty and profundity by repetition. It runs somewhat as follows:

"Let not the setting sun reach the western horizon, nor close thine eyes in sleep, before thou hast gone over all the events of the day just past, and hast asked thyself: What have I done today that has been done amiss? What have I done today that has been done aright? Have I injured anyone? Have I failed in my duty? Let not the setting sun reach the western rim of space, nor let thine eyelids close in sleep ere thou hast asked thyself these questions."

If only men and women would conscientiously follow that simple rule, ninety-nine percent of the world's trouble, heartache, sin, and anxiety, would be nonexistent, would never happen. The reason is simple. The world's troubles arise from our weaknesses, not from our strength; and if we would increase our strength, and do away with our weaknesses, every human being thereafter, in proportion to his inner evolution, would become a power for good in the world. And you see what that would mean. It would cut the taproot of most of the thoughts and feelings and acts that bring misery amongst us.

Universality and the Esoteric Tradition

H. P. BLAVATSKY WROTE GRANDLY of the secret doctrine of the ages, and she pointed out that this secret doctrine has come down to us from time immemorial in the guardianship of the great teachers, in all their various grades. She showed that this wisdom of the gods was originally handed to the first human protoplasts by spiritual beings from other spheres, from other planes. But it seemed to me that with all the grandeur of her teaching and the high plane of thought to which she led us, there still remained something to be given which should guard the student against the intrusion into his mind of false ideas, false teachings, doctrines leading him away from the central Fire. In other words, men lacked a standard, a teststone, against which they could lay a teaching presented to them and find out whether the teaching were pure gold or only brass.

What is this infallible touchstone, this instrument which you can use if you recognize it? It is universality. Any teaching presented to you which cannot stand that test, which can be shown to be only a purported communication from other spheres, and which has no basis in the great philosophies and religions and sciences of the past given to mankind by masters of wisdom — any such teaching is fraudulent and has no right, no place, in the court of our conscience. The gods taught man in his childhood, and led him on, and bred him up, enlightened his mind, so that it could receive and understand and pass on *in secret and open tradition* the archaic god-wisdom, the god-teachings, the secret doctrine.

In getting this idea, this conception that truth, reality, has been communicated to mankind, that it is now on earth ready for us when we prove ourselves ready for it and worthy of it, we understand that it is traditional, that it has been given forth in larger or smaller measure and in varying manners from age to age by the greatest men, the titan intellects, of the human race; and therefore that this tradition, this Qabbālāh, this Brahma-vidyā, can be found in all the great religions and philosophies of the ages.

In accepting this view, you lose sight of the mere author of whatever book may be in your hands. You forget the personality, the individuality of the teacher, and you look to what he brings. If he is genuine you find, not the vague frontiers upon which structures of falsity may be erected by scheming minds; but you understand that here is a glorious and mighty tradition coming down to us from the universe, from the heart of Divinity.

It is this tradition, this secret doctrine, which gave to H. P. Blavatsky the title of her masterpiece; and it was for this same reason that I chose these actual words, the esoteric tradition, as the title of my latest book. It is esoteric because few have as yet understood it; it is traditional because it has been handed down from immemorial time. Thus *The Esoteric Tradition* is an attempt, feeble it may be, but very honest and sincere, to do what our teachers are trying to do with us: to instill into our hearts and minds a reverence for and a worship of the truth before us; to awaken in our hearts the divine fire of love for all that is, which becomes constricted and restricted and usually degraded when it is fastened solely on an individual accepted as a teacher.

The suggestion in the title of this book is that a teacher should receive reverence, but only in so far as his teaching is truth. In losing sight of the person, you see the message. Is there not need of just this touchstone, particularly in the Theosophical movement today? Is it not absolutely accordant with all that H. P. Blavatsky taught us: to look within, to look up, to forget yet to revere the hand which gives, to take the message? Inspect it; take from it what you find good; reject the balance if you wish. You may make a mistake in so doing, but you are exercising your prerogative of choice, of discrimination, of intuition. By so exercising it you give it strength; and as time passes it will grow very powerful, and you will then take back the cornerstone which you rejected, and in so doing you will receive the teacher with the teaching in your hearts, and in the proper way.

One lesson I have learned: that it is the teaching and its magic working upon me which counts; for when the teaching enters my heart my reverence for the communicator grows. Is not your reverence for the masters infinitely greater when you realize that they awaken in us the noblest and best? It is just this noblest and best in us which, when awakened, enables us to see them. And that is what they want: not to have us see them, but to have us awake, our hearts beating in steady rhythm with the heartbeat of the universal heart, and our minds fired with the truth which they communicate to us and which we value precisely in proportion as it is impersonal.

I think the Theosophical movement will suffer from no more fakers, no more false teachers, now or in the future, provided we can remember that the touchstone of anything that may be offered to us for a teaching is universality, and the appeal to the conscience, the appeal to the voice within.

Where the Masters Work

Do THE MASTERS HELP, inspire others than theosophists, than the Theosophical Society? I should be awfully ashamed of any theosophist who could not answer that question instantly. Of course they do! Why, it is one of our A B C thoughts, teachings, that the masters aid and help and inspire anywhere where there is an open door to their entrance, in other words, where the soul is not surrounded with impassable frontiers, keeping the light out, the help away. Why of course! And if the masters' influence were not felt in other organizations than the T.S., as indeed it may be felt, it would be in this case because they had lost touch, had enclosed themselves with the impassable barriers of the frontiers of thought and feelings. The truth is that the masters work *anywhere* where the doors are opened to their entrance, and where the conditions propitious for their work exist.

Just take one thought which has been one of the dreams of my life from childhood. If the Christian church or churches could go back to the *original* teachings of their great master, to really primitive Christianity, the masters would be working through them as one of the greatest channels in the West today to help men. And if they don't so work therein, it will be because the help is barred out by frontiers of thought and feeling.

And the T.S. — as I have often pointed out, it will depend upon us whether the masters continue to work through it as an instrument as now they are doing, or abandon it. They will never abandon us as long as we keep our hearts and minds open; but if we begin to put frontiers around our consciousness, *we* do the work of exclusion, not they. The gods, said the old Greeks, visit the houses of those who open doors to them. Think what that means. Why not try to entertain divine and divinely human guests?

The whole trouble with us and with civilization is that we build these frontiers around us. They are not placed there by nature. They are built by ourselves, frontiers of exclusion in thought, in feeling, in tradition, in everything. What happens to the man who shuts himself up in a cell and lives there? Who loses? The world, or the foolish man? Such a cell is a frontier of consciousness. And the man (or the civilization) is great precisely in proportion as he can break through the barriers, the frontiers, with which habit and custom and he himself have surrounded himself, and move out to ever loftier houses of consciousness, ever receding frontiers of consciousness.

What makes a religion successful? The building around itself of frontiers of thought, frontiers, barriers of exclusion? Why of course not. The answer is obvious. Destroy the barriers, the door is open to all.

Prayer and Aspiration

WHEN WE ARE ASKED the question "Do theosophists pray?" I for one answer yes and no; it depends upon what the questioner means by prayer. If he means getting down on bended knee and addressing a petition to a god outside of himself, purely imaginary, which the intellect has enormous labor in attempting to conceive of, and therefore which is not instinctive in the human heart as a reality, then we must answer: no, not prayer of that type. That is an abdication of the god within the individual denying its own rights and appealing for help outside itself. That is mere supplication, mere petitioning, a mere begging for benefits. It is purely exoteric.

True prayer is the rich, deep, spiritual humility of the human self envisioning the ineffably grand. It is a yearning to become like the heavenly Father, as Jesus phrased it; yearning to become a son of the divine. It is almost a command of the man to himself to arise and pass on to higher things, upwards towards the divine, of which a spark pulsates in every human soul. When we come into sympathetic relationship, into identic vibrational frequency, with this inner heartbeat, this pulsing of the divine, then our lives are made over; we are completely reformed. We become no longer mere men begging for favors, and thereby weakening ourselves; we begin to recognize our identity with the divine. Dignity steals over us and enfolds us like a garment. And what prayer is nobler than this: for the son to yearn to become like unto its divine parent?

I, for my own part, never sleep at night, never arise from my bed in the morning, until at least once I have raised myself and attained the experience. And prayer of this kind is not merely an attitude of mind. It is a way of life, a way of living, clothing him who falls in love with it, and follows it, with dignity, enriching his mind with understanding, making him sympathetic to all else that lives.

> He prayeth best who loveth best
> All things both great and small.

Yes, for this is a becoming at one with all around us. It simply means progressively making your consciousness greater, expanding every day a little more, to include a little more, to encompass, to embrace a little more of the world around us. Our consciousness, after this way of prayer, of living, of thinking, of feeling, grows ever larger, until finally some day we shall be in our thoughts and feelings able to encompass the universe. Then no longer shall we be merely men; we shall be god-men, and after we die we shall take our place with the gods, the cosmic spirits, archangels, angels, powers — if you like the Christian phrase.

What is the difference between the ordinary man and the genius? The ordinary man is one who lives in the small, circumscribed shell of personal consciousness; he cannot go beyond it. He has no intuition, no inspirations. The man of genius is the man who has broken this shell. He wanders out in consciousness and feeling to the surrounding universe. He vibrates in synchronous frequency with the universe around him, and then come inspiration and marvelous ideas. He sees, he feels — and men say, "A genius has arisen."

This then is the prayer that puts us in touch with all things. It gives us qualities that have been latent in us before but now have an opportunity to evolve, to unroll, to expand. And by true prayer we mean not only enlarging the personal consciousness towards becoming at one with the universal consciousness, but putting this experience into practice. And this is a pleasure just as exquisite: to practice what we preach. Otherwise we are but as tinkling cymbals and the rolling bellow of empty drums — *Vox et praeterea nihil*, "A voice and nothing more." But when you *practice* prayer, then you reinforce your own powers by exercise. What you have yourself felt, you begin to practice. You see the light of understanding flash in the eyes of others, a new and secret sympathy springing up between man and man. It is a new life force. This kind of prayer is likewise a way of life; it is likewise science; it is philosophy; it is religion.

We are children of the infinite, of the divine. Our deity is intracosmic and yet transcendent, in the same way as a man is not only his physical body, and not only his mind or his spirit. He is body and feelings and emotions and mind and soul; but above these he is transcendent; there is something in him which is greater than all this. That is the spark of the divine, the spark by which man is linked with the invisible, with divinity. That spark is the most important, the most powerful element in us. It is the predominating and governing factor in our destiny, and if we want to grow grander and greater and nobler and higher, we have to raise ourselves up towards that spark, we have to raise ourselves by living what we know. And then our life will become grand. And finally, when practice has become relatively perfect, the vision of genius will steal into the mind. For genius is cosmic wisdom. With genius, understanding grows and grows, and finally we begin to realize that we are not merely a person with perhaps a postmortem life in heaven or hell, but that our destiny is the destiny of the infinite All: that we are endless, coeval with duration, with cosmic time, that the boundless universe is our home; that we are here on earth merely for a day-night; that this is just a phase in our evolutionary journey upwards and onwards.

This is what we aspire towards, this is what we pray for: an ever enlarging consciousness by aspiration, by study, by living the life we profess — an ever enlarging consciousness towards that ultimate, a unity with the divine. We pass through all the kingdoms of nature, grow from being a man to becoming a superman; from a superman becoming a demigod; from demi-godhood to godhood, to supergodhood, and so on and up the endless ladders of life. What a marvel! What a conception!

That divine spirit of which we speak so glibly — because it does represent an intuition, an answer to that yearning, that ineffable hunger within every normal man — that divinity we realize is but our human conception of something still more wonderful, vaster, and that we can never reach an end; that it is growth and advance and enlarging genius of consciousness forever and forever.

Do theosophists pray? In the way that we try to make our daily lives a prayer in action. We have the Ariadne's thread, we have the key, and we are trying to use it. And do you know what this key is? It is the god-wisdom. And do you know what the lock is? It is we ourselves, taking this key. By inserting it into our own consciousness, turning it however slightly, magic streams forth from the slightly open door, from the ineffable mysteries hidden within, drawn from the cosmic font. No one can ever name it. It is nameless. Names but degrade it. Aspiration towards it always and forever — that is prayer. By living it we grow. What hope and what peace! What increase of understanding comes to one who from within himself, from his own consciousness, has got the end of the Ariadne's thread. This, in its steadily progressing stages of experience and growth, is what we call initiation.

The Only Way Out

MODERN MEN AND WOMEN, both older and younger, form a generation which we can, I believe, adequately describe as a lost generation; and the cause of it, the reason for our mental wanderings and emotional gropings, is the loss of our understanding and hold of a common or universally accepted ethical and intellectual standard. This is shown by the babel of voices surrounding us everywhere, by the hungry human hearts, and even by the eager human minds searching for truth and not knowing where to find it, nor its guidance: human minds searching for a sufficient and satisfying inner light, for something that will guide us in solving the problems facing us. We *are*, indeed, a lost generation, and it is not the youth only who are "lost"; in fact it is the elders who are even more perplexed than are the youth of today. Our whole generation is blind, walking in darkness, not knowing whither to turn for the longed-for light; and the babel of voices that arises from the immense human crowd is something frightening and significant in its clamor and confused insistence upon panaceas and nostrums of various kinds, political and otherwise.

One hearkens vainly while lending an ear to this turbulent babel, which too often is mere babble, in order to find constructive suggestions which are of universal application. It is rare indeed to hear voices speaking with the authority of knowledge; and I will venture to suggest the reason of it all.

If there is a common struggle or fight in progress and you go down into the arena of turmoil intending to fight those already fighting there and to outshout them, the chances are small that what you have to say will receive attention; the probability is that you are going to be hurt. This is because the would-be reformer simply descends to the level of the shouting squabblers. Such is not the manner by which to bring about anything that is universally and definitely constructive in idea, or attractively new or helpful, or that will explain and solve the problems causing the universal disturbance. You are simply descending into the battle yourself, trying to overcome violence with violence, force with force; and this procedure never has succeeded, and it never will.

This does not mean to imply that force is always to be ignored in human relations. Sometimes it is necessary wisely albeit kindly to use force, but always without violence, and in order to overcome an evil. Such employment of force or power should always be a merely temporary event or procedure, and should never be used save in an impersonal and upright manner, and for a good cause, and for the common weal. Justice to all is never gained by descending into the arena of battle and "fighting it out" there. Justice is rarely gathered into pockets, so to say; and very rarely indeed is it wholly on one side of a question.

Our generation is lost, intellectually and morally, because it has lost its vision. Without a vision the people perish — an old Hebrew saying based on a comprehensive view of human psychology as demonstrated in history, and therefore a saying which is full with truth. It is invariably a vision or an idea, or a body of ideas, which guides men upwards to glory or downwards to the pit. Plato was fully right: it is ideas which make or unmake civilizations, build up or overthrow established institutions; and it is grandly universal ideas, and the *will* to follow them — ideas and ideals which all men feel to be true — which men today lack. It is just because we today lack vision, an inner knowledge of the right thing to do, of a clear way out of our troubles, that as nations we are where we now are.

We are presently at the end of one form of civilization which, like the Roman Empire in its time, has reached its term, its breaking up, and we are facing the opening measures of the cosmic drama which is now coming in. It will depend upon the innate wisdom and sense of high justice inherent in men's hearts and minds, whether our present civilization will go down in blood and despair, or whether it will take breath and time in order to recover itself; whether, with the dawning of a new intellectual and moral perception of justice and reason, it will stop its descent down the declivity and begin to rise to new heights overtopping the finest that as yet racially we have attained. This latter can be done; and it is man's higher nature only, his intuitions and instincts for justice and reason, nothing else, that will bring it to pass with surety: man's innate sense of justice and of right, and the common recognition that reason and not violence is the way out — and upwards to safety, peace, and progress.

History with its silent but tremendously powerful voice shows us that there is absolutely no other way out for us; that there is no other complete solution, nor one which will be satisfactory to all types of minds, to all types of human character. Freedom for all; each people seeking its own salvation on its own lines, but in ethical directions accompanied by reason and a desire to do justice. Even an enlightened self-interest, with its always keen eye for individual advantage, must see the universal benefits and securities of such a plan. All stable institutions are founded on these intuitions and instincts, and upon naught else; for were it otherwise, then our sense of order and law, our very respect for our courts of law, international or national, were collectively a monstrous deception, and an ignominious and miserable farce; and all sane men realize that our laws are based on the rules of justice and impartial reason, tempered with impersonal mercy.

I am not one of those gloomy pessimists who say that man is but a poor worm, with instincts born of his association with dust, and intuitions that are unfounded in fact, and that therefore he cannot solve his problems adequately. He can solve them if he has the *will* to do so. We are indeed approaching the end of our civilization, and are fascinated and hold our breath as we watch the phenomena of its breaking up; but all too often we forget that this has been a civilization of matter almost wholly, where things of matter often counted as the only ones permanently worth while. There are no longer new lands to which we may send our young people to colonize, for they all have been preempted or taken. The rule of force and of material values has prevailed almost universally, rather than the rules of international justice and common human rights. For eighteen hundred years, more or less, it has been the rule: let everyone grab what he may; let everyone hold what he can. The conduct of the peoples of the earth has been largely based on this purely materialistic and selfish foundation. We sowed the wind; we are now as a body of spiritually bankrupt peoples reaping the whirlwind.

Is it not time that the more farseeing and superior minds of the world should see to it that calmness and reason and impartial justice shall henceforth prevail? Is there any other and better way out of our troubles and difficulties than by solving them wisely? If men deliberately refuse to listen to reason, if men deliberately refuse to wish or to *will* to do justice, then it seems certain that down we shall go, and our civilization, our great cities and the manifold works and labors of millions of hands through the years, shall be dust and ruined heaps. No god will step into the arena of human pain and willful ignorance and pull us wretched mortals out of the world mess that we have created for ourselves, mostly through rabid self-interest and through our willful turning away from the paths of justice and peace. We alone must save ourselves; and when we begin to do this in the manner pleasing to the higher powers, then we shall make an undeniable appeal for their aid and guidance; and we shall receive it. Hercules helps the wagoner, indeed; but only when the wagoner begins to help himself — and *in the right way.*

It is the sheerest foolishness and the most blatant of all ethical and intellectual poppycock to aver that man's destiny, now that the waste places of the earth have been taken, is blocked; that there is no future for those who were not in at the beginning. Such an attitude is contradicted by every page in the annals of universal history. We must remember that no thing, no institution, is unchangeable, eternally the same; and that the shifting and continuously varying scenes of human history in the past — a certain fact of truth — promise that the future will be as full as the past has been with the shifting of cosmic scenery, and the changing of human interests and fields of activity. The greatest peoples of the earth have not been those possessing the greatest extent of territory, but precisely those who have been foremost in the reception of ideas and in the application of progressive ideas to the upbuilding of human institutions based on and usually proclaiming, if not, alas, always following, the ideals of impersonal justice and trained reason; for these are spiritual qualities — which in fact are universal.

Let us fill our hearts with eternal gratitude to the watching though silent cosmic powers, that the horizons now before us in all parts of the earth, and without distinction of race or creed, are spiritual and intellectual horizons, beyond which there are for us unknown regions of infinitely vast extent waiting conquest by human genius, when we shall give rein to the instincts and intuitions of the soul. Look then at what lies before us if we *will* to bring justice unmotivated by self-interest and the love of honor and truth to work amongst us!

One of the main causes, and perhaps the foremost, of our troubles both national and international is that men commonly — with many grand exceptions — are still holding to the belief in force, in violence, as being the way to solve our troubles. Such procedure never has succeeded permanently, and never

will. Violence breeds violence; violence grows by violence.
Hatred breeds hatred; selfishness breeds other selfishness.

It is one of the objectives, let me say duties, of the Theosophical movement to show men the simple precepts of reason;
that life should be governed by the grand ethical instincts of
the human soul, which are based on no human conventions but
on the orderliness of nature's own structure and processes. Out
of these ethical instincts spring the directing precepts of reason
and our will to do justice, teaching us that the way out lies
within ourselves: not in our armies or in our navies, or in all
the dreadful methods of mutual destruction which man's evil
genius has invented. These last are not even temporary remedies
and bring no satisfactory adjusting of troubles. At best, the
machinery of defense should be used as police machines; for
then their use becomes justified, because then they would be
employed in the cause of justice and used with reason only.

Our problems will never be solved by our mad rush in
competitive armament, bringing about universal distrust, fear,
anxiety, and crushing the peoples with taxation which threatens to grow beyond their power to meet, and almost making
them hate the conditions under which they live their lives. It
is the old folly, now recognized by all, to argue that by piling
up armaments and inventing new devices of horrible destruction, and by increasing the use of violent force, by and by war
will become so horrible that men will shrink in fearsome terror
from it. Of all the fallacies and stupid arguments, this is the
worst that has ever been inflicted on the suffering minds of
mankind.

You will never succeed in stopping war by organizing yourselves into associations or societies swearing to refuse service to
your government, and defying it in case of war. That procedure,
in my judgment, is abominably wrong. We may admire the
idealistic courage and ideal thoughts of the young men and
women who, it seems, are doing this. But they overlook the fact

that they are merely announcing their declaration to declare war of a kind upon their own government and country, if war should come, thereby introducing disorder and strife among themselves.

Let the youth of the different peoples of whatever country set the example of fidelity and loyalty, each youth to his own government, thus proving the strength and worth of the moral ideal of citizenship; yet, on the other hand, as the world badly needs the idealisms and chivalry resident in the younger generation, let youth express these likewise by raising its voice loud and insistent, powerfully declaring itself for universal justice and reason, and do so by the measures of established law. In this manner, the voice of the world's youth will penetrate into all places, closed and open; for their insistence upon their rights as the coming generation soon to shoulder the burden of the older, will reach sympathetic ears too numerous to count. *Novus ordo seclorum!*

I should like to see complete disarmament of the peoples take place, by mutual compact and convention, to be replaced by an international navy, officered and manned by men drawn in rotation from the different maritime or even inland peoples of the globe, and trained for this purpose. I should like to see the armies of the world reduced to relatively small national police forces solely. The duties of the international navy would be the policing of the seas, the repressing of piracy, and the making of the high seas and coastal waterways safe for the commerce of the peoples of the world. There is not one thing to prevent this double achievement of constructive genius — except a psychology which everyone detests and all fear: a psychology that has merely grown up to be a habit of human thinking.

One may pray and hope that the prominent men in the world today, those who hold the destinies of the peoples more or less in their hands, will hearken to the heartbeat, the unexpressed and growing will of the peoples for a permanent solving of their troubles. If they do so, these men will go down in history; they will be remembered not so much by statues and monuments in stone, but their names will be emblazoned in perpetuity in the perduring fabric of human hearts. Their memory shall remain for ages to come as the fire of love and gratitude burning in human hearts.

Again I repeat: a brotherhood of the peoples based on reason and justice and functioning for the common good, for the progress of all, is both practicable and practical, and will some day be seen to be inevitable. Why not therefore lay the foundations of it NOW!

Where Two or Three Are Gathered . . .

THERE IS AN OLD SAYING that where two or three are gathered together in my name, that is, in the company of the spirit, the spirit is present with these two or three.

There is a great occult truth in this, and if you will multiply the two or three fiftyfold or one hundredfold, and realize, or try to realize, that the force of a unified spiritual will and understanding can do much good in the world, and keep this before you as an ideal of help and comfort, then I think you will feel with me that it is not merely for ourselves that we gather together in theosophical meetings for consolation and comfort and light, but that wherever these meetings are held we gather together as aspirants to join the highest elements of the human race.

In these words there lies more perhaps than may appear on the surface.

The Direct Road to Wisdom

JUST WHAT IS THE DIRECT ROAD to wisdom? I think that this is the most important topic of thought that can be addressed today. Is anyone able clearly to define just what this direct road to wisdom is, as contrasted with what I may call the indirect road?

The indirect road may otherwise be described as the road leading into our consciousness from outside of ourselves: the road of instruction, the usual way of the churches and the lecture halls; helpful perhaps, stimulating it may be, to certain minds at times; but can we really define this road or path as the road to *wisdom?*

The direct road to wisdom is the road or path of inner light, understanding, arising from inner striving and experience; and it has been outlined, at least briefly, by every one of the great teachers of the human race. It might otherwise be described in mystical phrasing as achieved when the man himself becomes at one — more or less in fullness — with the god within himself. This is the direct road.

What ails the world today? What is the cause of its manifold inner troubles, of its hesitancies, of its loss of confidence? The answer lies in the fact that men are largely inwardly empty; they are, as multitudes and as individuals, relatively empty vessels: there is no inner fullness from which to give to others, no inner and filled richness of understanding through and by which we may receive and solve the problems confronting humanity, and thus wisely help ourselves and others. Instead of the unity and understanding of action which would accrue from such inner richness, there is opposition, strife, quarreling, and the inevitable consequent wretchedness combined with galling poverty and keen pain. Hence I say that the inner spiritual richness arising in an inner unity of life is the direct path to wisdom, for all that makes life worth while and grand is there.

Most men and women are unensouled, or relatively so. This does not mean that they have no souls, or that they are "lost souls." It means rather that the soul within is not showing through us and in our lives its transcendent powers. Keep ever in mind that the spiritual soul is within-above us, attempting always to inspire and to infill our lives and thus make them rich and strong and full and beautiful. But most people are not thus ensouled. "We elbow soulless people at every turn," as H. P. Blavatsky pointed out. More than anything else it is the duty, the high and lofty labor and privilege, of the Theosophical Society to help to recall to thinking men and women the realization and the assurance of the fact that they are and should be ensouled beings.

How this, if achieved in multitudes of our fellows, would change the face of the earth! Everything would change. Happiness would come to replace unhappiness; peace would replace strife, understanding and mutual consideration would replace the hatreds and contempts which now disgrace us all. For men would be infilled with the inner light, with the inner power, bringing understanding and mutual sympathy and kindliness and instinctive brotherhood; and there would be a universal yearning for peace and goodwill.

The majority of men and women today, being unensouled, are empty vessels, instead of filled ones — filled with inner power and light. Instead of being guided by the spirit within, and by its irresistible mandates, they follow brain-mind schemes of selfish considerations. It is always: "Number one, and the devil take the hindmost."

Now the indirect way to wisdom does help no doubt to change these conditions. To be just, one must say that it is perhaps helpful to certain weak and stumbling ones. But it is devious and roundabout. It lies in trying to receive things of spiritual and intellectual value from outside of us alone, without the attempt to arouse them in ourselves. We treasure these gifts from without perhaps; and this is good. Yet they are but feeble staves in the hands of us pilgrims. The staves are not strong. But once the inner life, once the emptiness within, is filled with the richness and holy power of the spiritual Reality within us, then we have wisdom: we *know*.

It is said of H.P.Blavatsky that once when she returned from taking exercise after her morning's work, she had tears streaming down her face and walked the floor of her room in a perfect torture of inner agony. The reason of it came out afterwards: "Oh, they are unensouled, these multitudes. In their faces are emptiness, prejudice, ignorance, lack of knowledge, lack of wisdom. They yearn, they hunt for truth, they cry in vain, they attempt to fill the aching void from outside instead of from the perennial springs of inspiration within their hearts!"

To do our utmost to fill this emptiness in human hearts, more than anything else I believe to be our duty: to teach men the direct path to wisdom, to make the inner emptiness a filled richness, a richness of wisdom and of quick and understanding sympathy, so that by it their lives may become grand and strong and true. Then we shall work justice, and gentle reason will preside in all our doings. Much if not all of human ignorance will then have fled; the light of wisdom will guide our steps.

What Is Old Age?

WHAT IS OLD AGE, the scientific rationale of old age? Disease as everyone knows is disobedience to the laws of nature, the laws of health, of which disobedience we are all guilty more or less. And death is simply the withdrawal of the finer powers from this physical plane in order that the peregrinating ego may journey on in its egoic fullness to other adventures when the call and attraction of this earth have temporarily ceased. Books could be written on just these two points. But, after all, what is old age?

First, have you ever wondered about a very simple fact, that most human beings die more or less within a certain framework or cadre of years? Barring disease and accident, the average life span is pretty much the same all over the world: we don't live to be a thousand years old, and unless we are taken away to the other spheres by accident or disease of some kind, we live more than ten days or one hundred days. Why is it that the average life span for the average human being is something between fifty years and eighty; let us say one hundred, if you will? It is still so short. Now why is it? Are we just like sheep that we accept a fact because it happens and don't think about it and ask ourselves why it is? Why should the turtle or tortoise live to be nearly two hundred years, and we human beings are commonly reaped by the Angel of Death before we attain our one hundredth year? So rare is it for a man to go beyond the hundredth year in physical life, that they keep records of those exceptional cases where human beings have attained 105, or 130 or 140 years.

I will tell you what it is — it is habit: the habit that we have of acting and reacting in the evolutionary stage in which the human race finds itself at the present time. We talk about the planets and how they govern the life span of man. Perfectly true; but how is it that the planets allow a man to pass what might be called the critical period and continue living, and only take him when he may pass it again? He may have happened to pass it several times previously in a life. Why does it catch him at a certain time? These are facts, fascinating, interesting, and I ask you why. My answer is: it is a habit of nature due to our past karma, feelings, thoughts, our past thinking. We have framed for ourselves a framework of psychic and intellectual habit which causes the Angel of Death to call for us more or less within this short span of between one and seventy or a hundred years.

How did this habit arise? Was this habit always so? Will it ever be just the same? In other words, did our forebears of let us say 120 millions of years ago live to be only 50 or 60 or 70 years and then die? They did not. They lived to be several hundred years old; and you have records of this in all the scriptures of antiquity, as for instance in the Jewish Bible when Methuselah lived to be 900 odd. Now I think that is an exaggeration, but it is an illustration and we can let it pass. And then the days of men were shortened on the earth because they sought evil and loved evil and its hot and fetid breath; and as evil is an increase of the vital tempo, the vital reservoir is exhausted before its normal time. So the lives of men were shortened. It is a true explanation, and when the human race through millions of years acquires a psychic habit, the very atoms of man's body respond to that habit, obey it. So it is with all kinds of habits, such as waking every morning at a certain hour. One can get a habit of overfeeding or starving himself. He can get all sorts of habits; and every thoughtful physician knows perfectly well the physiological habits that the body automatically follows in birth, in healing, even in disease.

However, that does not still quite answer the question: why is it that man lives a life of only 80 to 100 years, which is so short compared with endless time? Just a brief flash, and gone! Look at the stars, consider even the other creatures on the earth, many of them much more long-lived than we humans are. Why should it be just so? Now here is some occultism which, whatever you may think of it, happens to be true. This habit was acquired not only because of our past karma, which means the things we did and the thoughts we had and the feelings we underwent and followed, or did not follow, in all our past series of lives; but it also means that the human race in its evolutionary journey towards a far greater perfection than that which now it has, is only at about the middle point of this evolutionary journey of what theosophists call our planetary chain. In other words, it has reached in its series of seven rounds just a little past the central point which is the point farthest down in matter. The call of physical stuff is therefore the strongest.

Now then, if you watch old age you will notice several things: that in the cases of those whose old age is the most beautiful, they never lose their powers until within a few days or a week or so of death. Their powers remain intact, not the bodily ones because the body is aging rapidly, but the real powers which make a man man. Merely to have a physically strong body is not the mark of a true man. Sometimes gross animals have bodies that are far stronger than those of the highly intellectual civilized human. It is the powers within that make us human beings, and it is these powers that the finest old age retains, because these men and women are the finest, the most evolved at the present time. It is as if, because of this fineness of evolutionary status even at the present time, they took tentative steps ahead of the race into the future and its greater glory, and could retain this evolutionary forerunning until death came — forerunners, as it were, of the racial habit.

We are at present in what we call the fourth round, just

about at its central and lowest point. When we have reached the fifth round, death then will not come so quickly; the human life span will be far longer than the three score years and ten which the Hebrew Bible gives us as the normal span of human life. When we shall have reached the sixth round, the life span will be still longer. When we shall have reached the seventh and last round for this planetary imbodiment, the span of life will then be at its longest, there will be no old age, there will be no future for that particular planetary chain, no best men as it were who could step a little ahead of the norm, for all men will retain their faculties until death comes. During this seventh round the human race will have become relatively a race of Buddhas or Christs. Death, as the Christian system has it, the last enemy to overcome, will then have been conquered, disease will be nonexistent, for human beings then will live by a habit that is absolutely in accordance with the laws of nature; and what we call death will be simply a falling asleep, to awaken in higher realms. I mean just that — no wrench as at present, whether the wrench be kindly or harsh, but simply a falling asleep.

So you see, we look forward to the future millions and millions and millions of years hence, when man's life will again be several hundreds of years long, when health will be his in relative perfection, because all the laws of nature will become automatically obeyed by mankind. And death when it comes will come like a gentle sleep when there is release into the inner worlds; or, if you wish, in those days human beings will step out of their bodies at will, leave them behind if they are tired, and take a new body at will, or go on into other spheres, for we then shall be conquerors of death. There will be no death as we understand it. That is what evolution has for us in the future — a wondrous picture! Then, instead of old age, men will be in fullest possession of their faculties, not merely physical powers such as they have at, let us say, forty-five; but their intellect, their spirituality, their vision and their mind, will be at their highest. That happens even today occasionally amongst the finest exemplars of the human race, those who are a little ahead of their evolving brothers trailing along behind them. They intuit, they have intuitions, as it were, like a child taking tentative steps towards something still unknown. Nature pushes them ahead so that their old age is a picture of what the future will be for all men, visions of the future casting their shadows back to us here.

We approach old age now as we do because of our pasts; but in those far distant aeons we can say the older a man grows, the stronger and more powerful he becomes in everything about him, even his body. But we have not reached that yet! Our old age is a copying in us in the small, of all that the race has attained up to the present time. It has become a racial habit.

I will point out something else: mere physical old age is by no means something to long for. When you think what the old age of so many millions of human beings is, it is pitiful — the loss of intellectual power, the loss of spirituality, the loss of course of the physical powers, the loss of the psychological insights, and the loss of the mind to a large extent; and yet they live on because the physical vitality is so strong. Who wants that? The ideal old age, which we can strive for even now and gain in proportion to our effort, is to face death when it comes with joy, for it is the beginning of a marvelous adventure; and from birth until the time of its coming so to live, so to think and to feel and to aspire, that while the body inevitably will become more or less enfeebled as old age comes upon us, the mind remains unimpaired, spirituality grows and glorifies what is so inadequately called the sunset years. This is the ideal of old age: a man increasing in inner power, in inner vision, in mind power, in intellect, in spirituality; so that up to even a few hours of his death, he is with every advancing day a bigger man than he was the day before or the year before. It is no impossible ideal. Live aright. The guerdon is such.

Yet there are karmic things in the lives of many people which bring about disease, disease which can be traced back far into past lives. Therefore in these things we should do wisely to remember the fine old rule: Judge not your brother lest you be judged. You never know but what your brother may be going through some terrific retribution in this life for a misdeed let us say ten lives back which, like a seed of trouble lying hid, is now blossoming. Judge him not, he may be far ahead of you — when once this life is ended he may have a new body and a new karma far better than anything you could look forward to.

We have many mountain ranges of experiences still to climb, but what joy there is in all this wonderful adventure. Look at the future imbodiments in all kinds of races, and in all kinds of lands, some of them to come up above the surface of the waters, as ours then will have sunken or be submerged: new lands, new languages, new experiences, new adventures, and always going onwards and upwards, and always growing better.

But here is a consolation for present conditions: that the race as a whole has passed the central point. From now on it will go no longer downwards into matter, but will be on the slow climb upwards to the very end of time for this earth. Death will be no more, and this evolutionary habit which the human race is in at the present time and which limits the life span to its ridiculously small number of years will have changed. Death will have vanished, birth will be brought about in other ways. Human genius will confabulate with the gods. Inspiration will be the common heritage of all men. There will then be no more poverty, no more suffering, no more sorrow; for the sun of truth will have risen in men's hearts with healing in its wings!

Work Out Your Own Salvation

THIS IS THE TEACHING of the great sages and seers of all the ages: work out your own salvation. Exercise the powers within you with which you are endowed. Does the fact that we are bewildered and often troubled with questions of conscience signify that we have been left without guidance? Don't you see that this very fact is a call to us by nature to exercise the powers latent within us? By the exercise of judgment and discrimination, judgment and discrimination grow stronger. If we do not exercise our own godlike right of spiritual and intellectual judgment we grow weaker and weaker. It is by this exercise that we evolve, bring forth ever more the godlike powers within us.

Look at the great, the magnificent examples of human spirituality and genius with which the annals of human history are built. These are indeed glorious and give us courage and show us how, since others have attained, so may we. These are signposts along that mystic path leading to the mountains of the spirit. But it is we ourselves who must tread that path, and we ourselves who must make our own judgments and abide by them. Just there is their great beauty.

As ye sow, ye shall reap — not something else than what you have sown. Think what this means. When men become convinced of this, their judgment will be broadened; they won't leap to points of conclusion, they will not lean negatively on others and thereby weaken their own judgment because no call is made upon it. They will accept the magnificent examples of human history as encouragements. "What he has done as a son of man, that also may I do by exercising within me the same powers that that grand figure of human history exercised." Their lives are a perennial example for us. But it is we ourselves who must grow, and by exercising our powers we do grow; and with each exercise the discrimination becomes more keen, the judgment becomes more sure, the light brighter. Then when the test comes we know which way to go.

The Touchstone of Truth

How CAN YOU KNOW any facts about the after-death state? Too often in a question like this there lies latent the supposition that knowledge of things which are not visible cannot be had — not visible, not attainable. Of all the follies that the human mind is unfortunately addicted to! If you study the history of religion, of philosophy, of science, you will discover that a frequent disinclination to recognize facts is one of the saddest traits of human nature. Think a moment: the things which you can touch and see are precisely the things which are the most misleading because first you have your senses with their imperfections to contend with — touch, sight, hearing, etc. — and then from these imperfect organs of report to the mind, the mind itself is not a perfect instrument of judgment when it has to make deductions.

But there is something in the human being which can know at first hand. Call it the spirit, call it the intuition, call it by whatever name you like. The fact remains that the only knowledge you can ever trust is not in what you can touch and see, but what comes to you from within. You do not know anything except that. Other things you have ideas about, or you read the ideas of other men.

Do you realize that practically every great discovery that has ever been made, in science or out of it, in any field of human endeavor, has come from some man who has been thus inspired? And when he gives this wondrous gift to the race, the race is elevated. Every such gift has been brought forth by man's inner genius. Every great invention has been a flash of inspiration first; first the idea, and then perhaps years of work in bringing it forth and in persuading others to understand it.

You can know truth by that power within. But if you want to find that power then you will indeed have to do a lot of hard work.

To Those Who Mourn

THE BEAUTIFUL MESSAGE that theosophy has to give to those who mourn, those who sorrow, applies not only to death and those left behind by the passing ones, but just as much to those who are not yet touched by death, to all those who have to live on this earth where there is more of sorrow and trouble and weariness of spirit than of happiness and real peace. For I wonder if any tender-hearted man or woman can really be happy in a world like ours, when we see surrounding us on all sides the most awful proofs of man's inhumanity to his fellowmen. How can we retire into our watertight or spirit-tight or heart-tight compartments of life when we know what is going on around us, not only among humanity, but among the helpless beasts: suffering and pain and sorrow, and on every side the cry of these martyrs raised to heaven!

We talk about those who mourn and restrict it, each one of us, to our individual selves. How then? Do we not love the hand of kindliness extended in sympathy and understanding to others, who sorrow in loneliness? Death itself is nothing to grieve over. We have been through death a thousand times and more on this earth. We know it well. It is an old experience; and here we are back again. But we feel for those who mourn while they live: mourn for the loss of beloved ones; mourn for the loss of fortune, so that they are in difficulties to give even the physical bread to the bodies of those they love; mourn over the difficulties to find work so that they may work like men and women and feed the mouths of their hungry children; mourn because they have lost friendship, lost love, lost hope and, perhaps most awful of all, lost trust in their fellowmen.

Every son and daughter of man mourns, or he or she is heartless. The man who cannot mourn and who does not mourn to my mind is inhuman; and so great and wonderfully is nature built that it is precisely this divine capacity for mourning that gives us sympathy for others, and to the mourners the hearts of understanding; and, strange magic of the human spirit, mourning, sorrow, suffering is our wisest friend. How these enrich our hearts! What priceless treasury is the expansion of consciousness that comes when mourning sets its often burning but always healing hand on our hearts. We sacrifice; but in this sacrifice is purification, is the awakening to the greater life. It is in sorrow, it is in mourning, it is in the evocation by these of pity, of compassion, that we learn truly to live. Even little children know what sorrow is, and how blessed it is for them that they may learn life's greatest thing: to learn and become enlarged by it, made grander by it.

How pitiful is the man who cannot feel for others and is enwrapped solely in the small prison of his minuscule self. Where in him is grandeur? You seek for it and find it not. But the man who has suffered feels for all the world. On his heart each cry of mourning falls like a scalding tear, and he is made grand by it. Nature here works a magic, for in this process is born rosy hope, a starlighted inspiration that comes from the enlarged consciousness.

Blessed peace, the most exquisite joy and happiness that human hearts and minds can bear, is the spiritual heritage of those whose hearts have been softened by suffering. They who never suffer are the hardhearted ones, unripe in their own restricted consciousness. The man who has never suffered knows not what peace is. He has never entered into it. The man who has never experienced sorrow knows not the surcease nor the blessedness that comes when quiet comes.

It is to those who mourn — which comprise really all the human race — that theosophy brings its ineffable doctrine of hope and peace, and this because it teaches us to understand. The French have a proverb: *Tout comprendre c'est tout pardonner*, the meaning of which is: if you *fully* understand you forgive all.

Isn't it clear to us that inner grandeur comes from enlargement, and that enlargement of our consciousness, of our understanding, and of our heart, comes from suffering? Joy too can bring the smile to our lips and the light of happiness to our eyes; but isn't it a mere truism that all of life's ordinary joys turn to ashes in the mouth? Isn't it also true that the joys of life all too often make us selfish? We grab the joys to us, afraid lest we lose them. These commonplace joys often narrow us. But fellow feeling, sympathy brought about by suffering, make the whole world kin. The man who has known naught but joy in life perhaps does not mind inflicting sorrow upon a fellow. He is not awakened. He does not understand. He is misled. He is ignorant. But the man or woman who has suffered, who has mourned, these are they who are great in their gentleness, who are great in their understanding because they comprehend, take in; they are enlarged, they are magnified. And the extreme of this is glorification in its true original sense: they become glorified, the next thing to god-men on earth.

So our blessed message to those who mourn is this: fear not the bright and holy flame. It will make you men and women, not mere males and females. What is the great and outstanding characteristic mark of the god-men who have come among us from time to time? It has been the understanding heart, so that they could speak to the woman in trouble and help; to the man in ignorance and bring him succor and peace; to the little children and bring understanding. For the great man's own simple heart speaks to the simple direct heart of the child before it has been sophisticated, spoiled by the falsities which it all too often learns as it grows up and has to unlearn in order to be truly a man, truly a woman.

To those who mourn comes the blessed gospel: let the holy

flame enter into your hearts as a visiting god. Treat it very friendly. Welcome it. Receive it as a guest; and that guest, sorrow-clad, will cast off the habiliments of mourning, and you will realize that you have been entertaining unawares a god. And that god is you. Then you have entered into your own.

The Giving of the Self

THERE IS NO FREEDOM so great, no happiness so large, so wide-reaching, as the giving of self in service. It is the hero who gives himself. If he did not give himself utterly, there would be no heroism in it. It is the giving which is heroic.

So is it with love. Where there is questioning about it — not uncertainty because uncertainty is always very natural in these things; one wishes to be sure — but where there is a question about the values involved, where there is a selfish searching of "what *I* want," there is no heroism, no love, no self-giving. There is not the ghost of a shadow of a chance there for the godlike, heroic quality of self-renunciation.

When the year begins, when it opens, the one mantram I always make to sound in my own heart and mind is this: a new year is opening. Can I give myself a little more than last year? I pity from my soul the man or woman who has not learned the exquisite joy of giving of the self. There is not anything on earth that equals it in beauty, in grandeur, in sublimity, and in the peace and richness it brings to both heart and mind.

Why Not Laugh at Yourself?

MANY PEOPLE TALK ABOUT the heroism of self-conquest — something with which we all agree; but I sometimes wonder if our ideas of heroic battling with ourselves are not just a wee bit hysteriac, even foolish! I do not mean the heroism part of it, but this lower self of us, poor little thing! It plays havoc with us all the time, simply because we identify ourselves with it and always try to fight it and make it as big as we are. Is it heroic to fight a ghost of our own making?

How about wise old Lao-tse? If you want to conquer your lower self, make it ashamed of itself, make it look ridiculous. Laugh at it; laugh at yourself. So long as you pay attention to something, you dignify it and put it on your own level; and then when you attempt to fight it you are actually fighting another part of yourself which really could be enormously useful.

I have heard it said: kill out the lower self. Well, suppose we could do that? We should then be most unfortunate beings; in fact, we should not be here. This lower self when kept in order is a good little beastie. It helps us. Our duty is simply to keep it in order. Now when a man has a fractious dog or a horse or a cat, or some other pet, whatever it may be, he does not kick it and beat it and hit it on the head in order to make it good. He would be apt to make it rebellious, cowardly, and vicious; he would be degrading it. Thus the lower self should be neither degraded nor clothed with the false dignity of an adversary erroneously raised to the position of the spiritual self. It should be kept in its place and treated with kindness, consideration, and courtesy, but always with a firm and governing hand. When the lower self begins to presume, then put it in its proper place, but neither by brutality nor by dignifying it nor by fighting it. Ridicule your lower self, and you will soon see the lower self reassuming its proper position because full of temporary shame and loss of dignity — loss of face, as the Chinese say.

Just so with the dog. Have you ever seen a dog stick its tail between its legs when you laugh at it? Dogs know when they are laughed at and it is one of the finest ways of handling a beast.

I do believe Lao-tse of China was wise in his statement which runs to the effect that one of the best ways of conquering a foe is to make him look ridiculous.

Now that does not work as between man and man, because it is often very harsh and cruel, the two being on the same level. You can hurt a human being horribly and unjustly by placing him in a false position through ridicule. No; but try it on yourself. The next time the lower self wants to tell you what to do, laugh at it; don't dignify it; don't give it position and power and strength by fighting it; on the other hand, do not abuse it or make it weak and vicious and cowardly. Put it in its proper place by ridicule and, indeed at times, a gentle contempt. Learn the greater heroism. Laugh at the thing which bothers you!

The role a sense of humor plays in life, which means in human thought and feeling and consequent conduct, and the role that humor plays in spiritual things is all too often overlooked. We may define a sense of humor as seeing the harmonious relations between apparently incongruous things, the congruities as among incongruities, arousing a sense of the funny in us.

The ability to see humor in what happens to ourselves is a spiritual attribute. After all, humor is at the very root of the universe; and I think that one of the greatest tragedies of individual existence has been the lack of the ability to see the funny side of things when troubles come. When disasters befall you, just try to see the funny side, and you not only save yourself in all likelihood a lot of trouble, but likewise you get a great kick out of it.

I remember the great kick I got out of a discussion between myself and my dear old father when I was a boy. My father had read an article in a theological magazine by some eminent Christian clergyman who pleaded for the existence of a sense of humor "in Almighty God." I said this was simply grand; because although our sense of humor is human, small because we are small, yet is it possible for a part, a human being, to have something which the almighty whole, which the divine, lacks? So of course if divinity has a sense of humor, I said, it is a sense of divine humor, but it is humor all the same.

There is a great deal of sound science and philosophy in the old Hindu idea that Brahman brought forth the universe in play, in fun. The words are different from those of the Christian clergyman, but the idea is the same. In other words, the bringing forth of all things was not a tragedy; there was beauty in it, there was harmony in it; there was humor in it; and those who are in this universe can see the humor in it if they will.

Look at the religious wars and squabbles that never would have occurred if people had had a sense of humor. If people nowadays would see the funny side of things, then they would begin to live together, to love together, to laugh together, and to take counsel together instead of distrusting each other.

The Guardian Angel

I ASK YOUR VERY REVERENT attention to a profound and beautiful fact of nature. To me this thought is one of the most beautiful of the theosophical doctrines. It is that of the "angels" guarding us, or what the Christians call guardian angels; but this wonderful doctrine, which is such a comfort and help to men in time of stress and trouble, is no longer understood by the Christians of this day, because they have lost the original meaning of it. They seem to think that it is an angel outside of oneself deputed by Almighty God to be a kind of protecting parent over the child; and some Christians seem to think that when the child attains adulthood the guardian angel departs. This doctrine of protective and guiding spiritual influences in the world is a very old doctrine of the wisdom-religion. It was taught in Persia, India, Egypt, amongst the Druids; in fact, as far as I know, everywhere.

It is simply this: that there is in and over man a spirit or power guiding him, instilling hope and comfort and peace and righteousness into his mind and heart; and that he who is ready to receive this and does receive it will guide himself by the inner mandates, and do so openly. He will be more or less conscious of the companionship of the guardian angel, be conscious of this companionship as a helper, with him day and night, never failing, always guiding, teaching him to save himself. But the mind and heart must be ready to receive, otherwise the brain does not catch the guidance and the inspiration.

What is this guardian angel? You may call it a dhyāni-chohan. Our own particular name for it is Sanskrit: *chitkāra:* "thought-worker." You remember it was stated of the great Greek philosopher, Socrates, that he was guided by his inner *daimon,* his constant companion, which in his case strangely enough never told him what to do, but always warned him what not to do. It is stated of him that frequently when he was undecided as to what course to pursue, he would go apart and close his eyes and remain quiet, trying to free his mind from all the debris, claptrap, noise, and hurly-burly of tramping thoughts — in other words, cleansing and emptying the brain so that the guardian angel inside could penetrate into the brain-stuff. Such in his case was the guardian angel.

Again, what is this guardian angel? Is it outside of man? It is a part of man's spirit, pertinent to his pneumatology; not the human part but a part of his spiritual being. You can call it the higher self, but I prefer to call it the spiritual self, because the phrase "higher self" in theosophy has a meaning containing certain restricted ideas. Thus, man's inmost entity, the guardian angel, this spiritual self, is like a god compared with the man of flesh, the man of this brain. Compared with his knowledge it has omniscience; compared with his vision it has vision of the past, the present, and the future, which three really are but one eternal NOW in the ever present.

This guardian angel will always strive and is incessantly striving to guide its willful errant child, the man of flesh. If you can make your mind pervious to this inner monitor, and follow its mandates, your life will be safe and happy and prosperous. Of course, you have to go through whatever your karma has for you, that is, whatever you have wrought in the past; it will have to work itself out. If you put your finger in the fire, it will be burned. If you catch your foot in the machine it will be crushed. But the inner warrior, the guardian angel, once you come into its fellowship, in time will prevent your putting your finger into the fire, or placing your foot where it could be crushed. As for myself, my own life has been saved six times by this. I only blame myself for not having begun sooner as a younger man to try to cultivate and to try to bring about an even closer consciousness or self-realization of this wonderful guide, this divine spark, this spiritual self in me: the very stuff of divinity. Compared to me my guardian is an angel, a god.

The only difference between the ordinary man and the Christ-man and the Buddha-man is this: that we ordinary men have not succeeded in becoming absolutely at one with the guardian angel within, and the Buddhas and the Christs have. The Buddha or Christ is one who has made himself, his whole being, his heart, so pervious to the entrance of the guardian angel within him that that guardian angel has actually imbodied in him so that the lower man is scarcely any longer there: it is then the guardian angel that speaks with the lips of flesh, it is the bodhisattva, the inner Christ.

These are some of the forgotten values in human life, and I know no values greater than these two. First, you are one with the universe, one with divinity, inseparable from it. Then it does not much matter what happens to you. Whatever comes is a part of the universal destiny. You become filled with courage and hope and peace. And the other forgotten value is what I have just called *chitkāra:* let that guardian angel live in you, and speak through you, and as soon as may be. I speak what I know, not only with regard to saving from trouble and from peril, but from dangers of all kinds. It will instill peace and comfort and happiness and wisdom and love, for all these are its nature. These things are especially needed in the world today by poor mankind, most of humanity feeling that all the trouble in the world has happened by chance, that there is no way out except by a lucky fluke of fate. That is all tommyrot. This world is a world of law and order, and if we break these rules of law and order we suffer.

Oh, that man would realize these simple verities of universal nature! They are so helpful. They give meaning to life and inject a marvelous purpose into it. They give incentive to do our jobs and to do them like men. They make us love our fellowmen, and that is ennobling. The man who loves none but himself is constricting his consciousness into a little knot, and there is no expansion or grandeur in him; whereas the man who loves his fellowmen and thereby begins to love all things, both great and small — his consciousness goes out, begins to embrace, comprehend, to take in all. It becomes finally universal feeling, universal sympathy, universal understanding. This is grand, and this is godlike.

Strength through Exercise

Our destiny lies in our own hands, and we can make or mar ourselves. No god forbids, no god imposes; we are children of the divine, and therefore partakers of the divine freedom of will; and in our own feeble way as only partly evolved souls, we work out our destiny. As we shape our lives, so those lives shall become good, bad, shapely, distorted, beautiful, or ugly. We make them such. There is no fatalism in this. All nature surrounding us is not only aiding us but, at the same time strangely enough, to a certain degree restricting us so that it gives us an opportunity to exercise our strength against opposition, which is the only way to develop a good pair of biceps!

Exercise brings out strength. If nature gave us no chance to prove the god within us, we should never grow. Therefore nature is not only a beauteous, helpful mother, but also a stern nurse watching over us with an infinitely compassionate eye, and insisting by her operations and reactions to what we do or follow with our own will, that this will shall grow in strength through exercise; that our understanding shall become brighter and keener through use.

The World's Trouble and Its Cure

WHAT IS THE TROUBLE with the world today? It is this: the desperate desires that men have to make other men accept their views. That was and has been the trouble with the Occident since the downfall of paganism. It was the scandal of the Christian church — and I say it with reverence for the many noble hearts who have lived in and brightened that church with their lives. The great fault of men from the time of the downfall of Rome in all the European countries, and in these two continents of ours, has been the desperate effort of men to force others to think as they do — in religion, in politics, in society, it matters not what.

It is this which has lighted the pyres of the martyrs. It is this which has sent murdering, marauding bands out for the killing of other men. It is this which has made and signed treaties, and imposed them on nations. It is this which troubles us today. You see it everywhere. You see it even in countries at peace. You see it in our social relations among ourselves. Western men and women do not seem to be happy unless they are trying with more or less success to impose their will upon others, their thoughts, their ideas of what is right: the way the world should be run, the way things should be done, and especially the way other people should believe and feel. When you realize how greatly we value the sanctuary of our own hearts, the freedom of our own lives, and our right to think freely, you can see how tragical the consequences always are.

Why, I have seen the same evil strain running even through the minds of theosophists who seem to think that other theosophists are all on the wrong path because they do not accept *their* opinions — theosophically, this is simply repeating the same old evil desire to make the other fellow think as you do.

Now, try as you may, you cannot completely succeed in this. You can kill men, you can shackle their bodies, you can defile and distort their minds and their hearts. But you cannot enchain the human soul. It will break free. And then the same old tragedy is repeated. It is pathetic; and the pathos of it lies mainly not so much in the great human suffering brought about, but in the immense loss to humankind of the treasures repressed and defeated in the hearts and minds of others. Think! what is more beautiful than for a man to study the mind of his friend or his fellow, to bring out what is there, to see it grow, to see unfolded the treasuries of thought? This is productive. The other is destructive. The one enriches the treasuries of human thought and human feeling; it brings about gentleness and peace and mildness in men's dealings with each other. The other brings about hatred and suspicion and a seething resentment and urge to throw off the slavery of imposed beliefs, ideas, or forms.

Do you know why all this happens? Simply because people, most of them, are unensouled. I do not mean they have no souls; but their souls are not active, are not working, are not productive. They are asleep. Thus men and women mostly live like human animals; in fact, worse, because animals are governed more or less by an instinct which holds some measure of respect for other animals. But men have planning and tricky minds, and when planning and tricky minds are endowed with reason, we have tyranny, religious, social, political, any kind. We have, I say, tyranny: the attempt by minority, or by majority, or the one upon the many, or the many upon the one, to impose ideas and thoughts and modes of conduct to which the others must submit — and we call that the "freedom of the Occident"!

Freedom! One of heaven's most blessed gifts and the one that we have most outrageously abused, for we have considered that to gain freedom is the causing of other men to accept our beliefs, is the obliging of other men to accept our institutions and our ways of doing things. And the result: the crushing down of the flowering of millions of human souls which otherwise would have produced abundantly, brought forth nobly their contribution to the enrichment of our common human treasury.

Am I revolutionary in these ideas? Never. For that would be just myself trying to repeat the moral crimes I speak of, trying to impose my views upon others. Evolutionary? Yes! Appealing to human hearts and minds always to remember that they can never be ultimately happy, or produce their best, or allow their fellowmen to produce their best, if they fight others. It never has worked. It never will. It is against the laws of human nature. It is against all the laws of psychology, both the higher and the lower. It is a man's duty to obey the laws of his country. No matter what country it is, no matter what laws it may have, as long as he lives in it he should be obedient to its laws. But let him in his own life be an example of an ensouled man, and if he die a martyr in the cause of justice the world will hear of his example and it will be, as the old Christian said, "the seed of the Church"; for it is a curious fact in human psychological thought, that even though a man die in a poor cause it is a seed of propaganda.

The greatest wisdom in human life as taught by the masters of wisdom is sympathy for the souls of men, and making your own life an example of what you preach: justice, brotherly love, sympathy, pity, compassion, helpfulness, refraining from doing any unjust act to whomsoever it may be. Your example will be followed by others because you will stand out like a beacon light on a dark night.

That is the ideal; and I shall always hold it before me as an ideal. For I have found, and I found it even in my boyhood, that the most interesting thing in human association, in human relations, in the give-and-take of daily life, is the bringing out of what the other man has within him, wants to show, wants to express. It is fascinating; and the quickest way to kill that, to check its growth, is to impose your ideas on him. For then you kill something wondrously beautiful; you bring about the destruction of the noblest thing in human life instead of sympathetically aiding in its flowering. It is a crime to do this. Contrariwise, if you can bring out what is within a man's soul you can enrich him and yourself, both. And this is the essence of real leadership. It means leading the hearts of men; bringing out the best in others, so that they themselves come to love the beauty thus brought forth and become fired with enthusiasm. To impose ideas on others is tyranny.

We are living under a rule of force; there are forcible repressions everywhere. You know what that means in mechanics; similarly does the crushing of the aspirations of the human soul, the forcing down of what must come out some day, produce explosions. Can you wonder that the greatest men who have ever lived have taught us that the way to peace and happiness and growth and prosperity and riches and all the good things of life is love and justice? Love for the souls of men, sympathy for the souls of men; doing not unto others as you would not that they should do unto you — this negative form is the wiser one. Doing unto others what you would they should do unto you — "saving the souls of men" — is a rule which admits of the abuses of ignorance and fanaticism.

Treat others — put it in the positive form if you like — treat others as you want others to treat *you*, and by and by you will grow to see the flowering of their and your ideals. A man who does this is an ensouled man: one in whom the qualities of the soul predominate; who loves because love is beautiful; one who, enriching the life of his fellows, enriches his own life; one who treats others generously and gives to others the first chance. This is not only chivalrous, but also it increases one's own power and strength, for it requires willpower to do this continuously.

It is a process of ensouling oneself ever more. The greatest men in the world have been the most ensouled in this sense. They are those whose hearts have held the most love, whose minds have been the keenest, the quickest, the strongest, the manliest; whose ethical sense has been the most subtle, the most quick, the firmest. They are those who have refused to impose their will upon others, but instead have led forth the beauty in the souls of others.

Guard Your Thought Processes

I HAVE OBSERVED my own processes of thought and I have noticed that many and many a time I have been saved from drawing a false conclusion by being reluctant to accept that conclusion until I have examined it. That is an excellent rule that we all try to follow. But I likewise have observed that if I am cowardly or lazy, and refuse to face a thought or a problem squarely, nobody suffers but me. I am the loser. So I have learned to think, and to try to think clearly, to be afraid of thinking no thought whatsoever, but always to strive to see that the thoughts that pass through my mind as the instruments of cogitation shall be high ones; not to give in to snap judgments, not to be led astray by emotional volcanic outpourings, nor what is worse, I think, led into judging others with injustice. This is an exercise the Hindus would call yoga. It is an exercise I recommend to anyone who wants to improve himself. Watch your thoughts. Watch your processes as you think those thoughts. Discard the thoughts you do not like. But be careful in so doing lest you refuse to receive a divinity knocking at the door of your heart when you are at first too blind to perceive its divine character.

Initiation and Suffering

ALL INITIATION IS REALLY A TEST or trial, but the preparation for that test or trial is daily life — from January 1st to January 2nd to January 3rd, and throughout the days to December 31st. What we call initiation is simply the showing by the neophyte in the tests then and there laid upon him, whether his daily life's training has been sufficiently strong to make him fit to hitch his chariot to the stars.

That is why the masters have told us that no especial tests whatsoever are put upon chelas; only when initiation comes and they are given a chance to face the trial. The tests come in daily living. Do you see the lesson to be drawn from this? Fit yourselves while the day is yet with us and before the night comes. Do you know what some of these tests are? There have been all kinds of romantic stories written by people about them. These have been mostly guesswork, but the fundamental idea is often true. The tests are these: Can you face the denizens of other planes and prevail with them in peace? Do you know what that means? Are you absolutely sure of yourself? The man who cannot even face and conquer himself when required on this familiar plane where he lives, how can he expect to face with safety the habitants of other planes, not only the elementals — they are not by any means the worst — but the intelligent creatures, beings, living on other planes?

Now then, anyone who has mastered himself, perhaps not completely, but who knows that if he sets his will to it he can control anything in his own character, and knows it by proving it, is ready to go through initiation. When this knowledge comes to him then he is given the chance.

So many people seem to think that initiations are privileges granted to people who pretend to live the holy life and that kind of thing, but I will tell you something more that I myself know because I have seen it in my fellow human beings: there is more chance for the man or the woman who has striven honestly and has fallen and risen again, in other words for the one who has eaten the bread of bitterness, who has become softened and strengthened by it, than there is for one who has never passed through the fire. So compassionate and pitiful is universal nature, that it is precisely those who stumble on the path who are often in the end the richer. Holiness comes from the struggles with self fought and lost, and fought and lost, and fought and *won*. And then compassion enters the heart, and pity, and understanding. We become gentle with others.

You see now why it is that the quick one to judge the faults of others is precisely he who himself has never stumbled on the path and therefore is not fit and ready. Compassion, pity, are marks of character, of strength gained through suffering. "Except the feet be washed in the blood of the heart" — there you have it! Look how compassionate the Christ was and the Buddha. Let us learn and do likewise.

I have often been asked or written to as to what my opinion would be concerning one who has been unhappy on life's pathway, has wandered from the straight and narrow path, and I have wondered how any theosophist could ask me a question like that. Is it not obvious that it is precisely those who have learned through suffering who are stronger than those who have not? — and I here mean those who have suffered and conquered self. "Judge not lest ye be judged." The one who has been through the fire never judges one who is passing through it. He knows what it means. It is the immature, the spiritually undeveloped, those who have never been through the fire of pain, who are quick to criticize and judge others. Judge not, lest ye be judged some day.

The Weighing of the Heart

OUR LIVES, OUR HUMAN destinies, are not the flotsam and jetsam of an arbitrary fate, but as symbolized in the Egyptian ceremony or rite of the Weighing of the Heart of the Defunct: all that we think and all that we feel and all that we do is weighed in the scales of destiny. And these scales weigh two things, as this Egyptian ritual so ably demonstrates: in one pan of the balance is the life center, the human heart of the man who lived but now is dead; and in the other pan of the balance is the feather of truth, of reality, that naught can bribe, that naught can sway, that naught may persuade or induce. We therefore see in this symbolic ritual a wonderful exemplification of the doctrine of karma, inescapable destiny which none and naught in infinity may change, for it is divine law itself, which we call retribution when our evildoings receive it, and compensation when our goodness or good works receive it. But under the majestic atmosphere around all this ritual, the man depends on no judge or sentence nor is there any pardon. He depends on naught but the very laws of being themselves. Utter true the balance weighs, naught sways it, naught causes it to rise, naught to fall. He is weighed — think now — he is weighed against truth it-self; and have you ever heard of truth being bribed or swayed or persuaded or changed or modified or influenced?

This is the doctrine of compensation and of retribution which we call karma: that what a man sows, that he reaps, not some-thing else; and he cannot escape the reaping of it, for he him-self, symbolized by his heart in the pan of the scales, is weighed against truth. When the heart and the feather of truth have an even balance, the heart is of the lightness and spirituality of truth itself, akin to truth. But when the heart is weighed down by evildoing and attraction to the lower things of earth, it falls; and the rising feather in the other scale is the witness, the testimony, against the earth-charged heart which cannot rise to make an even balance.

There is something truly majestic about this symbolic ritual. It is filled with wonderful meanings, and I think the noblest is its effect on us as human beings in our daily lives. What ye sow, that shall ye reap. There is not a word about pardon, and if there were any pardon in the universe, the universe itself would be thrown out of the gear of infinite justice. No mere man can commit an infinite sin, for neither his spirit nor his soul nor again his strength is infinite in compass. His sins are human and therefore the weighing in the balance is human; and the retribution is human in magnitude and the compensation is likewise human in magnitude. This is the infinite justice of Mother Nature, nature which is spirit, which is divinity, and the nature around us, for they are one.

When a man is persuaded of this greatest of facts in human life, his whole life as a man is thereafter changed. He begins to feel concern for his acts, he begins to feel concern as to what his thoughts may be. He feels concern as to how he allow his feelings to run; for he, before his passing and what men call death, is himself the holder of the scales, the balance; and into his heart by his thoughts, and into his heart by his feelings, and into his heart by the actions, by the consequent actions following upon thought and feeling, he burdens his heart with these weights. And after death he is weighed in the scales, not by any theatrical weighing such as is given in the symbolic picture, but weighed in the scales of destiny, those very same scales which bring me or you into this body or that, into this country or into this land or that, strictly according to what each man in former lives has built into himself in thought and feeling and aspiration and all the other human feelings and emotions. These things are not chance or haphazard.

Now then, is it not clear that when a man realizes these things, and they begin to flow into his heart and work upon him, his conduct thereby is of necessity changed? Precisely as the child who, in his infantile innocence, puts his finger into the candle flame — does he not learn? He has learned. See the immense moral import of this symbolic representation of a man's heart, which is his selfhood, being weighed in the scales of cosmic justice, which no prayers can sway, which is utterly true, for the feather of truth is in the other pan of the balance. No man is unjustly condemned ever, nor suffers a hair-weight which he himself has not merited; and no man is ever unduly compensated for what he has not earned, for this would be ridiculous; and the universe is incomparably sane and beautiful.

The weighing of the heart, which is the man's own self, in the scale of destiny likewise shows us that we build our lives to grandeur or to debasement strictly in accordance with our own wish and will and aspiration. Our destiny lies in our own hands. One man is not credited with the x power to succeed and the next man credited with a y power to fail. We are all sparks of the divine heart, we all have an equal chance, and eternally have an equal chance; and if we fail it is we who fail and pay the penalty; but once the penalty is paid, we begin anew with a new hope, another chance: I have paid my debt, I am now free, I begin again. See how manly this doctrine is, and what encouragement it gives to us. It is a doctrine of hope, for there is no human destiny so low or so base which cannot from this instant of beginning be altered marvelously for the better, if you will; for the heart, when you wish to order for the better, begins to work and to work upon you, and to fill your mind with ideas nobler than those which have lived there, and feelings which are higher and sweeter and purer by far than those you have passed through.

This is a wonderful symbolic picture of reality. And what are these scales, and how does nature do her work? Why, we see it around us all the time. How did I come into this body and incarnation? Through many chambers of the Father, as the avatāra Jesus would phrase it. I came from the heaven world, the devachan, into this world through many planes of being, dropping downwards to this material world because I am attracted here. Who is the guide and the leader? Horus, the divine spirit, the chief guide of my footsteps, when I allow it — following the Egyptian ritual. And it is all done as it were by the same forces which prevail in these material spheres, which cause the suns to radiate and the celestial orbs like our earth to rotate, and which cause all with confluent motion to pass from one sphere of the cosmic planes of destiny to some other plane. It all happens because it is all within the law of nature, the laws of nature.

Thus, how do I find my way through this life? By attraction, by what I have made myself to be. I am attracted here, and that attraction won't allow me to go elsewhere. I myself have carved my own destiny, and I am carving it now, and in the next life I shall carve it anew; and let us hope more symmetrically than in this present life I carve this one.

What are these halls or chambers through which Ani, Everyman, of the Egyptian ritual, has to pass before his heart is weighed against the feather of truth — light as a feather, yet holding the universe in bonds that are never broken? What are these chambers and halls through which the divine soul passes? They are the various planes, the various worlds through which men after death find their way. How does the defunct soul, when it comes to a portal and knocks for entrance, know the proper word? By exactly the same instinctive knowledge and attraction that the incarnate soul coming from the devachan finds its way into its present family and into its present body. It cannot lose its way. And what is represented by the knock of the defunct — a beautiful symbol again? It is simply, as it were, its approach to a new plane, a new world, a new stage of its way on its peregrinational pilgrimage, and it knows instinctively how to approach it, how to enter, according to the Egyptian ritual, how to say the words of power. They are in the soul itself. It is experience, intuition, knowledge, the same thing we are using here now in understanding each other, and speaking to each other and reading together and studying together. We understand each other; but to one who did not understand what understanding is, how could you explain understanding? When I say words that knock at your mind, when a speaker knocks at your heart, it is done with a thought, it is done with feeling, it is done with knowledge; and the portals of understanding fly open wide, and ideas and thoughts enter into your minds, into your souls. The right knock has been given.

That is what is meant by the chambers or halls through which the soul passes and comes to the different portals, and gives the knock of power; and when challenged gives the words of power which allow him to pass. When you have built these words of power into yourself, you pass unchallenged. If you have not evolved to the point, or are unworthy, if you have not built them into your soul, you are challenged, and stopped, and back you go.

It is an old truism of the god-wisdom that from the human heart come all the greatest issues of the world. They do not reside in the brain-mind, for the brain-mind is the great separator of men, the great deceiver. It is the heart that is the unifier of men. And the reason? Because the heart speaks a universal language which needs no words. But the brain-mind speaks a language of words which have to be interpreted from mind to mind. Therefore is the heart so much the greater. Out of the heart come the great issues of life, for in the heart are love and intuition and discrimination and understanding and self-sacrifice and pity and compassion and purity and goodness and truth and troth and honor; and out of the mind of man come disputes and wranglings and quarrelings, disinclination to understand the other man, hatreds and all the other foul brood of man's lower nature, because it is about things out of the brain that men are continually quarreling. They never quarrel about the issues of the heart, for they are things of our common humanity.

Example: I love truth, so does every human being in this room. That is a statement directly from the heart. The mind immediately says: well, what kind of truth, what do you mean by truth? Tim's truth, or Charles' truth? You see, it flops right down and begins to argue and quarrel and spread around and to dispute about mere details; but the heart simply says: I worship truth, and every other human heart in the audience understands. The heart says: I love it. The brain-mind immediately begins to argue about it, and all kinds of men and all kinds of women have different ideas about what love is and how far you should go and how far you should not go, how much you should trust and how much you should not trust, what kind of person I love and what kind I do not love. The heart is infinitely beyond this. It simply says, I love. It is a universal language every human being understands. You don't need to argue about it. You accept it. The brain-mind is the former of arguments. The heart says troth is one of the most beautiful of actions in human conduct, to be full of troth. Where do we love this and admire it? With what part of us do we give allegiance, pay homage? With the heart. It speaks a tongue universal; therefore we say, out of the human heart come all the great issues in human life.

I will go a little farther. I will tell you that the human heart is the temple or dwelling or tabernacle of a divinity; it is the dwelling of Horus, to follow the Egyptian ritual. Every time a man gives you his word and keeps it, especially at loss to himself, that man is by so much acting as an ensouled man. Every time a man gives you his word and breaks it because it is convenient for him to break it, that man for the time being is unensouled. His soul is asleep. Every time a man takes advantage of a fellow human being, by so much his soul is asleep within him, it is not working. He is not ensouled. Every time a man does some deed or thinks some grand thought which is of help to others, he is a man, for he is ensouled. And when a man is fully ensouled, as all men on this earth shall some day be, when a man is free of soul we no longer have a man, we have a god living amongst us. I think the most beautiful sight that we human beings can perceive ever is the light of ensoulment that dawns in the eyes of a fellow human being. If you have never seen that and never understood it, it is because your own soul is asleep, for in these things spirit calls to spirit, spirit recognizes spirit, divinity recognizes divinity, the man in me recognizes the man in you, and this is ensouling. Oh, that all men and all women so lived that they might manifest the divinity within them, and by so doing acknowledge the divine source of their own inner light!

The Ensouling of Man

ON MANY OCCASIONS I have spoken of those Great Ones who are fully ensouled men, and also of the majority of men and women who are as yet soulless; and by this latter term I did not mean "lost souls." Now when you understand what ensouling is, you understand the meaning and substance of the chela path. The chela is one who is ensouling himself. The master is a fully ensouled man. The Buddha is a master with the light of the spirit illuminating his soul, one in whom the spirit with its refulgent glory increases the already great splendor of the ensouled man.

The path of chelaship is a process of ensouling "soulless" people. Such "soulless" people fill our cities, our towns, our hamlets, our homes. Every one of us in those moments when he is no longer a "soul," but lives only in the four lower principles of his being, is for the time soulless; that is the meaning of it: the human monad is no longer active in him. A lost soul, on the other hand, is one who no longer has even the possibility of reunion with the divine, the spirit, the Buddha, the Christ, within himself. A lost soul drops to the Pit.

When the great Syrian sage, Jesus, said, "He who gives up his life for my sake" — for the sake of the Buddha, the Christ, within himself, within each one of us — "shall find his life," he meant that even in the most ordinary of us, feebly in the beginning, lives the Christ within, continuing to live as an inmost being; and that as time passes, and the man draws nearer to the inmost center of his being, he becomes gradually ensouled, a leader; then a Buddha; and upon the Buddhas shines the light of eternity. It is as simple as that.

Soulless people are not wicked. They are just drifting, sleeping, unawakened. They live more or less in the four lower principles of the constitution. But the chela is the man who begins by will and effort and thought and devotion and love for all that is, great and small, to ensoul himself; and he rises along the chela path precisely in the ratio in which he ensouls himself ever more greatly.

I use the term "ensouling" because it is a simple term amenable to understanding. I have deliberately avoided using a term which might require lengthy explanatory comment. The desire is to suggest rather than to give an explicit teaching.

I will try to give you what to me at least seems to be a graphic illustration of what ensouling means. We human beings are composite entities. We have a divine and a spiritual and a human and a beastly side to us, as well as the physical body which suffers so often unjustly because of the crimes committed upon it by our erratic, vagrant, wandering, passionate, lower human aspect: the lower emotional and mental principles in us. These four lower principles are the *human* animal. Being a *human* animal it is superior to the beast-animal, because throughout the former there is an instinct of humanity. Nevertheless this human animal, when the man lives as a man, should be ensouled by the humanity of the man. When a man lives solely in his four lower principles he is less than a true man. He merely vegetates. He exists. He has no chance for immortality, none whatsoever, because there is nothing immortal in the four lower principles of us. But the human monad, the vehicle of the spiritual monad or, to put it otherwise, the human soul, the vehicle of the spiritual soul, has a great chance for conscious immortality.

When a man lives in his human monad the four lower principles are ensouled. He is a full man then, consciously living and happily living in such fashion as to bring no bitter regrets. There is the test. It does not mean a man who is perfect, or that the man has no temptations. Certainly not; because we are all human. The four-principled man succumbs to temptation usually because he is not ensouled by the humanity of himself. The humanity-part of ourselves, to use easily understood language, the human monad, *has more chance of conquering temptation than of succumbing to it;* and when I say temptation I do not mean physical passion only; I mean all kinds of temptation. Overweening ambition, only to be gratified at others' cost, is one common vice today; selfishness in any of its manifold forms; egoism, a hydra-headed thing; uncontrolled anger — all these things are the lower human; less than the higher human, less than the truly human.

So then, ensouling means living those things which we intuitively and instinctively sense belong to the better part of us. That is all there is to it: living in the human soul instead of in the human animal soul; to speak technically, living in the buddhi-manas instead of in the kāma-manas.

Our streets are packed with soulless beings in this sense, vacillating in character like the winds of heaven, without firmness of will, without even convictions, moral convictions especially, changeable as weathercocks, pulled hither and yon by every passing gust of temptation of any kind. They are less than human. They are soulless — which does not mean that they have no soul; but it means that the soul within them is not operative; it is not active; it does not manifest itself. Look into the eyes of these people: there lacks the wonderful shine of the soul which, once seen, you will always recognize.

Every kindly act you do marks you as by that much ensouled, if it is an act which springs from the heart and not merely from the egoistic wish to show off. Every time you conquer a temptation, which if yielded to you know perfectly well will debase you in your own eyes, even if your fellows do not know of your fall; every time you conquer it you live in the human soul, you are by so much ensouling yourself. Every time you conquer an impulse to do a selfish act, a deed with selfish thought for your own benefit, then you are by so much ensouling yourself.

We shall be fully human, fully ensouled, in the fifth round. At the present time we can be so by effort and aspiration. The vast majority of mankind are soulless in the technical sense that we understand. The soul is there but they won't live in it; they won't make it themselves. They prefer to live in the animal. And mark you, the animal does not only mean sex. That is only one side of it and a relatively unimportant side. The animal means the grasping, acquisitive, selfish, appetitive, indulgent, part of us, running after this and running after that, without stability of character, in other words without soul.

Set about ensouling yourself with the soul which is *yourself;* that is the chela path. The man who succeeds in doing so is a chela. The path is the same for all men, yet distinctive for each individual. Find it.

Overcoming Doubt

YOU WILL NEVER HAVE any doubts about the god-wisdom if you study. This study is so persuasive, it leads you captive. Once you understand it, your doubts go, and the study includes not only the intellectual digestion, assimilation, and of course appreciation of these godlike doctrines, but it means living the life. As long as you are not godlike in your inner nature, you are bound to have doubts, and be torn to shreds by the pursuing hounds of thought and feeling, as the Greeks phrased it in their way, the man pursued by the divine vengeance. The hounds are his lower self, what is within himself: the inability to weave his soul, his spirit, into one compact divine unity, one thing, alliance with the divine; the hounds are the indecisions and the doubts and the horrors and fears.

The Essence of H. P. Blavatsky's Message

WE SPEAK OF RENDERING homage. There are various ways of so doing. There is the homage of words, and there is the homage of the heart which leads to emulation. The homage of words is good when the heart is behind it; but the homage imitating grand action is finer and higher still.

I think the best homage we can render to H. P. Blavatsky, outside of the words with which we express our deep gratitude, is by copying her, copying her life and her work for mankind: being as like unto the example she gave to us as it is possible for us to be. She indeed said the same in regard to her relation to her own teachers: they teach, I follow. My message is not my own, but of those who sent me.

In the theosophical world since her passing there has been no small amount of talk about the successors of H.P.B.; and all this has seemed to me to be so perfectly trivial, a trifling with words and with the most sacred instincts and impulses of the human heart. For every true theosophist is a successor of H.P.B. and should be glad of it and proud of it. We are all successors of H.P.B., every one of us without exception whatsoever. And the least is often the greatest amongst us. Here is a case where it is not conceit or arrogance but the impulse of a loving and grateful heart to come to the front and serve, and dedicate one's service to the cause which our teachers have served and which they still serve. What is grander than this? Actually it is the abdication, the rejection, of the low and the personal. It is the forgetting of the personal and the sinking of the self into the immensely greater self of the universe. When we forget ourselves, then something supremely grand is born in us; for the spiritual then, of which we humans are such feeble examples, has a chance to come forth in us, to speak and to work in and through us, because then it begins to find its channel in and through the human heart and mind.

It has always seemed to me that H. P. Blavatsky's great work was to ensoul men — words which are profound and very meaningful; to give men and women a philosophy-religion-science which should so mightily persuade both mind and heart that they would come to realize that the universe is alive and conscious, and that we, her children, perforce and from that fact, are alive and conscious also, and are coeternal, coeval with the universe, from which we come, in which we live, and into the spiritual parts of which we shall again return.

When you get this simple thought in your heads and in your hearts so that it amounts to a conviction within, you are already becoming reensouled. The soul, nay rather, the spirit within you, is beginning to take command of you, and from that moment your lives will be changed. New and grand vistas will open to your vision, vistas which your intellect and your intuition will show you are realities, and you will begin to govern your life in accordance with the living, flaming thoughts that will thereafter make their shrine in your hearts. You will begin then really to live. You will no longer be what Pythagoras called the "living dead" — those alive in their bodies and relatively unconscious in their souls. You will then actually be imbodied souls.

This to me has always been one of the loftiest and most beautiful parts of H. P. Blavatsky's work that she came to inaugurate: to ensoul men so that they might live anew with the vision glorious and with eternal hope.

No man will act against the dominating impulse within him. Let him change that dominating impulse from self-seeking interests to altruistic service for all, and life will take on a grandeur that up to that moment he had never seen or understood. Such a man is becoming truly ensouled. He sees the reason for his life. He sees the reason for the universe around him. He sees the reason for his own thoughts. He understands causal relations and effectual consequences. He sees vast and utterly grandiose visions opening before his mind's eye; and he knows that all he has to do in order to attain still greater vistas, and to be of greater service, is to put the strength of his intellect in these intuitions and lofty feelings, center his power of action upon them and thus grow in ever enlarging stages of inner grandeur and inner understanding. His life will then have changed because he will have changed. He will have been awakened; and he will then so rule his life and coordinate it to the life of the universe around him and to the lives of his fellow human beings, that universal brotherhood will be his first instinct and the controlling impulse in both his thought and action. This to me is the essence of the message of H. P. Blavatsky.

The Yoga of Theosophy

THEOSOPHISTS USE THE WORD yoga as a convenient word, but we do not use it so much in order to express the theosophical discipline. Why? Because in the West the word has come to signify one or other of the five different Hindu schools of yoga; whereas the theosophic yoga discipline includes them all, and tops them with a nobler, a sixth.

Now, what are these five Indian yoga schools? They are these, beginning with the simplest and lowest: hatha-yoga, the yoga of physiological psychical training, dealing almost wholly with the body and the lower mind; next, karma-yoga, from the word *karman*, "action"; third, bhakti-yoga, the yoga of love and devotion; fourth, jñāna-yoga, the yoga of wisdom or knowledge, of study; fifth, rāja-yoga, the yoga of self-devised effort to attain union with the god within, the yoga of discipline, such as the kings of the kshattriya or warrior caste were supposed to exemplify as the leaders of their states; and the sixth, which theosophists add, is the brahma-yoga, the yoga of the spirit, in practice including the other five.

It is a sheer absurdity, taking human psychology and nature into account, to think that India is the only land that has ever known what yoga is — *yoga* here meaning discipline, training, in order to attain self-conscious "union" with the god within, with the inner Buddha, or the immanent Christ, call it by what name you like.

Take karma-yoga: something of this form of discipline has been known for centuries in the Christian church, as "salvation by works." It is a well-known training in the Christian discipline, as is bhakti-yoga: known as "salvation by devotion," or "love," "self-dedication" — exactly the same things that the Hindu and the theosophist mean by these words, and which arose spontaneously in the heart of Christendom, as they did in the heart of Hindustan, or in any other country. Then again there was the training of the Stoics — these and others are all different kinds of yoga. They did not call these trainings by the word yoga. That is a Sanskrit term pertaining to, belonging to, Hindustan; but the disciplines were known. The Christians called them "salvation" by this and by that; the Hindus said "union" by this discipline and by that, etc.

The theosophical occult discipline comprehends them all, because these different types of training or union correspond with the five main types of human minds or psychology, some men finding salvation in works, using the Christian term; others in love or devotion; others in theology or high thought. Why, even Christendom, in the monasteries especially, has known in the past a kind of hatha-yoga in their physiological training — their flagellations, whippings, the wearing of sackcloth, and other practices of mortification and self-denial — in order, as they expressed it, to control and subordinate the lower passions and the body. These are typical examples of hatha-yoga of the lowest kind. However, when a man has the fortunate type of mind which will lead him into the training of the inner life, he does not have to bother with breathings and postures, flagellations, and tortures. We know that to do our duty, we must work reverently, dedicate ourselves to duty, to effort, in the simplest things. This is karma-yoga. We must control the body from within, as well as our psychical impulses and our emotions, and keep the body clean and healthy, so that it be a fit instrument of the human spirit, and of the human soul. That is the real hatha-yoga. We likewise know that to do our duty by ourselves and our fellowmen and by the movement to which we have dedicated ourselves, we must learn to give ourselves in devotion, in utter love, to the sublime objective — and this is bhakti-yoga. In order to understand life around us and our fellowmen, and our own selves, and the glorious truths of the laws of nature upon which nature herself is built, we must study the sublime god-wisdom intellectually — jñāna-yoga. We likewise know that to practice all these lower yogas we must arouse the feeling of love for self-discipline, finding marvelous joy in the fact that we can control ourselves, that we are human beings striving to be masters of ourselves and not slaves. We do not need to think twice about that idea. Look at the one who can control himself, and look at the one who cannot control himself: master and slave.

Yoga when properly understood is what we might call the moral, spiritual, intellectual, psychical, and the occult training that the theosophist has, if he is worthy of the name. Of course if he merely accepts the philosophy because it appeals to him, because he thinks it is logical and fine, and that nothing has yet overthrown it, he is simply what Pythagoras and the great men of his school would call *akousmatikoi*, "hearers," "listeners." This stage is indeed something, much, but lacks greatly of the higher degrees of understanding and development.

The final yoga, the sixth, brahma-yoga, is the one that most chelas, disciples, aim for. It means taking all the best in the lower forms of yoga that we have just spoken of, unifying them into one, as it were, carrying them all up and nailing them as it were to the spirit within. The thought, the emotions, the wish, are fixed like the flag nailed to the mast. It cannot be hauled down: brahma-yoga, union with brahman, the spirit, the ātman.

I would like to point out one thing more: how is it that these particular forms of yoga exist always in India? All yoga in India is discipline, as stated, methods of training; and these arise mainly in the key thought contained in what the Hindus called the greatest, grandest, most comprehensive verse in all the Vedas, III, 62, 10, of the *Rig-Veda* called the Gāyatrī, or often the Sāvitrī. This the Hindu recites upon rising in the morning, after he makes his ablutions, before he sleeps at night. The *Rig-Veda* is the chiefest of the Vedas, and the Hindus reverently regard these two lines as the heart of *Rig-Veda*. In Sanskrit they run thus:

> Tat savitur vareṇyam bhargo devasya dhīmahi,
> Dhiyo yo nah prachodayāt.

And they mean this — I will give a translation, slightly para-phrased so that you will get the heart of the great Rig-Vedic verse out of which sprang all Hindu philosophy and all Hindu yoga:

"That lofty inner soul of the god's sun, may it unite the thoughts of us, its offspring, and urge us into that union, the union of the lower with the superior, of the individual with the spirit of man, with divinity." When this union or yoga is won, achieved, then we have those grand cases of god-men, or men-gods: Jesus the avatāra, Krishna, Buddha-Gautama and all the other Buddhas, Apollonius of Tyana — there have been hun-dreds. When this union is less complete, we have the great teachers, less great than those just spoken of, but great.

Out of this one phrase, this one yoga of the *Rig-Veda*, sprang all the philosophy and religion and occult science of archaic India, all the systems of training by which men have sought to ally that divine solar spark with themselves, to become in indi-vidualized union with the cosmic spirit — first with Father Sun, and then with the spirit universal. For so reverent were these ancients that to them naught was divorced from divinity. Every atom, every stone, every animal, every man, every deva or god, whatever it be, high or low or intermediate, was a child of the cosmic heart of Being, and could by degrees rise higher and higher into self-conscious union, yoga, with That. And when this glorious consummation is achieved, then you have a man-god, a god-man.

These thoughts are not anything particularly unique in

Hindustan. On the contrary, they are commonplaces of archaic
and modern theosophy. They were commonplaces of the Stoics,
of the Platonists, and of other schools of Greece and Rome.
They have been known from immemorial time in Egypt and
Persia. Read the ancient writings of these folks.

Yoga therefore, is training, discipline, by which that holiest
of all human possibilities may be achieved: growth from manhood, expansion out of manhood into godhood, divinity, which
in our highest we already are. We simply become our highest
selves. That is yoga achieved. I and my Father are one. Any
Christ says the same. Any Buddha makes the same declaration.
When you understand the profound wisdom behind it, there is
naught of egoism in it. It is the spirit speaking through the lips
of devotion in man.

Beauty and Science

THERE ARE SO MANY BEAUTIFUL and holy and glorious things in human
life, and they are a balm to the hearts of men. They should be culti-
vated, they should be sought; not eagerly and selfishly for oneself, but
only that by ourselves becoming beautiful inwardly, we can shed the
light of our love with its softening and refining influence. Love is
always beautiful, and therefore is always grand, especially the higher
love, for it is universal.

I wonder sometimes if the great scientists, I mean those who devote their lives to the impersonal study of nature, realize that they are
cultivating within themselves an aspect of the beauty in nature, because, by the fact of losing themselves in their study, they are becoming
progressively more universal in their thoughts, less concentrated on
self. A selfish love can even damn, and this is the inverse case of evil
spirituality; but a beautiful love can raise.

The Understanding Heart

REVERENCE IS A GODLIKE QUALITY. I have a notion that the gods revere where we wonder only, and I think that the adult reveres where the child merely wonders. To me reverence is a mark of advancement in evolution; and the irreverent person is by so much short of wit, for it is vastly easier to criticize and to make fun, than it is to understand and in understanding discover reverence. Reverence grows apace in him who has the understanding heart.

Had we all the understanding heart, the most difficult points of philosophy would become easy to us. Further, I have discovered that when I am vexed, troubled, anxious, worried with a problem, I never receive help from the brain, but always from the heart. The head seems all too often to increase the burden, because it is full of imaginations and often vacuous problems; but the heart understands, for there is a higher intellect in the heart than in the head. For, if I might so phrase it, there is more intellectual power in heart-life than there is heart-life in thought.

It is small wonder that the ancients used to place the focus of man's ordinary attention in the head; but his real intellect, his understanding, his intuition, his spiritual capacities, his sense of ethical responsibilities, in the heart.

Thus the Egyptians in their hieroglyphic representations never showed the weighing of the brain or the head. They weighed the heart against the light feather of truth. It was the heart that was weighed; and it is a curious thing that in ancient occultism it is the heart that is supposed to contain the higher parts of the human being. These thoughts are rather new to the Occident because we retain only a little of the ancient ideal wisdom; although even today we have retained the truth that love abides in the heart and not in the head.

So mark you, just along this line of thought: if you are doubtful whether someone loves you, watch that person, and if you find that person governed merely by prudential reasonings — is it wise? shall I gain? what will be thought of me? — you can be fairly certain that that person's affection for you is not deep. There is a wisdom of the heart which is instinctive, immediate and unquestioning, and it is far greater a protection to the innocent and to the sincere than is the always broken-up and merely prudential thinking of the head.

I think that the greatest gift the gods can give to any of us is the understanding heart. It is eternally forgiving, it is full of charity, it is pitiful, it thinks of others before itself. It is wise with the wisdom of the ages — for it is the breathing within us of the god-wisdom.

And remember, the heart is not the emotions. Just there so many stumble on the path constantly. For the emotions are all too often connected with the head, as you will find, and perhaps have found; but the heart knows, and the heart is always hoping against hope that truth will be understood, that others will understand and help. The emotions are full of hot fire, of jealousy, suspicion, resentment. They have no vision, the emotions. So when we speak of the understanding heart, we never mean the emotions in which some people live and boast that it is a rich life. It is a poor life, thin and hungry, for the emotions are satisfied never. They are like the *piśāchas* of ancient India, described by the visionaries as beings of immense (or small) body, consumed with immense thirst or hunger, and with but a pin-size mouth, so small that a pin might not enter in; and they starve, and they thirst, and are not ever satisfied. This is figurative of the emotions; and it is a strange thing that it is just these piśāchas which are the astral imbodied kāma-rūpic emotions of dead men, built up during life on earth by those who have lived in the psychic nature, the brain-mind, and the emotions.

The heart is the center of the spiritual-intellectual fluids which in conjunction with the mānasic ākāśa filling the skull and permeating the brain, make the complete man, and the perfect man when they are fully harmonized and unified. Oh, pray the gods to give an understanding heart, and make that prayer real in your lives by yourselves opening the way for the gods that give it. Then your lives will be full of guidance, full of reverence, and rich with peace. All blessings will be yours.

Karma: Pleasant and Unpleasant

THE TITLE OF THIS BRIEF note on karma well represents, I believe, the manner in which people who are acquainted with this majestic doctrine look upon it: that karma is something which in itself is pleasant to us or unpleasant to us. Of course, as a matter of psychological fact, the viewpoint is natural because we all feel when karma impinges upon us that its blows are hard and unpleasant, or gentle and soothing or what we call pleasant.

Yet is it not rather the truth that karma in all its actions, inner and outer, general or particular, is considered by us to be pleasant or unpleasant because of our own reactions and attitude towards what destiny lays upon us? In reality, the laws of nature, of which karma is one of the most recondite, the most mysterious, and indeed the most comforting, are all of them absolutely impersonal, and in them there is neither variation nor variability nor any shadow of turning.

It is just in this perfect reliance on the fundamental justice in universal nature herself, that we find or discover happiness, peace of mind and, far more important than these, our indomitable resolves so to conform to nature's spiritual harmonies that our lives shall be lived in accordance therewith, and that thus we may become cooperators with nature, intelligent companions with her. When we advance into grander human spheres of activity able to become such willing collaborators with nature's plans, we shall then take our places by the side of the masters, and the gods of the Hierarchy of Light, who have become in their various evolutionary degrees instruments, conscious and willing, of the *lipikas* or "scribes."

Now these lipikas are extremely mysterious and occult entities in universal nature's structural harmonies, and indeed in the carpentry of the cosmos itself. Little has been publicly said of the lipikas, and yet the place they occupy in the universe is clear enough. They are in fact dhyāni-chohans of the very highest rank in the arūpa worlds so called; indeed, because they are the first channels or vehicles through which cosmic ideation manifests itself or flows, they become thereby the highest and most powerful instruments of karma originating from seeds held within the structure of cosmic ideation itself. Thus they are called the agents of karma; and furthermore, because they not only distribute cosmic ideas downwards to lower hierarchies, but carry karmic results upwards in order to deposit them so to speak in the treasury of cosmic ideation itself, they are, and mainly for the latter reason, called the scribes or recorders of karma, etc.

Essentially, karma is but a name we give to the operations or to the processes of the universal cosmic harmony seeking readjustments, moral and otherwise, that is to say, cosmic equilibriums throughout the universal structure.

From the foregoing we may easily deduce the highly important and significant fact that what we call our karma — whether we qualify it as pleasant or unpleasant — is actually results of manifold types or characters coming to us out of the past from what we and others around us, hierarchically speaking, have thought and felt and done in that past; and that in a precisely similar way our future karma and that of those around us, hierarchically speaking, will be what we are now, through our thoughts and feelings and actions, building as our future destiny.

Thus, as H. P. Blavatsky points out, it is not karma which arbitrarily compensates or punishes us in what we call the rewards or retributions of destiny, but it is we ourselves and those around us who have made ourselves in the past what now we are, and who are now making ourselves to be what we shall in future become. It is merely our present reactions to karmic destiny or circumstance which make us qualify karma as pleasant or unpleasant.

As a final thought, let me say plainly in connection with karma, that the karmic strokes of destiny that we call unpleasant, or perhaps harsh, just as often as not turn out to be very blessings of the gods coming to us in the guise and habiliments which for the nonce we regard with distaste, and it may be with fear. After all, it is but a truism to say that too much prosperity, too much happiness, can weaken the fiber of the best of us; but that when we find ourselves obliged to struggle or are driven to take action, often perhaps against our wish, we develop thereby not only willpower but intellectual and moral fiber because of the innate faculties and latent powers called forth and given exercise.

Karma in whatever guise it may come is a blessing, and let us never forget it.

Young People and Theosophy

IT HAS BEEN MY EXPERIENCE that the younger people take to theosophy quicker than we older folk do, with our sophisticated minds, often full of claptrap, of miseducation, full of wrong thoughts. It is these inner mental darknesses that keep light out. We are heavy with the fogs of centuries, lifetimes, of wrong feeling and wrong thinking; and this sophistication comes upon us as the body grows to maturity; we have built up an actual inner cloud of consciousness, a psychology, to which we unfortunately fall heir.

I have found, in the work for younger people in the T.S., that as frequently as not they recognize more quickly divine truths than do the older folk; and if people do not have success in interesting youth in theosophy, it is because the approach is wrong — the same principle exactly which brings about lack of success in approaching adults. You have to talk to people in a language they understand, if you wish comprehension on their part. You have to touch their hearts and minds, and you have to awaken something there. If a man, for instance, is tremendously interested in astronomy and you talk to him about folklore, he does not see the connection. He will after a time. But talk to him in his own tongue, and before you part you have made a friend and a brother in thought. It is the same with children. Their minds are unsophisticated, ready, clear, limpid. As a matter of fact, they usually have more intuition of the great things in life than we grownups have, with our blindness and sophistication.

Really the great man in life is the man who can refuse to be drawn into that mental miasma of thought which for each generation is its *Zeitgeist*, the "spirit of the age," the heavy astral-physical and quasi-spiritual atmosphere made up of the wrong, distorted, inaccurate thoughts, passing current for truth. No wonder children rebel, and younger folk also. I remember how I had rebelled with all my soul — not at the elders, not at the universe and its wonderful mysteries — I felt it keenly when I was sent to school and was almost forced to learn things that my soul hated, and that later on as a young man I found put into the discard. If there is any trouble or fault in teaching theosophy to the younger people, it is because our approach is wrong. We talk to them sophisticatedly.

I love young folk, because the human heart is perennially young. It never ages. It is our minds which age and grow crystallized, hard, so that we lack sympathy and do not understand the appeal in the eyes of the child and the youth. We try to interpret it with eyes blinded with wrong thinking and vibrations that absolutely put up a wall. When I speak to younger folk, I treat them as my peers. I don't embarrass a youth or a girl by speaking to him or her from on high as a learned elder. And why? Because my heart is akin to youth, and so is yours. Every normal man's or woman's heart is just the same. We approach most closely to truth when we can abandon the wrong sophistication with which our minds are filled, and approach simplicity, the child heart.

"Suffer little children to come unto me," said the avatāra Jesus, for they can learn. That does not mean years. The man, the woman, whose heart is that of a little child, simple, open, ready to receive and to pass on, who has conquered, thrown out, sophistication — those are the ones you can talk to and who will understand. Therefore treat younger people with the courtesy with which you treat your own compeers in age. How quickly they respond! Dignify your intercourse with younger folk by speaking to them of the things that you love. You will always find response.

No one need ever tell me that youth has no interest in the

universe, in science, in the wondrous discoveries that are taking place continuously. They are the keenest in research, the readiest to understand. It is the older ones who have to unlearn what they have been taught about these things, who find it more difficult to accept and understand than the younger, because of preconceptions.

My approach to young folk is to treat them with courteous decorum, and with the understanding that you give to those of your own age. I have not found it to fail. Naturally they lack a sophistication that the older ones have, but in some ways that is a blessing, for many of our sophistications we learn, and later unlearn after we have suffered from them; although of course on the other hand, our sophistications in the better sense are the things which enable us to support ourselves, to make a high and honorable mark in the world, at least to a certain extent, and to achieve and to dare to achieve better things. But this is only when the sophistication is enlightened from above by the simple, clear light from the spiritual sun within. It is not sophistication itself that is wrong, but it is allowing our minds to become slaves to it, for this last is verily our own creation and that of the world around us.

Interest young people by giving them theosophy on scientific lines, and note how quickly they grasp it, and how readily they hold it. You can present these thoughts to a young man (who is not just frivolous and pre-sophisticated before the proper age) and you will have made a brother and a friend: tell him that he himself is the pathway to the divine, that his highest life is the life of the divine, always unattainable in fullness because infinite, yet ever expanding and with a constant increase in understanding, in growth, in expansion, to something glorious within him. Name it not; that is sophisticating his mind. Get the intuition of it, the thought: something, some part of him, is a droplet, a sparklet of the divine. Therefore he is it. Just as science tells us that the chemical elements which compose our bodies are the same which compose these flowers, and the wood of this floor, the air which we breathe, the stones we crush under our feet as we tread our homeward way; the same that compose the stars.

How many times have I seen the flash of understanding come into the eyes of some younger person with whom I have conversed; and how many times have I not also received strange thoughts that have come to my mind from the mind of some youth, unspoiled intuitions before the mind has become crystallized, hard, with wrong thinking. Verily, we can at times learn something even from the little ones if we have the wit to receive, the openheartedness to receive, and we can rise above our sophisticated intellects.

Making Mistakes

I DO NOT BELIEVE it is ever wrong to make an honest mistake. Infinitely better for a man to have his motive right, to wish to do right, to render justice, to do grandly, and to make a mistake because he cannot see fully just the right way to take, than it is for a man who is all atremble lest he make a mistake; and because of his lack of inner strength, immediately proceeds blindly to make mistakes. That man will never easily rise. Better to make a mistake and learn by it and to bear the consequences manfully and be more of a man afterwards.

Improve your faculties by exercising them. Do not be afraid of making honest mistakes. Only let your motive be right, and then your mistakes won't injure others and you will soon correct them. You will be stronger, grow more keenly. Let your heart be filled with compassion for the mistakes of others, and the wish to do right, and you will never go far wrong. And each repetitive instance of exercising your inner power of judgment will be more sure, more certain, clearer. The light will be brighter. Then you are a man, a real man.

The Lost Cause of Materialism

THE ORIGIN OF THE Theosophical movement began not in arbitrary decisions by the powers that be, but because of conditions of cyclic necessity. Thus, when H. P. Blavatsky came, she came because of a need to keep alive in men their spiritual intuitions, and by so keeping them alive, prevent humanity from falling under the sway of a world ruled by brute force, in which might was considered right and in which the only justice was the booty of the strongest. She knew that the will of brutal power would govern mankind unless checked and stayed by those innate rules of right residing in the souls of men.

How came about this situation in our world? Because of two things: a religion which had become thoroughly materialistic, thoroughly; so much so that people no longer believed that this universe was run by spiritual powers enforcing the rule of right; and therefore that they could act pretty much as they pleased if they but rendered lip homage to an ecclesiastical setup. This idea coming from the religious side of man's knowledge, education, and social contacts, was more than strengthened by an equivalently evil power emanating from the ranks of modern scientists. And this latter power had incomparably more influence on men's minds than the dicta of the church and its hierarchy. Why? Because men had begun to believe that the noble research into nature undertaken by science gave us truth; and they were justified in so believing, for that is the real work of scientists: the investigation of facts and the collating of them into a comprehensive philosophic mold. A great many scientists do work most earnestly and with energy and most praiseworthy perseverance to that noble end. But it is a very different thing when men, who themselves had already lost all belief in a spiritual control of the universe, began to theorize and lay down laws of theoretic speculation regarding the origin of the universe and the origin of man, the working of the universe and the continuation of man therein, and the future of the universe and man's future in it. These were not scientific facts discovered by research. They were theories, speculations, hypotheses only, derived from the imagination of men who had lost a belief in a spiritual control of the universe. Sincere efforts these were, of course, but they were based on no spiritual belief, and therefore these scientists could not render into a comprehensive whole, a philosophic whole, the facts in nature which they had discovered.

Examine those early days of complete materialism beginning about the time of Voltaire and others. I use Voltaire as an example, not because he was the originator of this era, but because he was one of its earliest products and one of its noblest. He was a fighter against dogmatism of any kind. More glory to him! But his work likewise destroyed belief in a spiritual universe.

What were these scientific theories on the one hand, and religious theories on the other hand? That this universe runs itself, that there is no spiritual power in it controlling it or guiding it, and that things happen by chance, not by law. This was uttered out of one side of the mouth of scientists and out of the other side came the equally fervent statement: the universe is caused by the laws of nature. With one side of the mouth they preached fortuity and chance and with the other side they preached laws. It never seemed to strike them that these two preachments were mutually destructive.

What, then, were the factors that Darwin stated made evolution, or what were the conditions under which evolution took place; or again, what caused evolution? It was a struggle — a struggle in which the fittest survived, not the best, not the noblest, but the strongest. This was thought of as a law of nature. There was not a word in Darwin or in Lamarck or in

Haeckel or in Huxley, or in any of these great men so called, of the last century, about this world's being ruled by intrinsic moral sanctions, not a hint of it. It was a rule of brute force in which the strongest, the fittest survived, and the fittest meant the most brutally strong, not the best. Thus, a man and a shark in the ocean — which is the more fit to survive in case a conflict should arise between them? The shark will survive because it is in its element. He is the fitter in that element and he will kill the man. Yet the man is the nobler creature, the better, the more evolved.

That is what Darwinism is: chance action by nature in a desperate struggle to survive, in which the weak are eaten or go to the wall and brutal strength only is the cause of victory. These ideas are destructive of the soul-life of mankind, whether they are born from theology or science. Get these facts clear, and examine the lapses from logic in our scientific works, the lapses in the reasoning of our scientists.

It was into a world governed by a belief in brutality as nature's sole way of functioning that came the god-wisdom through H. P. Blavatksy, and, as she proclaimed, her first work was to keep alive in man his spiritual intuitions, so that he would react against this "rule" so called and miscalled, this "accident" in nature, this rule of brutal force. Look at the actions of the peoples of the earth during the last three or four hundred years. Look at the world today. The result of soul loss, of the stifling of the spiritual instincts of the human being. Indeed, theosophists have reacted with power against these teachings, whether from the theologic or the scientific side. We have faced the scorn and the ridicule of a day when even to speak of the human soul meant loss of caste.

Look what H. P. Blavatsky did. Almost alone and single-handed she challenged the thought-life of the world and brought about by her courage and her teachings the founding of the Theosophical Society, proclaiming aloud and to all and sundry that the world was ruled by moral law and that he who infringed that law, whether under the hypocritical guise of virtue or whether openly and desperately as the criminal does — *that he who breaks that law shall pay.* Today the world no longer believes that. It believes that the only way to make what they think is a criminal pay is to use greater brutal power than anyone else does. They no longer believe in the rule of spiritual law. They no longer believe that this universe of ours is governed by moral sanctions. They take the law into their own hands. Is this the truth? Is this religion? Is this philosophy? Is this science? It is not religion, it is not philosophy, it is not science. All these three in their essence proclaim the rule of law in nature; that this law is spiritual and therefore moral; that there is cause and there is effect emanating from that cause, and that these effects are ineluctable and cannot ever be avoided. They should, can, and will haunt your footsteps as the cart follows the foot of the ox which draws it — a magnificent old Buddhist statement of the *Dhammapada* written in a day when men believed that the universe was ruled by spiritual and moral sanctions.

Do an evil deed and, sure as the cart follows the foot of the ox which draws it, that evil deed will haunt you and find you out in this life or in a future one. This is religion, this is philosophy, this is science; especially science, teaching as this last does its doctrine of cause and effect, its doctrine that effect follows cause and is alike unto its parent cause. The world no longer believes in these things. The peoples no longer believe in them. Only those fine spirits whose intuition flames brighter than in the majority of our fellow human beings have disbelief in these teachings of materialism now dying: dying in religion, dying in philosophy, dying in science, but whose maleficent consequences afflict us like Atlantean karma even today weighing heavily upon us.

So it is important to support in the science of our time all those elements which uphold the belief in a spiritual governance of the world. It is important for us to support in philosophy those elements, those philosophic elements, which teach that the universe is controlled by intrinsically moral sanctions. It is important for us to support with deepest sympathy and understanding those elements in religion which, casting aside the materialism of the last 1800 years more or less, teach that divinity filleth all vessels, whether vessels of honor or vessels of dishonor; for to divinity neither the one nor the other is dishonorable. That divinity is the spirit universal out of the womb of which come all beings and things, and back into which celestial haven in due course of the revolving ages all things and all beings shall one day return.

The most needed thing for us today is to do our utmost to bring about a renascence, a rebirth, in the minds of men of the truth that this universe of ours is under the most strict cosmical moral law, in other words, of harmony; for what in the universe is harmony, in the human soul we call the ethical instinct. Remember that the man who is sincerely convinced that his thoughts and feelings are going to result in action and that he is responsible for this action, will take thought, and long and searching thought, before he acts. There you are. Just that simple law, a belief by us men that this universe of ours is not the product of chance; that it is infilled with moral power and that this moral force resides in the human soul and that this moral force in the human soul should be our guide in our daily conduct. If men followed just that simple rule our life here on earth would be a heaven when compared with what it now is. All too long has thinking man been under the illusion or māyā that he could take nature's laws into his own hands and in his feeble manner with his weak and shaky intellect attempt to administer cosmic justice.

How the gods must laugh at us! And if they weep, as some say they do, how at times their celestial eyes must be filled with the tears of divine pity for man!

The Virgin Birth

THE CHRISTMAS FESTIVAL, and the teachings which have gone with it from early Christian days, are not at all Christian in origin. They never were invented by Christian theologians or devotees, but were all based upon current pagan ideas of the Sanctuary. And this, very far from being an unusual event in Christian history, was a very common thing, for the Christians took over from the very philosophies and religions of the day — which later they scorned and rejected — the great bulk of the ideas that in later times became what was known as Christian theology.

The early Christians were brought up in the pagan world where it was an acknowledged fact that there was an exoteric religion or series of such religions, and a secret teaching kept only for those who had proved themselves to be fit and worthy to receive the teachings of the Mystery Schools, the secret things of the divine. All the exoteric faiths hid something wonderful, sublimely majestic, taught within the Sanctuary. Get this fact clear, because it is history; and early Christian historians always blurred over or forgot or passed by that idea, without even a mere hint, and yet that is the atmosphere in which Christianity was born. If you get this key and hold it in your mind, you will have something by which you may unlock what has been so difficult to Christian theologians not merely to understand but to explain.

As regards the virgin birth, this is not original with Christianity. The conception has been common over the face of the earth from immemorial time. Many peoples in the archaic days taught of virgins giving birth to great sages and seers, and you may read this same story of Jesus the Avatāra in other tongues and after other ways, but having essentially the same fundamental truth of a great man achieving manly divinity by a new birth. So common was this idea that it was even popular exoteric language of the streets and of the mart.

The Hindus spoke of a *dvija*, a "twice born," the idea being that of physical birth, born of the mother as all sons of men are, but when ready after training, receiving inner birth, inner enlightenment, which was the second birth of the man, a new birth into the light of the spirit. You see how grand this thing is once we throw the light of theosophy upon it. It becomes no longer Christian but universal, and see how it appeals to the human heart and to the human mind. How grand indeed shines the light of truth upon the face of the man whose heart is enlightened by the sense of his oneness with all; and what pathos there is when the sense of separateness drives him away from his oneness with others.

What did this teaching mean in the early days of Christianity? Precisely what it meant in all the other great pagan countries. It represented scenes passed in the Sanctuary where the neophyte or disciple after long training had so developed his inner being, his inner perceptions, that he was on the verge of becoming Christos, a Christ, or as Mahāyāna Buddhism has it, a bodhisattva. The next step would be that of buddhahood. Even in exoteric writings this wonderful truth from the Sanctuary was spoken of as virgin birth, a second birth; and all the saviors of man in whatever country, of whatever clime, and of whatever day, all the great ones, the sages and seers, the buddhas and bodhisattvas of highest rank, the greatest, were all born of the Mother, the holy spirit within. How beautiful, how true! It appeals to us instantly, and it is in strict accord with even the little that modern scientific research is beginning to tell us of what they call psychology. We all recognize it when a man's life is improved and raised by his own efforts and strivings to become greater. It is the first faint dawn in the Mystic East, the beginning as it were of the holy birth pangs whereby a man becomes superman. In time he becomes an incarnate god, the god within, and he thereafter manifests through the Christ-child, and the man of flesh becomes responsive to the inner flame, the inner light, the inner fire. See you not what dignity this lends to us human beings? What hope for the future for those who dare, who strive, who keep silent!

Here is a very significant thing in early Christian writings: if Mary were virgin, how could she give birth to children? In early Christian scripture there occurs a remarkable passage in the Greek Christian writings, and rendered into English it means: "My Mother, the Holy Spirit (for the Holy Spirit, the Holy Ghost, amongst primitive Christians was always feminine, never masculine as it became afterwards) my Mother, the Holy Spirit, took me by the hair of my head and brought me to the holy Mount Athor." Do you get it? Here is the spirit in me, the Holy Spirit, my Mother from whom I was born, born anew, no longer born of the flesh but born of the spirit: born first of water according to the flesh, then born of fire according to the spirit — the first birth and the second birth. This is indeed the virgin birth; for the spirit of man, a ray from the divine, from the ineffable, is eternally virgin, and yet eternally fecund, eternally productive. The cosmic Christ is born of the cosmic Spirit, feminine also in ancient time, and in the same way is the spiritual man feminine, and in the holiness of achievement gives birth to the bodhisattva, the Christ-child, and from then on the man is infilled with the holiness of the spirit pouring through him from the source divine.

What connection has all this with the sun? From immemorial time, Father Sun was looked upon with reverence — not necessarily the physical globe clothed with beauty and light and splendor and vital energy, the giver of light unto his own kingdom, but the divinity within and above and behind that sun as of all other stars. Our sun was an emblem of the cosmic spirit, for through that sun poured these floods of vital splendor and life and light: light for the mind and love for the heart, without which no man is man.

The Christians used to sing hymns to the sun, record of which is still extant, outside of other references, in a communication by Pliny, governor of Bithynia and Pontus, to the emperor Trajan in Rome. He said that in his jurisdiction the Christians seemed to be innocent and harmless folk, for they assembled every morning at the rise of the sun and sang hymns to that divinity. And in a collection of old Christian hymns we have one to the sun still extant, something I have often quoted. In English it can be translated thus:

> O thou true sun
> Shining with perpetual light,
> Image of the holy spirit
>   [not merely a creation of holy spirit but its image]
> Infill us full.

No Parsi or so-called sun worshiper ever created a more typical hymn to the sun than these early Christians did. These earliest Christians knew what they meant; they did not worship the physical sun, it was the divine light, teaching what the sun stood for. The sun was the emblem, the image, of the cosmic Christ, not a creation of god, but the image of the divine. O thou true sun — and the most common expression among the Christians was to liken their savior, Jesus the avatāra, to the sun.

I would that I had the time and could tell you more of the recondite mysteries of this teaching, but I will merely say this: that in man's constitution there is a solar element. Could it be otherwise? There is a lunar element, and an element derivative from every one of the planets. Even science tells us that we not only share in the cosmic light that reaches us from Father Sun, but also that the very heat we get from the coal or the wood which we burn originally derived from the sun, that the atoms which compose it are the same which passed through us, and that the solar body reaches not merely the earth but all the other planets. Of course there is a solar element in us and a lunar element and an element from each one of the planets. Otherwise we should be incomplete. Man has everything within himself that the universe has.

Even though a man have all knowledge and have not love in his heart, it profiteth him nothing; for it is simply a declaration that the man is incomplete, unevolved, because, being a part of the universe, he does not show forth or manifest all that is in the universe, everything that the whole has. I might have all the truth in the world, but I cannot understand it properly. I can reason and think about it, but I do not get the coherency of the reality because the heart is not yet awake within me. The magic key of love flames not yet in my breast.

Just ask yourself this question: two men you know. One has all the knowledge in the world, but he is heartless; and the other is a simpleminded man, is not sophisticated, but his heart is great with love's universal, all-comprehensive sympathy. Which of the twain would you choose for a companion and one to whom you can turn in time of trouble?

Let the Christ-Child Live

THEOSOPHISTS LOOK UPON CHRISTMAS in two ways: first, as the record of a sublime fact in occult history and life, a sublime fact that every son of man some day in his own spiritual history will repeat, if he climb successfully. And the other way is even more dear to me, that there is an unborn Christ in the soul of every one of us, the Christos, the Prince of Peace, the Prince of Love. As the cycling days bring the Christmas season around and the Christian world celebrates the supposed birth of the physical body of its Prince, its Chief, its Savior, we may take the words of the avatāra, the Christ, in their higher sense: that we humans are the "sons of god," of the divine, and that the spirit of love and consciousness of the most high dwelleth in the sanctuary of every man's heart — which means that there is a Christ-child in my heart, in your heart. Certain Orientals call it the Buddha, the Celestial Buddha in our hearts, but the idea is the same, if the words are not.

So when the Christmas season comes around it is a good time to let the Christ-child in our hearts speak, to attempt to understand it; nay more, to become at one with it so that with each new Christmas we may become more Christ-like, more Buddha-like, more spiritual, nobler exemplars of the Christ which lives in the heart of each one of us, so that one day, at the proper occult time, the Christ-child may be born as a Christ-man. Then the sun of healing will have arisen with health, with wholeness, in its wings, healing our sorrows, healing our troubles, effacing our woes, wiping the tears of grief from our eyes; simply because we as individuals shall have become at one with the spirit of the universe of which a ray, a bright ray, lives at the heart of each one of us. This is what we understand by the true birth of the Christ — quite outside of the other facts of the case.

Let the Christ-child live. Do you know, we have not ever tried it? We talk about it and dream it and debate it, but how few of us men and women live it, *live it*, come under its celestial influence? The one who does so is ten times the man he was before, keener of intellect, quicker of wit, larger of mind; for he is inspired by the very forces that hold the universe in order, in proportion as he becomes the Christ-child in his heart.

The Exoteric and Esoteric H.P.B.

INSTEAD OF TALKING TO YOU about what H. P. Blavatsky's work was, and what she has done, it might be interesting to try to give you a few important thoughts regarding H.P.B. herself: who she was, what she was, and why she came; and I shall try briefly to do this.

First, then, I shall talk to you on the exoteric H.P.B. There were two in one in that great woman — an outside which met the world and had to face the conditions of the world into which she came to work; and an inside, a living flame of love and intelligence, a flame of inspiration and holy light, and this latter was the esoteric side of H.P.B.

As you look at her face and study it, and consider the Russian features, the lineaments which proclaim the steppes of Great Russia: if you pause on these alone you will see little but a face in which there is not much of merely human beauty. Yet those who have eyes to see and who look behind the veil of the physical personality, indeed can see something else. They can see beauty, they can see intense pathos and a great sadness — not the sadness, not the pathos, of one who had a great work to do and who could not or did not do it, but the yearning, the pathos, the sorrow, that have always been connected with the figure called in the Occident the Christ. Just so! For behind these outer lineaments which some artists have actually called ugly, we see an ethereal beauty which no words will easily describe, but which every heart can sense, and which every eye which is spiritually opened can also see. There is inspiration in that face which is beautiful to look upon; there is self-dedication; there are thoughts divine because there is truth, and truth is nature's own divine heart. It is these spiritual qualities which shine out of the face of H.P.B. when we look at her picture, and which proclaim to us that behind the outer person there was the inner living esoteric fire.

Does anyone who has studied the wisdom-religion of antiquity imagine for a moment that H.P. Blavatsky came to the Occidental world by chance, outside of nature's laws and rigid concatenation of cause and effect which produce everything in due order? Does anyone imagine therefore that whatever is, has not its ordered and concerted place in the cosmic harmony? Of course not. This therefore means that she came in obedience to a law, one of nature's laws about which the ignorant West knows all too little, and therefore doubts, and because of doubting is blind — for doubt always veils the inner vision.

H.P.B. came because it was time for her to come. She was one of the series of teachers which human history shows us to come at certain stated periods throughout the ages, one teacher after the other, and always when the time is right and ripe, and never by chance. She was one of the links in what the ancient Greek initiates called the Living Chain of Hermes, the Golden Chain, in connection with the passing on of mystic and esoteric light and truth, and she came in regular serial succession to the teachers who had preceded her, each one of them sent forth from the great association of sages and seers, variously called mahatmas, the elder brothers of mankind, and by other names. These teachers, these leaders and guides of mankind, come and teach according to law, esoteric and natural law, when the time calls for their coming; otherwise how logically explain their serial existence?

The ages pass, and each age has a new generation, and each generation receives light from the generations which preceded it, from its fathers. But generations rise and they fall, physically in civilization as well as spiritually in light, and in the intellectual, the ethical, and mental courses which men follow in producing the civilizing influences of human life. And in these generations which follow each other, there is always need for guiding minds, for a light given anew from age to age, for a new lighting, phoenixlike, of the old fires. It is these passers-on of the light who compose the Golden Chain of Hermes.

Now what do these teachers bring to mankind? Doctrines contrary and antagonistic and opposite to the doctrines and teachings of those who had preceded them? Never, never, when their teachings are properly understood. Examine the teachings of all the great sages and seers who have appeared among men. You will find them essentially one, although expressed in different languages, expressed in different forms and formulations of thought appropriate to the respective ages in which each of the messengers appeared. Although clad in various garments, clothed in differing habiliments, the body of truth that they taught and teach is one.

Now what these sages brought, H. P. Blavatsky also brought. Examine, test, this statement, prove it for yourselves — and the literatures of the world lie before you enabling you to do this. If she taught anything that the great seers who preceded her did not teach, it will be to me a wonder if you can find it, and I believe that you cannot. You remember what Confucius said in effect: "I teach nothing new. I teach what my predecessors have taught. I love the ancients, therefore I teach what they taught." Details of the teaching differ, the clothing of the teaching varies of necessity, but the teaching itself is the truth of and about nature, about nature's own being, its structure, its operations, its carpentry, its characteristics, its laws. When the theosophist says nature without further qualification, he never limits this word to the physical world alone. He means universal Being, including divine nature, spiritual nature, intellectual nature, physical nature, astral nature — all the spiritual and ethereal realms and spheres and worlds and planes which compose what the great thinkers of both the Occident and the Orient have called the spirit and soul and body of the universe.

That is what she taught. That is what the great sages and seers taught: an open or outer teaching and an inner or hid teaching; an exoteric doctrine for the public, and an esoteric doctrine for those who had proved themselves capable of understanding it and ready in their understanding to hold it secret and sacred. For if it were proper to give this esoteric teaching to the public, it would be so given. Remember that the archaic wisdom-religion of the ages is man's natural heritage, and belongs to him by right; but we as individuals have no right to our heritage until we come of age, until we become mature of mind and are no longer spiritual and intellectual infants, ready to abuse what is indeed ours by right, but which nature and the gods and the masters in compassion and love and wisdom withhold from erring men, until they shall have learned to control themselves. Then men will be able to control what belongs to them by natural right. There will then no longer be a danger of misapplication or of misuse.

Grand and sublime ethics were the basis of what this noble messenger of the masters, H.P.B., taught. She showed us that ethics, that morals, are based on the very structure and laws of nature herself, that ethics and morals are no mere human convention, that right is eternally right no matter how men may argue about the details, and that wrong is eternally wrong. Right is harmony, and wrong is disharmony. Harmony is nature's heart of love and music and peace, for it is equilibrium; and disharmony is discord, lack of peace, unmusical discords in nature and throughout human life; for all nature is ensouled just as man is, and this doctrine of ethics is one of the noblest of the teachings which she brought. She taught us of our inseparable oneness, of our unity, with the heart of Being, so that death no longer is seen as a grizzly phantom, but as the grandest adventure that it is possible for a human being to undertake, a sublime and magnificent initiation into other worlds, into a nobler, a grander, and a greater life.

One of a serial succession of teachers, she came in the rhythmical order of the laws which control our planet. She came indeed at the beginning of one Messianic cycle of 2,160 years and at the end of the preceding cycle of the same term. She was the messenger for her age, that is, for the age to come — the one who was to sound a new keynote, which yet, mystically speaking, is as old as the ages, and in a certain very true but little known sense, she was an avatāra — an avatāra of a certain type or kind, for there are different kinds of avatāras. Every teacher who comes to teach comprises not only his or her body and an unusually received psychological apparatus, but is likewise at times infilled with the holy fire of a greater soul, and therefore is de facto an avatāra of a kind. Just as Jesus called the Christ was an avatāra of one kind for his age, so was H. P. Blavatsky an avatāra of another kind for her age.

It is usual among modern Occidentals, especially artists, to portray Jesus called of Nazareth as a man of wonderful physical beauty, of outstanding manliness, and of fascinating appearance; but was he really so? Is this picture true to fact? It is an idea or ideal of the Middle Ages and of our own times. Do you not know that the Christian Church Fathers often took pride in proclaiming the idea aloud to the world that Jesus was a man of mean appearance, insignificant in body and in physical form? Yet what has that, true or false, to do with the flame within, the flame of the spirit which shines through the mortal clay, so that the latter like a lamp becomes luminous and glows and gives light to those around? That is where the true spiritual entity is — within.

I will tell you the reason why H.P.B. — this present avatāra of the particular kind I speak of — had the form of one whose physical appearance is unhandsome. With her the causative reason has thus far succeeded wonderfully well. With Jesus, the Syrian avatāra, the same reason failed of effect in succeeding ages. What was and is this reason? This: an endeavor was

made by the teachers, is indeed made at each new appearance
of a messenger, to have that messenger make his spiritual and
intellectual mark on the world solely by the fire of the genius
within, only by the fire of divinity within, and to prevent later
generations from falling down and worshiping, through instinctive love of beauty, the physical body. It is against the instincts
of the human heart to adore ugliness, to pray to that which is
unhandsome. In the case of Jesus, in later times blind faith and
foolish adoration prevailed. In the case of H.P.B., the woman
unhandsome has saved us and her thus far from that fate. No
man or woman is drawn to worship ugliness, and this in itself
is right, in a sense; it is not wrong, because it is an instinct of
the human soul to know that inner beauty will produce outer
beauty, perhaps not so much in form, but in appearance. There
will be the beauty of manly and womanly dignity, the beauty
of the inner light shining forth in love and wisdom, kindliness
and gentleness. I do hope that you understand what I mean in
making these few short observations.

Two thousand one hundred and sixty years before H.P.
Blavatsky's birth the particular Messianic cycle began which,
as its centuries followed one the other, plunged European
countries into the darkness of the Middle Ages. Today, more
or less 2,160 years afterwards, a new cycle opened when she
was born, a rising cycle which should bring light, peace, knowledge, wisdom, to men; and it is the duty of theosophists, as
common members of the Theosophical movement, to see to
it that the message which she brought and gave into our hands
as a holy charge shall be kept pure and unadulterated, and shall
be passed on to our descendants of succeeding generations just
as we have received it. As I have received it, thus must I pass
it on, not otherwise. *Iti mayā śrutam* — "Thus have I heard."

I think that the greatest tribute that our hearts and minds
can give to H.P.B. is to know her exactly as she was, exactly
as she was in truth, not merely according to what anybody says

about her. The best way to see her as she was is to study her, and her books which indeed are she. Then you will know the real H.P.B., for you will use the test of your intelligence and of your heart, to judge her by what she herself was and by what she produced, not by what someone else may say about her. Let us carry on the torch of light that she gave into our hands.

H. P. Blavatsky came to a world which was in the throes of a veritable "dance of death," a *danse macabre*, in which might be heard, according to this medieval idea, the clattering of the bones of the dead, the hooting of the owls of despair, and where one might sense dank, evil-smelling odors of the graveyard wherein men had buried their hopes. That was the world to which she came and the time in which she spoke: a time when men had lost virtually all faith in recognizing that there could be a knowledge of spiritual things, a time when even to speak of divinity, of a lasting hope, and of things spiritual, was considered to be a mark of intellectual imbecility. The very word soul was tabu.

Single-handed, that mighty woman wrought a change in human thinking by the power of her spiritual knowledge which enabled her to work on human spirits and human souls, and in so doing she cast seeds of thought into human minds, which seeds swept like sparks of flame through human understanding. By the tremendous energy of her intellect she taught men and women to think of life and nature in a new way, for she showed to them that the doctrines of the dying materialism, which were then so fashionable and to which they had given the confidence of their hearts, were hollow-sounding brass and tinkling cymbals, and that they were not only foolishly burying their noblest hopes in the graveyard of material existence, but likewise were fashioning themselves inwardly to become like unto the graveyard towards which their feet were carrying them.

A mighty power came into the world and worked and wrought, and the weaving of the web which she wrought has

played a great part in producing the better conditions we find
among us today. The world today is beginning to think
theosophy, to think in a theosophical way, and hence the macab-
rian dance of her times has been stopped — that dance of death,
that giddy, soulless, thoughtless, dance of death in the graveyard
of human hopes — that has ceased!

There is a psychological wonder, a mystery, in H.P.B., for
H.P.B. was a mystery. Since she came and taught, what do
we find our greatest scientific researchers and thinkers telling us today? Adumbrations of many of the doctrines that
she taught: doctrines, so far as these scientific researchers are
concerned, which are based upon deductions made from the researches into physical nature that those scientists are following.
Before the scientist found the facts, she taught these facts, and
she taught them in the face of ridicule and scorn and opposition
from the church on the one hand and from science on the other
hand, and from the established privileges and prerogatives of
all kinds — social, religious, philosophical, scientific — which
surrounded her.

In her there was strength, spiritual strength, for she set
men's souls aflame; in her there was intellectual power, for she
taught men to think and to have a new vision; and in her also
there was psychological power, for she smashed the māyāvi
psychological wall which man in his folly had built around
his consciousness.

Now reflect upon what all this means. Could you have done
it? Would you have had the courage to dare it? Could you,
single-handed, face the world in a similar manner today? There
is a cause and a reason for the work that she wrought. We today
see the effects, we know the historical phenomenon of her life
and work; but what was the noumenal cause? It was the living
spiritual and intellectual fires within her. It was the *esoteric* side
of H. P. Blavatsky which enabled her to do what she did.

Do you think for a moment that H.P.B. was only an ordinary

woman? Do you think that the stories that have been told about her, such as Mr. Sinnett's *Incidents in the Life of H. P. Blavatsky*, contain all the real facts about her life, and do you suppose that even the statements that are therein narrated contain in themselves a full explanation of her? Don't believe it! The facts in themselves are against such a belief. Such a woman as Sinnett describes in his *Incidents* could never have moved the world as H.P.B. did. Do you think that the Russian girl that he describes, and that the Russian priestess, so called, that Solovyoff, her quondam friend and later her bitter foe, tried to portray, could have done it? Do you think that a hypocrite, that a false heart joined with an ordinary mind, could have gathered around her the intellectual and often highly ethical people whom she did? Of course not.

Take into consideration the facts in H. P. Blavatsky's life. Don't let your minds be swayed by the tales that have been told about her. Think them over for yourself, because thoughtful reflection is one of the first duties of a theosophist, and then draw your own conclusions. Indeed, the stories that have been told about H.P.B. interest us simply as a psychological phenomenon of the weakness of human thinking, because they describe the incapacities of the men and women who try to explain her. You might as well try to put the ocean into a teacup as to encompass the character, the constitution, of H.P.B. in the yarns professing to be biographical that have been written about her. At the best they contain certain facts gathered in random fashion from her own family — who understood her perhaps less than her theosophical friends did, and who said so — gathered together and strung along a certain thread of narrative. Is the reading of such tales the pathway to understanding one who did what she did?

H. P. Blavatsky was of course a woman in body, remember that; and invigorating and inflaming this body with its brain-mind was the inner divine Sun, the inner Buddha, the living

Christ within as the mystical Christians of today say. But between this divine fire and the receptive and mystically-trained and educated brain of the woman, there was a psychological apparatus, commonly spoken of in Western parlance as the human soul, which in the case of her — for she was an initiate of the Order of the Buddhas of Compassion and Peace — could at times step aside and allow the entrance into the vacancy thus left of a human soul loftier by far than even hers.

Thus was she an avatāra of her kind. It was this buddhic splendor which thus infilled the vacancy that she so gladly left for use, which in large part wrought the works of wonder that H.P.B. wrought. You may remember that in her writings she often makes a distinction between what she calls H.P.B. and H.P. Blavatsky. H.P. Blavatsky was the woman, the chela, the aspiring, learning, splendid, noble, courageous chela. But H.P.B. was the master's mind speaking through her. Body and spirit, one entity; then the intermediate psychological apparatus, commonly called the soul, temporarily removable at will. In fact, when H.P.B. was sent as the messenger, that psychological apparatus in large part remained behind. This fact accounts for the so-called contrarieties and contradictions of her character that the people who attempted to write about her saw — and saw very plainly, because they could not help seeing — but which they did not understand, and by which they often misjudged her and misunderstood her. But when the holy flame had infilled this vacancy, then there was H.P.B. the teacher, the sage, the seer, the teacher of great natural scientific truths which science today is but beginning to show to be true, the teacher of a great hope to mankind, the giver of a vision to men, the framer and former of a new philosophy-religion-science for men.

Shall we look upon H. P. Blavatsky merely as a Russian gentlewoman? If so, a most marvelous gentlewoman was she! The simple theory will not fit the facts — a Russian woman who had no education, technically speaking: no education in science, no education in religion, no education to speak of in philosophy, but who was educated in mystical lines; and yet the H.P.B. who lived and taught was an adept, and in her teachings was a master in all these lines of human knowledge!

Shall we look upon her as an incarnate mahatma? The facts are against that, all against it, just as they are all against the former theory. Let us take H. P. Blavatsky exactly as she was, not as she is misrepresented to be. Let us take her as we know her to be. Let us take her as we find her in her books. Let us take the facts, and no man's theories about her; and if you are wise enough you will see, you will understand, who and what she was.

There were times in her social life when she was the charming hostess, a *grande dame*. There were other times when she was a pianist of admirable and most exceptional ability. Again at other times she charmed people with her brilliant conversational powers, and she would fascinate a whole room, hold her audience spellbound. Men of learning, the laborer, the noble, prince and peasant, gathered to hear her. There were still other times, in her home, when things were quiet and her disciples gathered around her, when she taught some truths drawn from the Great Mysteries of the wisdom-religion of the past. There were other times when she sat at her desk, and wrote and wrote and wrote from morning until night, and then would lie down, and, as she herself said, for a little while went "home." She then had rest!

There were other times when she would hold her at homes, her receptions, during which she would receive scientists, philosophers, thinkers, controversialists of various kinds, philosophical, scientific, religious; chat with them; and they would leave her in amazement. "Whence comes to this woman," they said, "her marvelous understanding? How is it that she can tell me secrets of my own profession which I knew not before?

Whence comes to her the ability to show me that this is so?" All these moods, these sides of her character, were indeed there, and every one must be taken into account. Only the explanation of the facts themselves will enable you to understand her. At times she was the woman, and was tender and compassionate, with a woman's love of rings, of sweet perfumes, and of kindly friends. At another time she was the teacher and sage. At another time she was strong and virile, so that, as her friends said, it seemed verily as if man incarnate were manifesting through her — not any one man, but Man.

Now you have it: the body, the woman, the gentlewoman, well-trained, well-bred, ill-educated; the divine flame within her that occasionally seized her brain as it were — and then she spoke like a pythoness, like a prophetess, like an oracle at Delphi; and similarly so at other times, when she was infilled, as the avatāra, with the holy flame of one of the Great Ones. Then she was the sage and seer, and wrote her books, foreshadowing in these books what later has come to pass, and pointing out to men the dangers of a belief divorced from ethical rules.

Let us recognize H. P. Blavatsky for what she was; and mind you, my friends: we who have studied H.P.B. love her, are faithful to her in heart and mind, yet we shall set our faces like flint, like stone, against any attempt to worship her, to make a new Jesus out of her. You know what the Great Ones have told us: more than anything else do we desire a brotherhood among men, a brotherhood which will save mankind from the catastrophes which are facing it, brought about by its own folly. The catastrophes, the cataclysms, moral and even physical, which are even now facing us, will surely come upon us unless men and women change their habits of thought and, in consequence, their acts, their conduct. We shall set our faces like stone against any attempt to introduce a new religion, which our great teachers have already pointed out is one of the greatest curses and banes afflicting mankind at the present time: belief in an outside savior instead of fidelity to the divine spirit within. For there within indeed lie all truth, all harmony, all wisdom, all love, all peace. The inner god within each one of you as an individual is of the very heart of the heart of the universe, and concerning that heart of the universe, each one of you is It.

H.P.B. was indeed a mystery, but while she was a mystery, this does not mean a mystery in the sense in which this word is commonly used in the Occident. She was a mystery in the sense of the ancient Greeks, when they spoke of the ancient Mysteries and the ancient Mystery Schools — something which is hid, but can be known, something that is occult and holy, but which can be communicated.

H.P.B. can be understood; and when we understand her, we love her the more; the more we understand her, the greater grows our love, our veneration, for her. Let it never happen, therefore, that theosophists become so false to the trust which she gave to us that we shall turn our backs to the Mystic East, towards which she always pointed, and worship the avatāra. Let us be faithful to our trust. We can love, we can venerate, we can copy the example of magnificent courage and sublime hope that she gave to us. We can try to become like unto this great woman, and unto many others like her who have appeared in the past, who will appear in the future, others far greater than she, but let us never set her on a pinnacle as was done, alas! in the case of one of the teachers in the early years of Christianity.

No greater tribute could we render to our beloved H.P.B. than by continuing faithfully, and in our love of her, the work which she so grandly began.

The Vision of the Lord Buddha

WHEN I WAS A BOY of twelve I came upon a Buddhist quotation which fascinated imagination, mind, and heart. I think it was one of the things which in this life awoke me more than any other thing that I can recollect. It is pure theosophy and genuine Buddhist doctrine. It is this: the Lord Buddha is speaking, and I am paraphrasing his words in order to make them clearer: "O disciples, never let discouragement enter into your souls. See you suffering in the world, see you unhappiness and pain and ignorance, misery and distress which wring the heart? Disciples, all things are destined to pass into buddhahood: the stones, the plants, the beasts, all the component atoms of these, each and every one, aye, and sun and moon and stars and planets — all in future ages will become buddha. Each one will become a buddha."

What a marvelous picture! How it quiets the heart and stills the mind; for if one atom, one man, become a buddha, everything will, for this universe is one, broken into multitudes during manvantara or manifestation; rooted in that One, living from it, and by it. In it we live and we move and have all our being. Therefore some day, somewhere in the incalculable aeons of what we call the future, all now of the multitudes, suns and stars, planets, comets, gods, men, animals, plants, stones, atoms, elements, worlds, everything, each as individual, is destined for buddhahood.

When I read that, for nearly three months I went around in a daze of spiritual delight and inner reawakening. To this day I could not tell you whether I ate or drank or slept. I know I must have done so, but I have no recollection of anything except light; and the raising of the eyes inner and outer, upward and inward. Just that thought broke open the doors closed when I drank of the waters of Lethe, of forgetfulness, when last I died. The doors opened and the light came in, began to come in.

I think this extract gives us a most wonderful picture. Take the mineral kingdom: it is formed entirely of unconscient monads, that is monads unconscient on this plane, never unconscient in their own spheres. But what we call monads in the mineral kingdom are as it were the expressions of essential spiritual monads working and evolving down here on this plane, and going through these Gilgūlīm, as the Hebrew Qabbālāh has it, meaning these lower halls of life and experience, these worlds of the ceaseless evolutionary journey; yet each one is essentially a god, each one in essence a buddha, a ray of the Ādi-buddha or the cosmic Buddha. And so it is with all things.

Therefore, the Lord Buddha said: "Disciples, when sorrow wrings your heart, when pain and suffering are too bitter to bear, when you see others dying for the mere needs of life: be not discouraged. Look into the future. Every one of the multitudes some day will be a buddha, Ādi-buddha, therefore *a* buddha, stones and plants, and beasts and men and gods, suns and stars and comets and the elements of them all."

Yet this recognition of the essential divinity of all, and the certain future buddhahood of all, should never at any moment stay our hands from works of loving pity and helpfulness here and now; for it is here and now that lies our sublime duty of doing all we can to alleviate the world's suffering and need that are incident and necessary to the monads on their evolutionary journey.

Rules of Conduct

THE WAY TO BECOME LIKE unto the Great Ones is by beginning to become like unto them. Just that. Would you like a few rules? I will give them to you; but as soon as the brain-mind begins to think about rules, it begins to ask questions and make objections and exceptions. Nevertheless, here they are. Is your conduct in your daily life such that when you lie down to sleep at night, you can review the events of the day just closing and say to yourself: this I have done well; that I might have done better; that was not well done? and take your discoveries to yourself so to heart that when the next day dawns, and you may be faced with the same temptations, the end of the second day will find you reclining on your couch more at peace with yourself?

Tell the truth always, except when telling the truth will bring injury and suffering to others. Then be compassionate and suffer yourself in silence. In attaining what you desire, is there danger that you can obtain it, achieve it, only at the cost of suffering or loss to others; and even then that you can get it, attain it, only by double dealing, what is called the double-cross? Are you large enough to refuse to take that step downwards, it may be the first, towards the Pit? Do you realize that the next step, if you take that first step downwards, will be followed by an attempt to cover what you yourself are ashamed to tell? You become thereafter not merely a double-crosser, but a hypocrite; and the third step is easy, when discovery threatens to tempt you to cover your tracks by pleading charity, forgiveness, pity for others, and you acted thus for so-and-so because your heart ached to say aught.

Three steps: and have you noticed that each one of these steps is a distortion of your character, a twisting of your mind, and of the natural human impulses of your heart? That you thereby have made a definite mark upon your character which will perdure, it may be for aeons? How much better and simpler is it to do one's best to avoid having the feet mired in wrong-doing. Or if one is caught, to break free and ally yourself with the gods at any cost.

How many more rules might I not give. They are the simplest things in the world, these rules. They are so wonderfully occult, so simple and plain, that people won't believe in their efficacy half the time, and yet they are the rules made by the world's greatest sages and seers: live uprightly, speak the truth, let your life be clean, cleanly, so that you can look man or woman in the face without shame. Do unto others — I will put it in the other form — do not do unto others what you yourself object to having others do unto you. It is in this way that in due course of time Buddhas are born, the holiest men on earth.

Common Sense in the Home

IT IS MY MOST EARNEST CONVICTION that the so-called spiritual problems of the young are no greater today than ever they have been — not a whit greater; nor are they different or more embarrassing for children and parents alike. Human character does not change overnight. The Great War, supposed to have destroyed all old moralities, was simply the bursting of a dam, the flood sweeping away certain restrictions and limitations which nevertheless were good, and we have not as yet learned how to build up other fences of protection around our homes and our young people. But our young people are no worse and no better than we were, and the same fundamental problems of human character that faced us, face them. It is somewhat as an old boy that I myself write, for I believe that children are old folks not yet grown up, adults not yet matured, and that adults are still boys and girls.

I think one of the greatest spiritual problems for youth is their parents; and this is saying nothing against the parents, because they were youths at one time and had their parents. And the youth today will grow up and be parents equally relatively futile, and, alas, relatively inadequate! If there are any spiritual problems affecting the youth at any time, it is largely the fault of the parents, and I will tell you why I think so. The parents do not err from lack of love. They err from lack of common sense as to how to treat growing youngsters — just common sense.

If you want to correct a fault in some other man, you cannot do it by going to him and preaching at him, laying down the law. The chances are nine out of ten that he will resent it instantly. But by example you can make your words good to that man's mind and he will begin to admire you and respect you for exemplifying what you yourself talk about.

There is not anything that fascinates the mind of the growing youth so much as a striking remarkable example seen daily before the eye. It is worth years of talking and preaching, years and years of reading books that are stuck under its nose till it learns to hate these books. When it sees around itself in the home what is going on, snappy speeches from side to side, little selfish actions, unkindnesses done by father to mother, or vice versa, quarrels perhaps, short, irritable speeches, perhaps no words at all but the obvious habit of self-seeking in taking the easiest chair, the better light, the larger portion, in lack of courtesy to the other — when a child sees these things it remembers. These are the things which hurt the child. You older ones, put yourselves back into your childhood and remember whether you have not seen things in your own parents that hurt like the very dickens when you discovered them, and you wondered . . . And yet your parents may have been half saints — I do not mean to say that parents are bad. Not at all. But parents lack common sense. They wonder why their children go wrong sometimes. And here I am speaking of the normal child; if a child is born a degenerate, that of course is a cause for special treatment.

You have no right to have children unless you honestly feel in your hearts that you can bring them up properly. It is of infinite importance to make a child love and respect you, not for what it receives from you as gifts, which are often bribes to keep it from shrieking or making a noise, but love and respect you for what you *are*.

In my opinion, subject to correction by wiser minds than mine, the very best way to solve most of the so-called problems that face children is to let them see daily examples of unremitting courtesy at home. Just that one thing: unremitting kindliness and courtesy. Now what does that involve? It involves first of all self-control. Next, kindliness which means thoughtfulness for others. This is a wonderful discipline which a child understands and admires and loves to see. It sinks into the child's mind and heart; and these things are not forgotten. When a child is brought up in a home where there are lackadaisical conditions, slackness, not bad but little selfishnesses of the home, combined with emotional outbreaks of any kind, it in turn, because very imitative, becomes lackadaisical, emotionally unstable, unambitious to improve itself, slow in mind, discourteous to others, because too lazy to be courteous. It does not care. In a home where courtesy rules, everyone is happy. The child remembers the things it sees, and learns, because the example sinks into the mind. It becomes habitual in the child's thought, the child begins to pride itself on being courteous to others.

The whole root of the so-called difficult problem is this: we older people try to preach at the younger ones in giving them brain-mind thoughts; schemes to do this, and schemes to do that, which the children see the parents themselves do not practice. How can anyone respect something which is preached at him all the time and which he sees nobody else following or practicing? It is a very lovely idea, for instance, when parents want to have their children study beautiful books which give noble thoughts. They consider it a method of training, no doubt, presenting beauty to the mind of the child; but my opinion is — well, if I had children and I made them read for example the *Bhagavad-Gītā*, or any other similar book all day long; or if whenever they wanted to read they were given the *Bhagavad-Gītā*, before they were even fifteen years old, I know that they would hate that book like nothing else on earth. They would have to grow to be eighty years old before they would see the wondrous beauty of books like that. The child is quick to see that Daddy and Mother do not pass all their time when they have a little leisure at home in reading the *Bhagavad-Gītā*. They see that in their leisure they read other books, of a lighter character. There is an instance. You cannot expect your child to do what you yourself do not do. You as parents have to set the example. Now it is right to keep out of the home books which are obviously wrong, lewd or obscene or pornographic in tone. It is obviously wrong for adults or children to go to movies which picture the same ignoble things or precepts or examples. But I am not speaking of things which everyone condemns, nor am I decrying really good and elevating movies.

The minds of children are especially susceptible to suggestion and example. Precept is excellent, but precept comes afterwards when the child begins to ask questions: why? Then is the time to give the precept, to explain. But the child never forgets an example, and for the reason that children are old souls in immature bodies, souls coming to us out of the past, ages and ages of the past, having lived time and time and time again. They are wonderfully instinctive in catching things in you which finally become habitual in their thought and growth. They actually reason; and also commonly do they intuit things.

One of the greatest follies that parents commit is to bribe their children, is to talk to them and act towards them as if they were not reasoning beings. I believe it is all wrong. As a matter of fact I know it is, because I have seen how children despise in their hearts actions that their parents do in order to win acquiescence or approval, or a sweet smile from the child. What kind of love is it that the child gives to its parents, which has to be bought or bribed for? You don't need anything of that sort. The character of youth is intrinsically that of the hero-worshiper; it loves the ideal, the beautiful, what strikes it as strong and grand. I believe that youth loves these things more than we sophisticated older people do who have lost that appreciation.

Half the fear in the world begins in the home. It is a psychical injury to the child's mind, originated or brought about often by some circumstance or some ghastly thing that it has seen, that hurts, shocks. And the mind, by so much, is warped, hurt, injured, with fear. It is — I don't want to be uncomplimentary to the youth — but it is exactly the same principle by which a dog is trained, or a horse. You can make a dog or horse a vicious beast by ill-treating it. But if you treat a dog as you would a human being, in courtesy and kindliness and considerate action, you make that dog gentle towards others as well as towards you. That dog actually is in degree humanized. And the only difference in principle between us and the beasts is that we are far more evolved.

Make your homes centers of kindliness and courtesy — the parents to each other. That is the main thing. I do not mean manners only. That is only a part. I mean the actual instinctual wish to be kindly and courteous to the other; make this wish so strong in you that it takes action. The children sense it and see it and copy it, and they learn as they copy that it takes self-control to do it, to give up what "I" want in order to do a courteous act to others. This discipline teaches self-control, self-abnegation, self-respect; and when children discover that they win the respect of others for being this way, instinctively that self-respect is added to; they begin to see and feel that others have got the same feeling that they have, that others too admire and respect kindliness and courtesy. And then there grows in youth the feeling of fellowship, of brotherhood.

The old idea of a child honoring its parents and obeying them is a beautiful ideal, and is as valid in human conduct as ever it was. But the basis upon which this honor of parental dignity and standing should lie is the instinctive respect born in the minds of children and youth for their parents, because the parents themselves are seen by children to honor honor, respect respect, and revere reverence.

An Attitude of Balance and Vision

IT IS TRUE THAT THE WORLD is in a saddened and anxious state. But I think it unwise and spiritually and psychologically unwholesome to emphasize this, for it raises none to higher things but depresses courage, the courage to meet life and carry on in a higher and nobler way. See the beauty in and behind things, see the beauty in your fellowmen; see likewise the ignominy and the ugliness in life, although do not let these latter depress you or discourage you. There is no reason to lose our calm, our inner peace, in order to become like unto them of the mobs, passion driven, governed by prejudice. Such an attitude will not help us or those who suffer. But we can send forth into the world thoughts of courage and hope and an optimistic looking into the future: that no matter what happens through man's folly or infamy or infidelity to his inner god, to his spiritual essence, there are always right and justice which will ultimately triumph over all. The only thing is to be sure we are on the side of right and justice — and we cannot always judge by appearances.

The English poet Robert Browning expresses this thought, albeit in the theological language of the time, when he said: "God's in his heaven, all's right with the world." Those who do not like this optimistic outlook and conviction and who are trying to get down into the arena of hysteria and discouragement, mock at it; yet every sane man who keeps his mind cool and clear and can think for himself realizes full well that the mightiest forces in this world are cosmic right and cosmic justice, and that they in the long run will always prevail. There is no need to be discouraged. Avoid hysterias; on the other hand, avoid running at one and the same time with the hares and chasing with the hounds, which is what we all do more or less. Have your own convictions, and sometimes hide them if it is not wise to shout them from the housetops; but keep your own heart upright, in love with love, hating hate, always standing up for justice and innate right. Only be sure that when you stand up you are not standing up for the propaganda atmosphere around you, but for something that you in your own heart know to be right and true.

It would be a sorry thing indeed if there were naught to our world but what we see around us today, or have seen at particular intervals during the past; but every time and always the conscience and the sense of justice of mankind have proved supreme over all and risen above human feelings and follies, and marched onwards and upwards to balance and harmony. Don't be downhearted or discouraged or think the world is going to the devil because you don't like what is going on. You have a right to like it or to dislike it. But be sure that you, as an individual, on your part do not add to the hatred in the world, to its discouragement and unhappiness. That is my point.

Forgiveness and Karmic Action

THINK OF WHAT THE ANCIENTS meant when they spoke of men as the kin of the gods, the children of divinities, cooperating with the divinities in the affairs of the solar kingdom. It is true; and as time goes on and from manhood we pass into godhood, into becoming gods, our contributory efforts will be much better, much more beautiful, much wider, much richer, in every way grander. We are at present young gods at school, young gods at play. Our home is the solar system. It is likewise our schoolhouse, our university. This earth is, as it were, our schoolroom at present until we graduate to a higher schoolroom; but all our activity takes place in our university of life, which is the solar system. How wonderful a picture! And I can assure you that every human thought is registered for eternity on the deathless tablets of time. A thought of mine will touch with the most delicate finger of influence the remotest star in the galaxy and will affect that star by so much, just as I am affected by all thoughts around me.

Imagine two billion human beings on earth, the human race, that is, the imbodied portion of the human race. Suppose they are thinking, especially today due to the rapid improvements of intercommunication, all more or less at the same time about the same thing and pretty much in the same way — let us say it is a scare or a war hysteria or a great hate or a great emotion — do you think that that vast body of loosened psychic energy is not going to strike somewhere? Of course it will. And here is where karma comes in. It is an old, old teaching that the disasters that afflict mankind are mainly brought about by man, his own evil thinking and evil feeling throwing into the astral light or into the earth's atmosphere a simply terrific volume of energy, of force. You know the old English proverb, which is very true: "Curses like chickens come home to roost." They do not go and roost in somebody else's farm. Chickens come home. Thoughts of love, thoughts of beauty, thoughts of kindliness, benevolent thoughts and feelings: they likewise come like messengers from the gods winging their way back to us. Someday, somewhen, somewhere, we reap what we sow. If men and women knew and felt this great law, how differently would they not act towards each other! All feelings of revenge and hatred, and that diabolic fruit of self-seeking materialism that we must protect ourself at any cost against our brother: such things could never again find lodgment in our minds and hearts.

How true is the word of the old Hebrew prophet: "Vengeance is mine, . . . saith the Lord." What a warning! Theosophy shows us why and how. The man who suffers an injury would do infinitely better to accept and forgive, to take it manfully; his guerdon in recompense someday will be great, an injurer will become his benefactor; and if he stays his own hand, not only does he not add to the fearful weight of evil karma pressing on him, but he raises his enemy. An act like that is godlike. I say unto you, "Love your enemies." So spake the avatāra. Do good unto those who persecute you. Give not wrong for wrong, nor hate for hate. When will human beings learn this?

Capturing a World with Ideas

IT TAKES SOME COURAGE, I mean the true courage of the seer whom naught can daunt and none may stay, to oppose a world's thought currents, and for this sublime work are called forth the truest heroism, the sublimest intellectual vision, and the deepest spiritual insight. These last prevail always. Sometimes he who runs counter to the world's thought currents loses what the world esteems highest: reputation, fortune, even perhaps life. But his work — that is never lost!

This is what H. P. Blavatsky did. And this is what the Theosophical Society has been doing ever since. It is a strange paradox of our life on this earth that the noblest things call for sacrifice, and yet it is one of the most beautiful. The world is ruled by ideas, and an inescapable truth it is also that the world's lower thought currents must be opposed by ideas higher than they. It is only a greater idea which will capture and lead captive the less idea, the smaller. *Graecia capta Romam victricem captam subducit;* "captured Greece leads conquering Rome captive."

What is the Theosophical movement which was so magnificently voiced in some of its teachings by H. P. Blavatsky, but a series, an aggregate of grand ideas? Not hers, not collected by her from the different great thinkers of the world, but the god-wisdom of the world. She brought together the world's human wisdom in order to bulwark, for those minds who needed such bulwarking, the grand verities shining with their stellar light, and bearing the imprint of divinity upon them. Some cannot see the imprints of divinity. Forsooth, they say, it is to be proved! They must put the finger into the nail mark, into the hole. Millions are like that, they have not learned to think yet.

So the only way to conquer ideas is to lead them captive by grander ones; and that is what theosophy does. It is a body of divine ideas — not H. P. Blavatsky's, who was but the mouthpiece of them in this day, but the ancient god-wisdom of our earth, belonging to all men, all nations, all peoples, all times; and given to protoplastic mankind in the very dawn of this earth's evolution by beings from higher spheres who had learned it themselves from beings higher still — a primeval revelation from divinities. The echo of this revelation you will find in every land, among every people, in every religion and in every philosophy that has ever gained adherents.

When H. P. Blavatsky brought theosophy to the world in our age, she did not bring something new. I repeat, she brought the cosmic wisdom studied by the seers, as understood on this earth, which had been stated in all other ages preceding that in which she came: the same starry wisdom, divine in origin — science because voicing nature's facts; religion because raising man to divinity; philosophy because explanatory of all the problems that have vexed human intelligence.

It was an amazing world to which she came — the Western world I am now speaking of — a world held by one slender, yet in a way faithful, link to spirit, to wit the teachings of the avatāra Jesus called the Christ, nevertheless held to by faith alone and by the efforts of a relative few in the churches. On the other hand, millions, the major part of the men and women of the West, absolutely psychologized — by what? Facts? No! By theories, postulates, ideas, which had gained currency because they were put forth aggressively and with some few natural facts contained in them. Why, all the science of those days is now practically in the discard, and the later generations of scientists have themselves overthrown the overthrower of man's hope in those days.

It was in such a time that H. P. Blavatsky came, and almost singlehanded in an era when even in the homelife, in society, it was considered exceedingly bad form to speak of the soul in a drawing room; it was considered a mark of an inferior intelligence. Alone, she wrote her books, challenging the entire thought current of the Western world, backed as it was by authority, by so-called psychology, backed by everything that then was leading men astray. Today her books are being read by some of the most eminent scientific thinkers of our time. What did she do? Mainly she based her attack on that world psychology on two things: that the facts of nature are divine; that the theories of pretentious thinkers about them are not facts of nature, but are human theorizings, and should be challenged and if good, accepted pro tempore and, if bad, cast aside. She set the example; and other minds who had the wit to catch, to see, to understand, to perceive what she was after, gathered around her. Some of the men eminent in science in her time belonged to the Theosophical Society, although they rarely worked for it. They lent their names to it occasionally. But she captured them by the ideas she enunciated, and these men did their work in their own fields. That indeed already was much.

Consider her titanic task: that of changing the shifting and varying ideas of a body of earnest scientific researchers after nature's facts: replacing these shifting ideas, then called science — which had for nearly two hundred years been casting out *all* that innumerable centuries of human experience had shown to be good and trustworthy — replacing these with thoughts that men could live by and become better by following, thoughts that men could die by with hope and in peace; and bringing these back into human consciousness by the power of her own intellect voicing the immemorial traditions of the god-wisdom which she brought.

Karmic Results and the Bardo

I WONDER IF YOU CAN FORGET for a moment the matter-of-fact things in daily life and really feel or realize this fact: that you are going to be held to a strict accounting somewhen, somewhere, for everything that you are, which means everything that you have done, have felt, have been — karmic responsibility!

Most of us realize this and accept it as a philosophic proposition, but have not taken it into our consciousness as a serious reality facing us momently, daily, all our life long. We would be infinitely more careful than we are, not only in our feelings and in our thoughts, but of course in our actions. Whatever we do is not only going to mold our character, thereby changing our whole future destiny, but it is going to affect others; and others by that fact are going to react upon us. Action and reaction: nature's first law. That is all karma is: the doctrine of consequences, ethically speaking, the doctrine of responsibility. What ye sow, that will ye reap, not something else. The pathos of people who think that they can do what they want to do because they like it, or because they are afraid, too cowardly to do otherwise, and think they will get away with it! Never, never, never. You will pay for it to the uttermost farthing.

It is not only what happens to *you*. If you have hearts ever touched by the holy flame of pity, of compassion, you will realize that everything you think or feel will result in action some day, and this action will affect others, helping them, or injuring them. And *you* are responsible, no one else. And *you* will pay; yes, even if you fly to the uttermost ends of the earth, nothing can save you from resulting consequences.

By the same law, every gentle, pitiful act, every thought for others, every compassionate pulsation of the human heart, will have its holy recompense not only in the present gratitude of others, not only in their present friendship, sincere and given wholeheartedly, but even in future lives, for sympathy will have been set up between those others and yourself. How beautiful is sympathy! It is one of the things of this life of ours which not merely makes it endurable, but casts a glory around our living.

I think no man is so manly as when he does some act from compassionate urging, or refrains from acting because of the dictates of mercy whispering in his heart. A man like that is a true man and his life is beautiful. His guerdon in the *bardo*, as the Tibetans say, will be there for him to receive. Never think you may escape the consequences of your thoughts and feelings and acts. This truth is the lost chord in modern life; and the horrors we see in the world around us, or have seen or will see, might never have taken place, might never take place, if men could but once be convinced of this truth of the world, spiritual and natural: that you are responsible, held by nature's laws and habits to a strict accounting for all you do, which means all you think and feel carried into action. Nature's scales cannot ever be cheated.

Bardo is a word which means "between two," that is to say, between the end of this life or what we call death, and the beginning of the next imbodiment, incarnation. It means all the various things that will happen between the last physical breath of the one life, and the first physical breath of the next life, everything in between: the astral world, the kāma-loka, and the devachan.

The real teaching of the Tibetans regarding the bardo is identical with our own, because it came from the same source; but the Tibetan practices connected with the doctrine of the bardo are not our own. These practices came from the original Bhöns who were converted to Buddhism, and are often black magic. Yet it is unfair to call them black magic as the Tibetans practice them today, because the motive is good.

What are these practices? When a man is supposed to be dying or on the verge of death, lamas are sent for to come to his bedside, sit near him and whisper to him, telling him to have strong courage, to fear not, to keep his mind pure. And then they explain to him all the things that are going to happen to him when he dies. These are the practices that we would not endorse because they affect the departing soul, not necessarily adversely, but affect it in giving it a direction of thought, instead of allowing the karma of the last life to make its own aggregate of the last thoughts.

As a matter of fact in the more orthodox Christian churches they have something of the same idea. The clergyman or the priest will come to the bedside of the dying man, administering consolation and other things — all of which affect the mind of the dying man. If the dying man is rather simple, believes things easily, and all his life long has been an adherent of the church, and believes in it, probably no great harm is done.

But I merely point out that the Tibetans are not the only ones who have antemortem practices of that kind, as they express it, to speed the soul on its way. Infinitely better not! Let karma, let the voice of the silence, speak. Let the magic of weaving thought and feeling filled with the fabric of consciousness pursue its silent way undisturbed. Compassionate nature takes care of all, and it is infinitely better for those last holy moments of the departing consciousness to be in utter silence.

Beware then that at the bedside of the dying there be no loud noise, no weeping. Let there be utter silence and an atmosphere of peace. This is rich in kindliness and understanding. When the time comes when you die, you will remember this, and mayhap be thankful that those around you are not disturbing those last moments that you have.

The Guerdon of Self-Forgetfulness

THEOSOPHY WORKS A MAGIC upon us which is grander by far than merely telling us of the undoubted and beautiful truth of our essential divinity. It transmutes our weak and often evil manhood into godhood. It teaches us to forget ourselves for others — for the world. It so washes our natures and our hearts and our minds of the personal and limited that in time we are led on even to forget ourselves and live in the universal.

To me this is the lost keynote of modern civilization, whirling as it does around the egoisms born in us. If we can instill into the thought life of the world, of our fellowmen, ideas, principles of thought, and consequent conduct, teachings of religious and philosophical and of scientific character and value, which will teach men, enable them to learn, to forget themselves and live for others, then I think we shall have done more than teaching them the undoubtedly sublime verity of their oneness with divinity — one of my own favorite thoughts and teachings! For even that can have an atmosphere of egoism about it, of spiritual selfishness.

I really believe that if our sad and suffering world, hovering on the brink of disaster as it is — this world taken distributively as individual men and women — could learn the one simple lesson of self-forgetfulness, and the beauty, the immense satisfaction of heart and mind, that come from such self-forgetfulness, living for others, for the world, I honestly believe with all my heart that ninety-nine percent of humanity's troubles would be solved. Politics would then become an engine of human achievement and not of selfishness and often destruction. Works of philanthropy would be considered the noblest in the world, because they would be guided by the wisdom of an awakened heart. For no man's eye sees clearly when it whirls around the pivot of the personal self; but it will see clearly when its vision becomes universal, because then all in the field comes within the compass, within the reach, of its sight.

Am I not right, therefore, in believing that, beautiful as are the teachings which, as individual men, we can study in theosophy, and great as will be the advantage that individually we shall draw from these teachings, there is indeed something still higher which it teaches: that we reach our highest, our sublimest, peaks of achievement when we forget ourselves? And may we not find the same sublime verity at the heart of, as the essence of, the burden of, every one of the great religions of the past, provided we strip away the dogmatic excrescences born of the brains of smaller men?

Remember that true theosophy is a matter of the heart-life, and of the heart-light, as well as of deep intellectual understanding; but so many people do not realize this, and look upon theosophy as merely a kind of intellectual philosophy, which is only a part of it.

While the selfless life as taught in theosophy is considered by us to be the most beautiful because universal and all-inclusive, yet can we properly be living such a selfless life if we ignore those duties lying nearest at hand? In other words, if a man so yearns to help the world that he goes out into it and neglects duties that he already has assumed, is he doing the thing which is manly? Is he living the selfless life; or is he following a secret, selfish yearning for personal advancement? Is he even logical? Selflessness means never to neglect a duty, because if you do that, upon examination you will discover that you are following a desire, a selfish thought. It is in doing every duty fully and to the end, thereby gaining peace and wisdom, that you live the life which is the most unselfish.

"Vengeance Is Mine"

THERE IS NO ESCAPING nature's law that an effect follows upon a cause. There is no escape. No prayers, no petitions, nothing will change the sweep of the divine mandate: As you are and as your works are, so will be the fruits which you will produce. They will be your children. Do good: good will come unto you. Do evil: nature will bring the very same inharmonious vibrations and reactions upon the evildoer.

This is the meaning of the old Jewish Christian statement: "Vengeance is mine; I will repay, saith the Lord" — words that men have talked about and preached about for 2,000 years, and have not believed in sufficiently to trust in their power. In other words they have added evil unto evil by trying to check evil with evil, which is making the thing worse. Figure it out in the ordinary affairs of human existence. Revenge is no way to reform the evildoer. You are but convincing him that he is right after all: he is going to get his revenge and you are attempting to revenge yourself upon him. Restraint at times, yes, certainly. But you cannot check evil with evil, you cannot fight fear with fear, you cannot fight hatred with hatred. Foolish men have been trying it for heaven knows how many millennia, and have they ever succeeded? The world itself is the answer.

Even our ordinary human laws in civilized society won't allow a man to take the law into his own hands and retaliate. They recognize the idiocy of it, and that it produces more evil than good. The ordinary principles governing human society contain more good sensible wisdom than nations apply to themselves, or than humans as individuals apply amongst themselves. The law won't allow you to take the law into your own hands and seek revenge upon one who hurts you; and wisely, because the principle is based upon a profound teaching of wisdom. Nature won't tolerate it.

Men have forgotten that what ye sow ye shall reap — not something else. Think what this means; no matter how dark may be the day, no matter how desperate may be the situation, the worker of evil and the worker of good receive recompense in time exactly in proportion to the good or the evil they have wrought. People forget that you cannot think thoughts of hatred without distorting your own character, which means weakening it, rendering it less strong, less brilliant, less intuitive, less penetrating. It takes strength to be a good man and to follow the law, and that is a strength which grows mightily by the exercise of it.

Look what human society does; it protects itself. In accordance as human society is more civilized, the restraining of the evil is more humane. In proportion as human society is less civilized, the restraints imposed by it upon the doers of evil are cruel, harsh, and unjust. And they do not last. Why? Because men and women intrinsically are decent. I have found decency even in the heart and mind of a criminal — one with a desperate character. Even such a man knew what decency was, but he had become psychologized by the idea that it was utterly useless for him to try any more because no matter how much he tried there was his record against him; his life would be just one long hell.

What you sow you are going to reap, and what you are reaping now is what you have sown in the past. That is just what the world is experiencing now: the reaping of what it has sown. It won't last, it is not eternal, it is only temporary. What we call the iron ages of trial and sorrow are succeeded by a gentler and kindlier age, until men grow tired of beauty and harmony and invent the evil contributions and machinations of veritable genius; and then comes in a new dark age, a new age of horror, when men want to get all they can, and think they can get it without paying for it. They cannot.

That is a fine old saying: vengeance — no, not revenge; we can translate it as the bringing back of equilibrium, of justice, of harmony in the universe — vengeance is mine. No sane man doubts it. We all know that if we mistrust ourselves nature will demand retribution. If we abuse our bodies, one part of ourselves, even by such small indulgences as ordinary evildoing, it will not be long before nature will demand retribution, and we have pain, maybe disease. And all other disturbances of natural law and harmony have to be paid for.

This is the grandest doctrine that human genius ever brought forth from the womb of cosmic truth: *there is no escape.* See what a wonderful rule of conduct this brings into a man's life. You can never get away with it, even if you try. There is no escape. You pay to the uttermost farthing, and then your new chance begins. You have paid your debt. That is the doctrine of karma, and some people who do not understand it may think it cruel and unkind that nature should have her laws and exact retribution for disturbance of those laws, for the protecting of cosmic harmony. But think what would make you obey if it were not so. Why, human beings would have no protection, the gods would have no protection. There would be no law and order. The reestablishment of harmony is nature's greatest and most wonderful procedure. It is the great thought of refuge of the good, the great principle of conduct of the good, and the warning to the evildoer.

Take courage. Meet what is coming to you like a man, and if you have been at fault in the past you will pay your debt, and then you will be free with a clean sheet, to write upon it your new destiny. No longer will it be the warning of the Babylonian writing on the wall. But nature says: "yes, child, it is finished. A new path now opens before you, a new chance. You are now free. You have paid your debt. You are out of the prison of fell circumstance."

It seems to me that there is nothing so comforting and so

beautiful as to reflect that nature around us, by which I do not mean only physical nature, but the divine womb of being out of which we came in the dawn of time, is still our Mother, Father-Mother, that we are children of the cosmic harmony, and that in that harmony lie infinite peace and happiness in our own daily lives, and a code of conduct which will fail us never. Do good, and good will come back to you. Sow peace, and peace will come to you. Give others a little of the joy that is in your own heart, and joy will come back to your heart and in times of trouble the joy will bring peace. Sow evil in the world, and that evil, like the widening circles of destiny, will enclose you some day, and then it will be utterly useless for you to groan out to the gods: "Why did this come upon me?" You are paying your debt. It is painful, but once the debt is paid, you are free. Now isn't that a doctrine of comfort — sane, sensible, and comforting in every way?

Human Consciousness

ONE OF THE MOST INTERESTING things in the human constitution is what we call the consciousness, and it is a curious paradox that it is just about consciousness that the least is known. Everybody talks about it; everybody says consciousness, consciousness, consciousness; but when you ask a man: what do you mean by those words, he begins to hem and to haw. Shall we say it is awareness? Yes, that is one of the functions of consciousness. The only thing we can say is that it *is*, and we all know what it is; it does not need to be described. As soon as you begin to try to define it, you tangle yourself up in words, and you actually lose all intuition, all feel of what it is. Your consciousness goes as it were from your central consciousness into the low small consciousness of words. We all know of people who become so tangled up in words in trying to explain themselves that they actually forget what they are talking about because their consciousness just won't fit into details and words. They have lost grip of the main thing.

Now human consciousness is unitary and integral, that is to say there are not two or three or more kinds of consciousness in the human constitution. But it is a unitary consciousness which comes down into our brain-minds or into our ordinary consciousness from the spirit of us, the divine center where the truth abides in fullness; and this human center of us cannot transmit this celestial visitant fully because this human part of us is beclouded, heavy and thick with the sheaths of the lower consciousness. Our thoughts and feelings and emotions rise around us like a thick thundercloud under the sun. But behind the cloud is the one sunlight. So it is with consciousness.

Theosophical seers for many ages and belonging to different

religions and philosophies have classified human consciousness, for purposes of convenient understanding, into four divisions: *jāgrat*, the waking state, *svapna*, the sleeping state, *sushupti*, the utter dreamless sleep, the state of death for most men; and *turīya*, the state of the divine, which god-men and the great seers and sages have told us of, because to a certain extent they experience it. But it is all one consciousness. Jāgrat is the state in which we all here are now — unless there is someone asleep in the audience and, if he is, he will be in the svapna state, the sleeping state in which he is more or less dreaming. Sometimes people are half dreaming when they are in the jāgrat state. We call it daydreaming. I do not mean creative dreaming of thought; I mean just the lazy dreaming where the thought wanders. It is part svapna in the jāgrat state. Then comes the sushupti, which in sleep is dreamless. It is the state of most human souls after death: perfect, sweet, undreaming consciousness, in which a thousand days are as a day, and time exists not because the consciousness is not in these lower realms of time measured by clocks, watches, movements of the celestial spheres. Consciousness there is not in the time-state. Then the highest of this same unitary consciousness, the source of our consciousness, is called turīya. The Buddhists call it nirvana. The Hindus call it mukti or moksha. We use these terms also for they are so definitely descriptive. It is the pure consciousness of the spirit of man, a ray from the divine, or a spark from the divine.

Now then, here is the deduction, the moral to be drawn from these facts. All of us have this one state of consciousness manifesting to most of us in these three terms: physical waking, sleeping with dreams, dreamless sleep or the death-state for most people until they imbody themselves. Do you know what this means? It means that we are not alert to what is in us and what we can do. There is the key to the mysteries of initiation. First learn to be fully awake when you are in the jāgrat state as we are now — physical awakening. Learn to be fully awake. Next, learn to carry that state of self-consciousness when you sleep, so that you will be as self-conscious when you sleep as you are, or think you are, when you are awake. Third and next, the highest: learn to be self-consciously awake after death. For it is one consciousness working through all three states, and everyone of us has it; and everyone of us is subject to these three lower conditions or states of this one unitary consciousness.

Think what this means for our future evolutionary progress. Why should we not begin now? I remember a story that was told of the founder of the Theosophical Society, H. P. Blavatsky. One of her pupils came to her one day and said: "H.P.B., you know I am awfully tired; I have been working all day long." "So sorry," said H.P.B., "you had better go and rest. By the way, do you sleep when you sleep, truly sleep? Well, you are doing better than I do. I am working while I am sleeping." She had reached that point where she could keep conscious, in self-conscious awarement, while other men slept; in other words she could be self-consciously aware when most people go to sleep.

The third stage, as I have said, is to be self-consciously aware after death. When you have attained that, then the next is the state of the god-men, or the men-gods, whom the human race has known, the Buddhas and Christs, men like Śankarāchārya, Tsong-kha-pa, and Apollonius. When you reach that stage you have to be conscious all the time, waking, sleeping, after death, and until you return, for you will then have found yourself.

Have you never asked yourself why is it that after dreamless sleep or dreaming sleep, you awaken the same man? It is so common, so ordinary, it slips the attention of the average man, showing that he is not fully aware, not fully awake. But the genius sees this, and he recognizes that this most common phenomenon is precisely one that has never been explained by science, and yet the explanation is with us all the time. We return because we have never left. We rebecome our self-conscious selves again because we were never anything other. Consciousness is a continuity. We have not taught ourselves to be self-consciously awake when we sleep, self-consciously awake when we die. But the power is in you. It is yours for the asking. You remember that Pythagoras called those who were sleeping this life and death away, the "living dead." How long are you going to stand that for yourselves?

Theosophists and Prayer

PRAY NOT TO THE GODS, for hearing they may not act; for the gods themselves are held within the bonds of cosmic law from which they may not vary. Our prayers spring from our ignorance and weakness: ignorance of our own most real needs, and weakness because we want others to do things for us that we lack courage or will to begin to do for ourselves.

I pity those poor hearts who in their simplicity think that by praying to Almighty God their prayers will be answered. Just think it over. What is the reason that so many people like to pray? They really know by experience that their prayers are unanswered. But this is why they like to pray: because it brings peace, because it brings a sense of throwing their burdens upon some other; likewise because it strengthens the ineradicable feeling of the human heart that there are spiritual powers of enormous — what may I say? — enormous constant activity in the world, and that by thinking towards these beings, we come in touch with them.

Yes, it is thus far true. And were every prayer a yearning to come into closer contact with these spiritual powers, it would be beautiful. But change the picture: two armies meet for mutual slaughter, destruction, each side sending petitions to Almighty God for victory for its own army. Don't you see something horribly blasphemous in this, an utter lack of understanding of the divine character of the governance of the universe?

It is the petitionary prayer that theosophists disbelieve in: the asking God Almighty for physical and other benefits which the petitioner is either too lazy or too indifferent to his duties to endeavor to secure for himself. Such prayers are often downright immoral, secretly or even openly; as when one prays to God Almighty for selfish advantages over one's fellows.

But how the human heart longs for compassion, for sympathy, for beauty, for the understanding handclasp of someone else; and from our studies and our intuitions we keenly realize the living reality of great spiritual powers in the universe surrounding us constantly, and our infinitely faithful allies and helpers when we strive to raise ourselves spiritually and intellectually towards them. Indeed, we humans have something so much more beautiful and noble than prayers to nonhearing divinities — something incomparably closer to our hearts and souls, something wondrously beautiful, gentle, compassionate, always listening, always helping: the Brotherhood of Compassion and Wisdom. This Brotherhood extends upwards from us humans in an unbroken chain to the chelas and the masters, and on to the very heights of the ethery spaces. I know not how high the Hierarchy runs, certainly as high as the highest peaks of our own galaxy; and it is along this stairway that the chela, the disciple, climbs up, up, up forever more. And marvelous tale of occult meaning, he climbs most fast, most quickly, whose hand of compassion is extended backwards in help to those behind himself. Isn't that a strange marvel?

It is these helpers of humanity, the masters and their chelas, and those above the masters, who extend to us constantly the help of their always pitiful hearts, their strength, marvelous as it is, yet given to us freely. They are very wise in their giving, for the help they give is rarely known. "Let not thy left hand know what thy right hand doeth." I could tell you some of the things that the Helpers do for men, unseen, unknown, even by the recipients of their compassionate bounty and benevolence: lives saved in many a way, disasters prevented in many a way; those disasters which cannot be prevented, because invoked by man's own egoism and evildoing, softened so that their asperities and harshnesses hurt men less. Things like these are done constantly, and we men know little or naught of it. We simply see the results. This is why this Hierarchy of Compassion is called the guardian wall around humanity.

The selfish and lazy who make no efforts to regenerate their own lives do not climb the stairway leading to the Hierarchy of Compassion. Paradoxically, it is those asking the most who as a rule give the least. What gift is greater than a man's heart, than *himself?* Show me something nobler than that, something more practical, something that will bring about results more quickly. What is the matter with the world today? Men and women are distracted because of their own weaknesses; they have not willpower even to pursue a single path for a week at a time, or a month, still less a year. Their wills are asleep, their minds are weakened from lack of exercise and from depending upon help from without; their spirit within them has no chance to spread its wings and soar.

To say that theosophists disbelieve in prayer is a misunder-standing of the theosophical attitude. But most prayer, unfor-tunately, is petitionary, disguised or open, and prayer in this sense weakens the character. If I were the Christian God Almighty, I would say to the one who prays thus: "Son, you have the truth enshrined in your own heart. You have been taught it. Get upon your feet and *be*." The most beautiful prayer is aspiration transmuted into action. Then you have the real man, the real woman. No theosophists through the ages have ever objected to prayer if it consist in inner aspiration, the will towards self-regeneration to spiritual things, and the transmuting of this inner attitude of the soul into positive action on earth. Where you have this prayer-in-action then the whole life becomes filled with the prayer of the avatāra Jesus: "Not my will, but thine be done."

Strength and Balance in Occultism

THE HOLY MYSTERIES ARE NEVER publicized — never. You have to earn them and fit yourselves for them. It is obvious that if you are not fit to receive them, they never come to you. It would be a crime to attempt to do otherwise. It is the easiest thing in the world for a man or a woman to incur loss of the soul by following any other method of occult training than that of the masters, taught as they themselves in their turn are by the dhyāni-chohans, the bright and blessed gods. I mean it. If you want truth you must come to the temple for it, and you must come in the proper spirit; you must work upon yourself so that you will train yourself to be fit to learn, to be receptive. Otherwise you just can't receive it. You won't take it in. You can't take it in until you make an opening in which to put it — to use very plain, simple language. If your mind is set against it, like a closed door, it does not open to receive. You must train yourselves first. But if you do train yourselves and "live the life," there is absolutely no barrier which can or will prevent your going indefinitely forwards. It is exactly like a growing child. He cannot take in even the wisdom of this world until his mind has developed to the point where it can receive it and retain it; until it is trained to do it. It is exactly the same with occultism, with esotericism, with the Mysteries. They are indeed in the Theosophical movement, both the Greater and the Less. They can be had by anyone, but such a one must prepare himself, train himself, must be in deadly earnest. Then he can receive them.

The chief or fundamental rule of this training or discipline is the becoming receptive to the inner and higher part of one's own constitution, whose whisperings of truth and intimations of cosmic verities find no lodgment in minds willfully or ignorantly closed against their entrance. There is the whole, or at least the fundamental, rule of occult teaching and learning in a nutshell, and the reason for all the safeguards that have been thrown around it. I have myself known hapless students of theosophy who have literally gone crazy, temporarily at least, but nevertheless have been crazed, from an unwise and unguided study of some of the more recondite teachings. It is pathetic; the pathos lies in their yearning to learn and to become greater than their lower selves. The pathos likewise lies in the fact that they tried to scale the peaks before they had disciplined themselves to traverse the foothills of morals, of learning, and self-control. It is one of the perils that the masters and H. P. Blavatsky have had to watch out for, and to contend with. It is a very difficult situation. I have known men and women barely escaping the loss of health in merely brain-mind overstudy without the healing, saving power of selfless devotion: a most beautiful thing in a way; one's heart warms to them in admiration for their courage, for their insistence on getting truth; but it has been unwisely done. That is why we insist upon the all-round, balanced growth, a wise, shapely growing into knowledge and wisdom, instead of the distortions and ungainly malformations, mentally and even psychically, that come from unwise study of occult things.

It is for this reason that in our T.S. the inner, the secret, the occult, the esoteric, is so very carefully guarded and watched over and *never* publicized. The masters have no desire to have their students incur risks of soul loss, or mind loss, or even of physical deterioration, or any other human tragedy. Otherwise, having stated these things, just remember how beautiful and simple the rules of occultism are. Nothing in the deeper and more occult studies will ever interfere with your family duties, never, for those duties are duties; and it is one of the first obligations of a theosophist to fulfill every duty. He is no occultist if he neglects one, no matter what his temptations are. No matter if he tries to grasp the sun, if he neglects a duty he is a coward by that much. Being a coward and a weakling, he is no occultist. No injury should ever be done to another. If you do it you are beginning to descend, and you may walk into black magic. But there is a way and a chance to rescue yourself and to return to the strait and beautiful path. For it is a truly glorious path, and it brings a sense of the realization that man is akin to the gods and that the gods are present amongst us. Yes, I mean it: the gods even now walk the earth. But few are the sons of men who have trained themselves to realize it.

Now, the gods will associate with us, self-consciously to us, when we shall have learned first to know that they are there; then to make their approach to us mutually desirable. Let it, however, suffice for the main thought to carry home that the gods walk amongst us even now, as they did in far past ages, in the childhood of man, when he was still innocent and not so sophisticated that he thought he contained all the knowledge of the universe in his puny, little brain.

Let us, then, make ourselves presentable, and let us make our lives so attractive and interesting to the divinities, that they in their turn may be glad and happy to associate with us, self-consciously. There is a place, a geographical place on this earth, where not only is it common for the highest men that the race has produced to associate with the gods companionably, freely, friendly; but where the same relations of teachers and taught exist between gods and men, that exist today in our schools of learning. I wonder if you grasp what that means.

And at the heart — like this omphalos, or navel, or center, in the temple — in the holiest place there, the sanctum sanctorum, there is an invisible presence, the highest spiritual presence of this earth. Make of it what you can.

Fear, the Great Destroyer

THE GREAT DESTROYER IS FEAR, horror, apprehension of what is going to happen to *me*. Fear is destructive because it is based on egoism. Think how true this is. If a man utterly forgets himself, fear vanishes because he no longer thinks of the effect that anything may have upon himself. Fear is a concentration of attention upon oneself in an expectancy of disaster happening to one. Lose track of yourself, forget yourself, and fear will vanish.

Fear is often said to be a protection, but a protection only to the weak whose second nature is to fear; it is never a protection to the strong. It is horribly destructive. Of what? Of self-composure, self-confidence. It undermines will. It often makes one cruel in one's treatment of others. Fear is crippling. It stops the life forces; it makes one shrink and tremble, for, harboring it, one no longer has the daring, the vigor, the strength, and the power to go forth. Yet the timid man is always in far greater danger than the man who has no fear. Fear actually attracts danger. Your chances of safety are infinitely greater if you have no fear. Think it over.

Who would like to live in fear of his life, fearing everything that is going to happen, always slinking around the corner and running into cellars, and trying to go up, and yet afraid to go up for fear he will fall? All his life would be a continuous horror. Whereas the man who has love in his heart, who recks not of what is going to happen to himself, how happy and joyful he is; and he is strong and affects others with his self-confidence. If fear ever comes into his soul, it is because for the time being love is not there.

Forget yourself, and fear will vanish. Do you know the royal way to the forgetting of the self — utterly losing track of the thought of self in your life? It is to love all things both great and small; for perfect love casteth out all fear. Do you fear the things you love? Never. You want them, you long for them, you yearn for them. Learn therefore to love, and fear will go; and you become strong, for love is a mighty power enchained in the human breast.

Why is love so great a protection, outside of the fact that it casts out fear? Because its vibrations are infinitely harmonious; and fear is always shaken, distorted vibrations. The divine is perfect harmony, and all beneath it can arise to that. But fear is inharmony; trembling, shattering, undermining vitality. Look at the picture of a thoroughly frightened beast or man. You say to yourself: Where is the love in that man's heart which would give him peace, strength, and utter composure? He has lost it, he has forgotten it; if it were there, there would be no fear. And what is this perfect love which casteth out all fear? Why, it is simply living in that part of our own self which is universal. It is becoming allied with the divine. Therein lies perfect peace, perfect harmony.

Soul Loss and Insincerity

THERE IS A KIND OF SUICIDE which is rightly but infrequently so called, and yet it is a very real thing, and in world states like our own today, a danger, a grave danger. It is the soul loss — an idea which strikes the Occidental mind harshly, as being something unkind and cruel; for the Occidental mind in its ignorance supposes from wrong education that some divine power put us here, for our own good or for our ill, and that no matter what we do, we are to live forever and forever and forever. But there is absolutely no basis or reality in this idea, and this is shown by the very fact that the common sense of mankind has already rejected it in the land where it was born, in the West.

Now mark you, the soul is not the same as the monad. The monad is eternal for it is as it were a part of infinitude, of the cosmic ocean of life, inseparable therefrom. But the soul is the vehicle which it has built up for expressing itself on these our planes. If this soul be adequate and conformable to its divine prototype, you have a god-man on earth, and the soul may thereafter partake of the immortality of that divine prototype, because it becomes at one therewith, allies itself therewith. And we have a soul which has become not only the vehicle of the monad, of the divine spirit at the heart of man, but the very expression of it.

Take the contrary case where the soul is so distorted, so imperfect a vehicle, so imperfectly *evolved*, that even the terrific power of the spirit can hardly penetrate the density of its stuff, penetrate through the fogs of mind, through the whirlpools of feeling and of thought. The soul is here useless or virtually so, and is ultimately cast off, rejected, and a new soul has to be evolved through the ages. But this is not done solely on the part of the monad. It is the soul itself in which lies the choice, in the human soul. It can commit slow suicide by life after life of a deliberate choice of evil for the sake of evil, falling in love with evil for the sake of it. And when the point is reached where the rebellion of the soul against the divine ray streaming from above has become more powerful than the capacity or power of that ray to rule the rebel soul, we have the case of what we call moral suicide. A soul is lost.

This is a very real thing, and is not just words; and I think it is high time that theosophists talk straight from the shoulder about this. We have received our warning from immemorial time. All the greatest teachers the world has ever known have taught this same truth. "Live the life and you will know the doctrine." Live the life and you may be immortal. If you refuse to run with nature, refuse to obey her mandates, set yourself up in rebellion against her laws, it ends in soul loss — and the first steps thereof are so easy. *Facilis descensus Averno:* "the easy slide to Avernus." At first it is so easy. Why, we are all risking it every day of our lives: insincerity, failure to do our duty, to keep our promises, above all things failure to keep faith, failure to be trustworthy when we are trusted. We all know the inner reactions of the man who knows himself to be faithless, insincere. His very soul is becoming corrupt. In the worst cases I would say that the soul of a man like that is honeycombed with ethical rottenness. This is the way soul loss begins. Suicide, moral suicide, soul loss, begins in the little things. But grand is the man or woman who will keep faith, who is sincere and truehearted. There is grandeur in these things because the spirit abideth there.

A man is grand who will keep his word, who will be sincere at no matter what cost to himself — and this does not mean cruelty to others, it means being sincere with one's own heart, courageous in it. Thereby is self-respect born and inner peace and the respect of those one loves.

It is so easy to begin to slip. From insincerity is born falsehood, and then when the heart is false the tongue becomes false, and lies slip out easily. With each such step downwards the recovery is harder to achieve, and the next step downwards is easier to take. Do not flatter yourselves for an instant that you are safe. As long as we have our intermediate nature, what we call the soul, we must watch ourselves. Man has it within his own hands to make a god of himself, or if not so grand as that, to make of himself a man that others will look up to and have trust in; and what grander thing can be said of a man than that: he can be trusted! Just because we may rise, for the same reasons we may fall.

It is very difficult to give rules of conduct by which a man or woman may know whether he or she at least is on the upward path, extremely hard to give formal rules for these things; yet I do think that if you will honestly examine yourself, and after this scrutiny can say of yourself: "No matter what my mistakes have been, no matter how much I have stumbled on the path, I have kept faith; my tongue has not been polluted with falsehoods; I have not betrayed a trust; I have been true in my engagements to others and to myself" — if a man can say these things of himself, then he may feel that he is fairly safe. But if there enters into the heart upon such scrutiny the slightest feeling of self-satisfaction or the tendency to condone oneself and one's actions, when the heart knows that they have been twisted — look out!

I think the Egyptians in their hieroglyphic paintings of the heart weighed against the feather of truth, light as a feather yet almighty in its power to weigh truly and justly, had the right idea. I wonder how many of us, when our hearts are weighed, will find that the heart will weigh in the balance rightly. We too often think that the man is led astray by his brain — poor instrument. Here is where the demon works, here in the heart; and here is where the god lies also. The brain is used by the evil man to find excuses for the imaginations of a corrupt heart to injure others, scheming, scheming, scheming. But the impulses arise in the heart. The brain becomes merely the tool. I feel very strongly about this. I know that I myself in my job have forgiven betrayals many, many times, and I will tell you why. First because it is grand to forgive, and second because I saw that had I been in this or that person's place, in the betrayer's place, I might have done worse. And I have found the discipline of forgiveness good and helpful.

No human being is unconditionally immortal, none. You are immortal only if you ally yourselves with immortality, the immortality within you. Otherwise you are mortal, for you will have allied yourselves with the mortality within yourselves. So examine yourselves before it is too late, and if you find that in your heart you have been injuring others and doing so by translating the evil impulses of your heart into acts, stop it. Make amends. If you find in your heart that you are deceitful, deceptive, because you want to get something, or to prevent something, stop it, for you are going downwards.

Be always kindly; do not think for a moment that by being sincere you must be brutal, brutally frank to others. That is sheer cruelty. Sometimes silence is infinitely kindlier than speech. Sometimes you can tell more truth in silence, in remaining silent, than by speech. But whether in speech or in silence, keep faith always. Guard against insincerity as you would guard against all the demons of hell.

The Relation of the Finite to the Infinite

Question: What is the relation between the infinite mind and the finite mind according to theosophy? The trouble is if you say the finite mind is a part of the infinite mind, you must also ascribe to the infinite mind the vices of the finite. But if you say it is not a part of the infinite mind, then the infinite cannot be infinite.

Answer: The gentleman has asked a question which has been debated in all ages, among all races of men. It is the same problem which has vexed and harassed theologians, for it is obvious from the standpoint of theology, if God is infinite, and is nevertheless a creator, then everything that infinity creates must be infinite; but we see ourselves surrounded by an infinitude of finite things. How comes this? This is the same problem in theology that you, my dear sir, have spoken of as existing in philosophy. Now I don't know anything that can answer this question except the god-wisdom which today we call theosophy, and you will understand it is not so easy to answer, because one must be trained in esoteric thought before complete conviction comes of the full adequacy of the answer. Yet I will try to state the facts in simple language.

I have always looked upon the idea that the infinite is an actor as utterly wrong, for infinitude cannot be an actor, because an actor is a limited entity. Infinitude does not act as a being, for a being is a limited entity. We can only say therefore that infinity is action per se, life per se, not *a* life — that is limitation, that is finity. You take me as a man, you as a man, a celestial body like the sun or a planet or a beast, a plant, any limited entity: this limited entity, a finite being, in its physical expression lives and moves and has its existence in infinitude; it cannot be outside of it because infinitude has no frontiers, no boundaries, and no beyond. Therefore, that finite entity somewhere, somehow, in some part of it, has roots in infinity, infinity washes it through, so to speak, as the sea washes through all that its waves encompass, although of course infinity is a frontierless sea, so to speak.

Thus I, as a man, have my roots in the divine, that divine surrounds me everywhere, and permeates me throughout, in all my parts, in all my being. I cannot ever leave it. Therefore am I a child of it. Yet here am I, a man, in a weak, small, limited, physical body, with a weak, small, physical, limited brain as compared with the gods, a weak, small life, with a heart as we say, an ethical instinct, and whatnot. Yet I am a man. I have divine thoughts, I feel my unity with all that is. How? Why? That is the problem.

I will now hint at what esoteric theosophy says on this point. There is an infinity of finites, a strange paradox. In other words, these entities or beings which we call finite are infinite in number. I wonder if you catch that point. Thus the atoms of boundless space are bound by no frontiers, each one is a finite entity, and yet they exist in infinite numbers. We can conceive of no end because if our thought once says, there infinity ends, this is a limitation of the infinitude which has produced finites here, and we say, with perfect justice, why should, how could, infinity limit itself in any way? This thought is repellent, we cannot accept it. It is the infinite whispering of infinitude within me which enables my consciousness to catch this thread of understanding; this limited brain finds difficulty in holding within its small bounds an infinite idea. But I get an intuition, something within whispers, that is so. That is the infinitude breathing through me, washing through me.

Thus, there is an infinitude of finite entities, gathered together in distinct aggregated masses, whatever they may be — men, planets, suns, stars, stones, or whatnot — call them atoms, because all these things are formed of atoms, or things smaller than atoms like electrons and protons, etc. Indeed, all cosmic phenomena in the great or in the small follow the same general cosmic rule or pattern; and these are the phenomena of the universe as contrasted with the hid noumena or secret causes.

We see thus that Occidental philosophy has made a capital error in its philosophical researches in saying that infinity is around us, but that the finite is *radically* or essentially different from it. Strange paradox! Just because the finities are limitless, infinite numerically, therefore collectively as an infinitude they are a part of infinitude — indeed, in a sense the garments of infinity. They are it. In other words, we must change our outlook on the universe before we can understand why the infinite breathes in time as it does, in what we humans call boundless space. There is a manner in which even a human thought is infinite because it is one of an infinite number of thoughts, energies, living in the heart of nature, and never able to leave infinitude.

If you catch this very subtle, difficult thought, you will have precisely what the esoteric philosophy teaches, as also, for instance, the Vedanta, the Adwaita-Vedanta of India. What does it, as well as the sage of the Vedas, teach its disciples? This: *Tat twam asi:* "That — the Boundless — thou art." Because if That, thou, are different, then the thou is outside infinity, which is absurd, and infinity immediately becomes finite because there is something beyond it, which means that it is bounded, therefore limited, therefore noninfinite. Therefore that limited entity, that finity in this wondrous way is washed through with infinity, because in its heart, in its essence, it is of the substance of infinity.

Now turning to theology, this is just the reason why theosophists cannot accept Christian theology, although we accept the teachings of the avatāra Jesus. We look upon him as one of the greatest of theosophists; but the theology of Christianity was built up by smaller men later in time who had lost the secret

of the teachings of their great master. And when Christian theology says that God is a creator, that "He" created the world
out of nothing at a certain time in infinity, we say that is impossible, that limits "God." Infinity is no creator, it is not a maker,
not a demiurge — to use the philosophical term *demiourgos* of the
Greeks; just as the sage of the Vedas, as the Adwaita-Vedanta,
of India and as the esoteric philosophy say, it is That. We give
to it no concrete name, for such a name implies limitation. We
simply say it is nameless, That. "That" is not a title, it is not
a name; it is just an attempt of the human mind not to label
infinity, or to give it a name, or to put a ticket on it, but just
to use this term *That* as a means of reference in conversation.

And lastly, the esoteric philosophy teaches therefore, following these lines of subtle thinking, that even what we call
the physical universe is infinite because composed of an infinite
number of units, finities. And it is so from eternity — never
had a beginning, never will have an ending. Because infinity
has no beginning, has no ending. Infinity does not create and
produce these finities. Therefore they are always from infinite
past to infinite future, and are parts of infinitude. Strange philosophical paradox. Marvelous intuitions of the archaic sages!

I sometimes think that while it is noble of us to investigate
these recondite and difficult thoughts, because they raise us to
higher levels of thinking and enlarge our minds, I must agree
with the ancient sage who said that the answer, the most real
answer to such problems is found in the silence. How true that
is! It is words that mislead us, words which entangle us and
lead our thoughts astray. Yet we must use words to communicate with each other. If this gentleman is a professor or teacher
in one of the universities I sympathize with him, because I know
the difficulty he has in giving thought so subtle sometimes to
other minds. And yet he does so, teachers do so, because they
know there is something in the learners, in the pupils, which
can grasp at least an intuition of Reality.

I sometimes think that Western philosophy has lived under great disadvantages. It has suffered under a heavy handicap, and it is this, that Western philosophical thought has not had a real opportunity to develop and free itself from theological dogmatism. I know this perhaps is a ticklish subject to touch upon, yet it is one of outstanding importance for the freedom of human thought. Philosophy in the Orient has not been laboring for thousands of years under this handicap. The thoughts of Oriental philosophers and of the archaic Mystery Schools have had the freedom to grow and to develop; and I will now show you just what I mean.

In the esoteric wisdom, as likewise in the philosophical and religious thought of the Orient — a direct descendant and child of occultism, of theosophy — the Infinite or Boundless or That is not good, nor is it bad. These are human limitations, and can apply only by contrasts to limited beings. It is a man or an angel or a god or a deva who is good or bad. A spirit of good and a spirit of evil? This is a blind intuition which Christian theology has had. What actually is, is that in the bosom of infinity, out of it as from an eternal womb, come pouring forth hierarchies of lives, of monads as Leibniz would say, all spiritual beings in various grades and degrees of what we today call evolutionary unfoldment. Thus, for instance, we have the highest of the highest of the highest gods, and beneath them the highest of the highest, and beneath them the highest, and then the gods, and then the dhyāni-chohans, and then beings below them, until we reach us humans, and then beings below us on other ranges of hierarchies of entities, like the beasts and the plants and the elementals, all marching upward on their evolutionary way, higher and higher. Indeed, it is in this world in which we live that we find good and evil, and we see how beautiful good is, for it is harmony and love and peace and progress and development, evolution, expanding, and growth. We likewise see what evil is, restriction, constriction, suffering, pain, inadequacies, ignorance; in other words, imperfection in development often involving retrogressions or going downwards towards larger imperfections, until the lesson is learned by habit, and the entity begins the upward march. This is what the evil man does. He is going downwards and backwards for the time being, for the duration of his evil doing. So it is in the manifested things of the universe that we find beauteous good and the best, and horrid evil and the worst.

This entire series of thoughts involving the productions of the hosts of hierarchies of finite beings and things was called in ancient philosophy the doctrine of emanations, which Christian theology has condemned and scorned and mocked at, and which Western philosophy has never had a chance to understand because its teachers have been crippled. They have not been truly free, for they have not had the chance that the philosophers of the Orient have. I know. I have been through it.

So we cannot say that the infinite is good, because that is a limited term belonging solely to beings of emanated hierarchies; and when in the lower grades of these, we find them with less of the divine light. Then, as the Gnostics said — one school of ancient philosophy in early Christian times — they live in darkness, they are limited, they cannot see clearly, and that is evil, what we call evil, limitation.

So it is all wrong to talk about infinitude as being good, because if infinitude is good, how are we going to explain evil in the world? And there is lots of it! No, good and evil belong to the vast range of hierarchies existing in infinity, coming forth into manifestation in one great life-wave in some part of the universe, living their times, advancing and progressing; and when they have reached the culmination or highest point of their growth in that time period, then returning into the bosom of the divine for rest, at some future time to come forth again on higher planes, in loftier spheres. A process that we see in nature all around us, like the tree coming forth in the spring, bringing forth its leaves and shedding them in the autumn; just as we see a human being for instance, reimbody, part in the divine world and part in the physical, life after life, back and forth along the swing of the pendulum which is nature's law. We see it around us. There is the great book which we should study: nature, the things that are. And when I say nature, I don't mean physical nature alone, but all nature in the esoteric sense, the nature of the divine, the nature of the spiritual, the nature of the intellectual worlds, the nature of the physical worlds, the nature of the worlds beneath the physical. Who can, who dare, set bounds to the life in infinity and of it?

The gist of the answer to the question asked is, therefore, the following: every unit of the limitless number of finite beings, or of things living in and of infinitude, every such unit, I say, is in its highest, in its essence or fundamental substance, an identity with the substance of infinitude; but these points of infinite substance or monadic centers in their several expressions as cosmic phenomena are, or become, or appear, or show themselves forth as, the finite units spoken of in the question. Thus, every unit is in its essential substance of the very stuff of infinity, but all in their manifestations or emanated expressions are, or become, the discrete or "separated" units in their countless armies or hierarchies.

Misuse of the Free Will

I HAVE OFTEN HAD IT ASKED of me how it is that divinity is in and behind all things, and yet, at the same time there are all the horrible things that take place even in human life: wars, earthquakes, whatnot. These things are but proofs of cosmic activity. It is not the cosmic activity that is to blame; it is we, the channels through whom the cosmic forces travel and work, misdirected by us, by our free will — relatively free at least — by our choice, our choosings: sweet bells jangling out of tune, but they are bells just the same.

Everyone knows that a man who abuses his body will pay for it in suffering and disease. These things exist; and the disease and illness and sufferings are born from the original harmonies, if you please, otherwise there would be no contrast. They do not disprove the cosmic harmony; rather they prove that somewhere along the line somebody, something, has abused the god-given privilege of cooperation with the divine harmonies. When a man so cooperates in fullness, then he is what we call a Buddha, a Christ, or an avatāra. But when a man does not so cooperate and persistently uses his free will, born of the divine itself, to make disharmonies where it is his duty to preserve and perpetuate harmonies, what happens? It depends upon the plane where his mind is at work. In any case, if instead of following the upward path he chooses the downward, he goes down and down and down to the Pit. And this simply means the following: just as by continual abuse of your health you can ruin it and get a body which will be diseased, perhaps for more than one incarnation on earth, so with your mind, and so with your will. If you persistently fill your soul with thoughts of disharmony, hatred, evil, you will corrupt the inner fabric of that soul, and it will take on the pattern of your thoughts. You will be a workman shaping your inner self, making your future life to be according to the pattern your thoughts and feelings have given to yourself. The result is that as evil is always constrictive, the inner fabric of you, your free will, becomes less and less competent, more and more inharmonious with itself, weaker and weaker in power and energy, even in imagination and in feeling, because you are constantly becoming more and more constricted instead of widening and becoming universal. The result is that if you persist on this path downwards you will become as low as the beasts. You will have lost your humanity. Nobody will be to blame except you yourself. That is what we mean when we speak of dropping into the Pit.

The opposite of this is a continuous growth in faculty and power, by inclusiveness, by expansion, until we become finally divine, cosmic in our minds, in the reaches of our intellect, cosmic in our sympathies, widening with the universe.

"Lead Us Not into Temptation"

"LEAD US NOT INTO TEMPTATION, but deliver us from evil." When the avatāra Jesus made this beautiful statement to his disciples, he made it to help them. If you read the New Testament, you will there see that this prayer, as the Christians call it, was given to them for use. Therefore the entire prayer is based on psychology and must be read from the standpoint of psychology. I don't mean the psychology of the present age, which is little more than a kind of sublimated physiology; but I mean the psychology of the great seers, the titan intellects of all times, in other words, the science of the human soul, the intermediate part of man; not the spirit, not the body, but the soul.

The point is a subtle one: do you know that when you wish to avoid doing something that you realize is not good for you, one of the best things is not merely to face the fact, but to state it clearly through your own mind? Often the ugliness of the thought or of the action repels. The temptation is seen in its proper outlines. Thus it is never the higher self or the god within, what the Christians call God, which ever leads one into temptation. But the higher parts of our being, the spirit within, the god within us, is exercising upon us constantly the inner urge to do better, to be more, to strike out, to awake, to cast off the slumber and be and do. And often this wonderful brain-mind, which is not, however, as yet fully evolved, cannot get the true import of the inspiration from above, and therefore it distorts.

Remembering these facts which you have been taught, this is the import of the avatāra's speech. The very fact that you will say to yourselves in an uprush of aspiration: lead me not to follow paths which appear holy or which are veiled in the illusory colors or glory of what I want; lead me not to be tempted to what seems to be high, but deliver me from these things. These very thoughts in the mind make the temptation to lose all its seduction. The outline is seen for what it is.

You know the old fable about stripping off the garment which deceived the knight. He sees coming towards him the yearning of his heart; he is on trial, a knightly course of trial. Will he succumb to the temptation which seems to be the very yearning of his heart? Nobody knows. He is on trial, the trial of the knight. He steps up to the seductive illusion, pulls aside the enchanting veils and sees the death's head. This is the meaning.

The very fact that Jesus warned his disciples to take this as their aspiration every day showed that it had a psychological veritable protection for his disciples; in other words, they were to build up what modern psychologists call a framework or wall of thought around the mind.

Modern psychology has struck one truth, and it is that temptations come to us because of what modern psychologists have called schizophrenia, a long, ugly Greek word which simply means the good old-fashioned statement that a man's nature is often divided against itself. Schizophrenia means split mind, split personality. The good old saying was, a mind is often divided against itself, or, we are in two minds about it.

Now what is the psychology behind this? It is this: weld your mind together again into one and you won't succumb. Every decent man knows the truth of this if he examines himself. We fall into temptation because we allow our mind to become split, one part of the mind to bemean the other and then we scheme. "Can we not get away with it?" In other words, don't try to ride two horses.

Once the god within bathes our mind, our brain, with its holy light, with its love, schizophrenia becomes a horror of the past. Refusing to allow this mental division within ourselves, we become single-minded; we sense the inner divinity; and when this is possessed in extreme degree we have a Christ or a Buddha. These have appeared among us. There is no reason why they should not appear today.

Help from the Gods

ASSUREDLY THE GODS do help us. They are watching us as it were from their azure thrones, to help, and watching continuously; but does anyone think for a single instant that the gods are going to help in the work of destruction? Or contrariwise that you are going to receive divine aid or divine assistance, unless you yourself are a channel of divinity? Use your brains and your minds. Do not be led astray by religious propaganda talk. In order to obtain truth for yourself, strive to become godlike, thus becoming a fit channel for the godlike influences to pour through you; and you will not only be protected and helped, but you will do a divine work in the world. Think of these things. Be godlike, if you wish to have the gods help you, because you want to do godlike things. But you must be like unto the gods if you want that help. If you turn your back upon them, and do demoniac and diabolic things, particularly clothed with the habiliments of hypocrisy, that is not godlike, and you will get no help from the gods. Am I telling you truth, or am I telling you falsehoods? Am I telling you things that endure for aye, or things that are transitory and forgotten in five years? What is your standard of conduct? Have you principles or have you not? You have your answer. Don't cheat yourselves by thinking that the gods are helping you, because you will persist in running along your narrow human grooves, and then when disaster comes, raise impotent hands to the divinities, and say: "Why did this happen to me; what have I done?" Don't come to me and talk to me about being on the side of the gods unless you are, and working as gods, and doing godlike works, and keeping to the principles which you revere. Then you are on the side of the gods, and you will get the help. Otherwise you won't. Take the avatāra Jesus: look what his answer was with the money-changers in the temple and with the hypocrites.

Predestination

DO THEOSOPHISTS HAVE ANY doctrine similar to the Christian theological doctrine of predestination? Do we say as the Calvinists, and as many Romanist theologians believe in their hearts, that the divine foreknew everything before it came into being, and predestinated all and each and every thing before it happened? My answer is this:

The divine ideation of the *Monas monadum*, "the Monad of monads," let us say the hierarch of our solar system or, if you wish, the hierarch of our galaxy: the divine ideation foresaw, foreknew, knew before, knew ahead, the ways of the working of karma for the manvantara to begin, to unfold. But this was the knowledge not of an extracosmic God creating things and stamping upon these entities and things an irrevocable decree of fate, but merely the forevision of divinity of what the multitudes of monads forming the hierarchies within that universe would, each individual in its own measure of free will, do in the manvantara beginning to unroll. In the same way, perhaps as a parent or as a master might do: the parent for its little child, knowing the child's character, will say: I must watch out for this, this tendency or bias. Or as a master may say of his disciple, I see in him this leaning. I will be more watchful and helpful in that direction.

The divine ideation saw all that would happen; all that was present in the divine mind, all that would happen during the forthcoming manvantara, all that its children would do, how every one of those children would act according to its free will, and according to the divine urge or karma which it itself had effected in the preceding cosmic manvantara. In fact, divine ideation has not merely foreknowledge of macrocosmic and microcosmic events to be unfolded in accordance with that very divine ideation itself, which is the supreme law of the universe to come into being; but that divine ideation was (is), as it were, the very Architect's Plan* of the future universe to be, and of all in it up to the end of that universe; albeit each monad of the multitudes to spring into activity when manvantara opens, being in its essence a part of the divine life, and therefore an instrument of the divine ideation, acts according to its own inmost impulses, in the last analysis, through all the evolutionary pilgrimage in the university of life. Hence drawing its own free will from the divine life, its own proportion thereof — and when all is said, acting in accordance with the divine ideation, because acting contrary to it is impossible — we see therefore that there is no fatalism in this, and no predestined fate, i.e., the mandate of a power superior to the evolving hosts of monads. Each monad, in other words, acts out its destiny in accordance with its own inmost svabhāva or character, but nevertheless must obey the

---

*Plan in the sense that the Great Breath which will build the universe is guided and controlled in all its structural or building activity by the ideal outline contained in the cosmic ideation. This divine or cosmic ideation, philo-sophically speaking, is at once the past, the present, and the future, in the sense of an eternal NOW. The futurity of the universe, as well of course as its past, is therefore present in the divine ideation, and unrolls itself at the beginning of a manvantara along the lines of karma, guided by the *lipikas* working under the ideal compulsion of the cosmic ideation. This last of course contains all futurity, by the fact that it contains everything that ever shall be in the universe presently to come into being, from the beat of a mosquito's wing to the coming of the pralaya of a solar system. Thus while our destiny is indeed written for us not only in the stars, but likewise in the cosmic mind, seeing past, present, and future, yet every monad being a child of that cosmic mind, a portion of its own essence, has its corresponding portion of free will, and uses it. The misuse thereof instantly awakens the retributive action of karma; the cooperative use thereof instantly awakens the compensatory blessings of karma. "Help Nature and work on with her; and Nature will regard thee as one of her creators and make obeisance" *(The Voice of the Silence)*.

Thus while there is destiny, there is no fate, for every monad at its heart contains its portion as its own of the divine will and intelligence, and is free to use these as it pleases.

architectural plan of the divine ideation itself. Being, however, a spark of the divine life of which the divine ideation itself is but a manifestation, we have a picture, immensely grandiose and sublime, of all monads actually becoming cooperators in the divine plan, and acting contrary thereto only at their cost in suffering and misery. There is absolutely in this no blind destiny, no infallible kismet, no inescapable fate.

All monads when a manvantara ends, end as it were with a trial balance. As the Mohammedans phrase it rather poetically, a man's destiny is written in the Book of Destiny. His future is written in the Book by his own previous lives. And the divine ideation knew all this because that divine ideation — what is it? — is the all-comprehending hierarch, of whom we are sparks.

Thus we teach no predestination in the Christian theological sense, but we most emphatically teach destiny which each man is weaving for himself by his intelligence, and his will, from life to life, aye — from year to year, from day to day, with every thought, with every feeling, registering itself not only in his character and changing it, but in the astral light where molds are left, photographs are made.

As a spider weaves its web, so does a man weave around himself his own web of destiny. Often and often we human beings suffer for things for which we ourselves are not fully responsible. Think! Are you, am I, responsible for the wars that take place throughout the whole world? In one sense we are, as being part of the human race. Our thoughts in the past have helped to build up the astral molds in the astral light, but as individuals none of us made the bold strokes that lead nations into war. Yet these wars react on us, react on the unhappy peoples today living in fear and sadness. It was their own karma. They wove it in past lives to be in the midst of things. But as individuals not one of them is wholly responsible. This sounds subtle; it is really simple if we follow it. A war in any part of the world affects the whole world today — so closely is mankind knitted together. Prices rise, expenses rise, foods, luxuries are perhaps beyond the means of the majority or are prohibited. Positions are lost, anxiety, fear, rule everywhere. Did I do it, because I suffer from it? No; did my karma put me here by my own acts? Yes, and hence to some extent I am responsible. There are a great many things happening to us that we ourselves as men living in our quaternary — the lower part of us, the earth-child, the human soul — are not fully karmically responsible for. Yet there is a part of us that *is* responsible, and this is the dhyān-chohan within us, the rein-carnating ego. So there is no essential injustice in this.

I will try to phrase it in this way. The spiritual part of us is wholly responsible for everything that happens to us, for it is the reimbodying ego and has lived thousands of lives; but this human ego, this earth-child, the ordinary human soul, is not responsible for many things that the spiritual ego makes it suffer; and therefore so far as it is concerned undergoes unmer-ited suffering. Strange paradox! I call the attention of readers to H. P. Blavatsky's own words on this matter of unmerited suffering which will be found in her *The Key to Theosophy*, original edition, on pages 161–2 — especially perhaps page 162. It is in these two pages that H. P. Blavatsky in her incomparable style points out that while the reincarnating ego is responsible for all that happens to a man, good, bad, and indifferent, the earth-child or the merely reimbodied man, often undergoes what to him is unmerited suffering; but as she states on page 162, at the moment of death for a short instant the *personal* man becomes one with the spiritual *individuality*, sees and understands himself as he is, unadorned by flattery or self-deception.

> He reads his life, remaining as a spectator looking down into the arena he is quitting; he feels and knows the justice of all the suffering that has overtaken him.

While the personal man, the earth-child, the lower quaternary, does indeed undergo unmerited sufferings in this life for
causes sown in previous lives, and thus gets its recompense in
the bliss of devachan, yet the reincarnating ego or the true actor
in life's drama *is* responsible because the carrier of karma. Thus
when the *personal* man is united at the moment of death with
the reincarnating spiritual ego, even the personal man then sees
the perfect justice of all that has happened — suffering unmerited by the man of this life, but karmically the consequence of
the actions of the ego in past lives.

So you see, one part of us is responsible for what the lower
innocent part is not responsible for. It is this lower part of us
that after death gets its recompense in the devachan for all the
unmerited sufferings and sadnesses and sorrows and hurts that
it has had, or experienced, in life; in other words, the things
that it itself in that life had not willingly brought about, but
were brought upon it because the reincarnating ego unlike its
child, the lower man, *is* responsible.

No wonder the masters tell us that one of the greatest things
in human life is the cultivation of the spirit of compassion, of
pity, of sympathy, sympathy for the souls of men. When we
have it we rise out of our earth-child soul still higher. The
spiritual part of us sometimes leads us into sorrow and suffering
and trouble for our own good. It itself becomes responsible.
So, do not be so ready to blame others, do not be so ready to
say, Oh, it is his karma! Precisely that is just your chance to
give a helping hand. Inactive in a deed of mercy, you become
active in a cardinal sin, as H. P. Blavatsky nobly declares. And
you will be held to account. This lesson does not mean doing
things blindly and rushing around in a wild emotion of compassion. It means using your brains. There are plenty of crooks
in the world, and they are making a terrible karma in the world.
But when one does know that someone needs the helping hand,
it is a criminal act if we withhold it, and we shall suffer karmic

retribution for our inaction. Think what it means to us when we in desperate need feel the warm clasp of a helping hand. The courage that flows back to us, the feeling that we are not alone in the world; that there is at least one person who has given us a kindly thought. One touch of the divine heals and strengthens the whole world.

So in answer to the question, does theosophy teach predestination? the answer is an emphatic negative. But we do indeed teach destiny, which every man weaves for himself, around himself, and from which there is no escape, for it is the fruiting of the seeds sown by our own volition or choice. We do teach the doctrine, sublime and grand, as already stated, of man's free will, relatively so at least, dependent upon his evolutionary status, and of the inescapable destiny that dogs the footsteps of the evildoer, and showers blessings upon the doer of good. The one, retribution, is as inescapable as the other, compensation for the good that we have sown.

It is a marvelous thought to reflect that the divine ideation at the opening of the manvantara has, as it were, a plan of all the future time of that manvantara, predestinating nothing, reprobating nothing, but, as the Silent Watcher sees it in his glorious wisdom, what its children in that manvantara will unroll from themselves: the destiny woven in the past. It is very largely in order to carry out the plan immanent in the divine ideation that the avatāras of the gods from time to time come amongst us to direct our vision towards the laws of Being, and in doing so to guide as well as comfort and aid us human pilgrims.

What Is Truth?

How may we find truth, or distinguish as among different teachings calling themselves truth, as to which is the proper or the best? What is truth? Do you remember Pontius Pilate, when he was examining Jesus, putting the question: what is truth? I ask you the same: what is truth? Do you think that any one of you can have all truth within the small compass of your mind? Don't you see what a preposterous question this is? All we can know of truth is partial cognizance of the laws of the universe, an ever-growing cognizance, an ever-increasing range of consciousness and feeling, a growth in wisdom and inner power. But if any man could encompass the whole truth within the small compass of his mind, of his brain, what a sad outlook for all the future there would lie before him. He has ended, he has finished, he has it all! He has infinite truth — all of which is fortunately impossible.

Truth is relative, because what men call truth is just so much as each individual man can understand, take in, receive and digest, of the laws of the universe around us; and by that I mean the spiritual universe even more than the gross physical one that gives us our bodies. Truth is relative, I repeat, which means in the simplest way of speaking, that what is truth to Jack may be false to John. Charles may see where Jack fails and where John fails, and have a vision of a still higher truth; and some other man with a vision and a penetrating power of intellect larger than that of Charles, may see more and feel more.

Be therefore generous in your feelings towards others. Learn to respect true convictions, if they are indeed convictions; and learn to understand mere opinions for the paltry value that most of them have, opinions that are as changeable and uncertain as the moonlight.

Truth per se is infinite wisdom, and what man has it? Even the gods themselves have only portions, but portions vastly greater than we have. So you see how futile such a question is after all, and how distressing it is that questions like this have given rise to so much human ill feeling among men, not only in religion but in every aspect of human life. Instead of having kindliness and sympathy towards others, and an endeavor to understand your brother's viewpoint, there is a constant clash of opinions and warring of words, leading to unhappiness at the least, and to desperate misery at the worst — all very foolish and, indeed, childish, because unnecessary. The old simple rule of brotherhood and kindliness solves all these problems. Remember that your own growth in wisdom is steady, your own growth in understanding is constant. Learn then to be charitable to others.

Of course, on the other hand, some systems of thought have much more of truth than others. This is obvious, because some men are more evolved than others, are wiser, have a more penetrating mind, and see farther. Learn therefore to be charitable, but to be always ready to receive a new truth and to follow a teacher whom you believe to have that truth, thus recognizing that it is possible for someone else to know a little more than yourself. It takes a big man to follow some other man; and I don't mean blind slavery or servile obedience. I abhor them. I mean an honest conviction in your heart that someone else in the world knows more than you do; such a conviction dignifies a man, clothes him with manly dignity.

Truth dwells within, in you and in me. There is a secret fountain of truth and consequent wisdom within every son of man, at which he may drink; and this secret fountain is his own inmost being, his link with the divinity which is the heart of our universe, for that same heart is his heart, for we are of its substance, of its life we are children, of its thought we are offspring. The very physical atoms which compose my body are mere guests therein, and I am their host. They come to me from the farthest ranges of the galaxy, dwell a while in my body, and give it form, and pass on. And I, alas, perhaps dirty their faces when they come to me in trust, or mayhap, peradventure, I cleanse their faces. But whatever happens, those same atoms will return to me some day in the infinite whirling of the wheel of life, continuous throughout eternity.

> The big wheels move by the grace of God;
> The little wheels move also!

You know the old Negro spiritual — a wonderful truth in that fact!

So then, truth is merely as much as the spiritual being within you can take in from your study, from your intuitions, from your living with your fellowmen, and above all from your inner inspiration. Does truth dwell in science? Does truth dwell in the churches? The answer is obvious, isn't it! Does truth dwell in the philosophical lecture halls of our universities? The same answer. You will find in church and lecture hall and in scientific laboratory only as much as individual men bring there; and these individual men know only as much as they have evolved from within themselves.

You see how futile this question is as among the different sects and societies. Where may truth be found, and how may we know when we find it? Here is the touchstone: *within;* because there is truth within the heart, within the core of your being, the divine center which is identical with the divine center of the universe, for we are children of it, of its essence; and just in proportion as a man comes to know and to become this divine spark burning within his own being, does his grasp of truth grow greater. The more he can vibrate in unison with the vibra-tions of that spiritual sun within himself, that spark which is the light from the divinity of the galaxy, just in proportion does he know truth.

But in a practical way be kindly to those who differ from you, recognizing that your own understanding is limited also. Do not resort to sarcasms, a sure mark of small minds. Use irony if you like, but not unkind sarcasms. When a man resorts to sarcasm, it simply means that he cannot think of anything more clever to say. Be kindly towards others; respect others' convictions; and seek continually that fountain of wisdom within yourself where in its inmost we may indeed say that truth abides in fullness.

We Have No Dogmas

WE HAVE NO DOGMAS or creeds in the Theosophical Society nor in its work; and thus it is that we have Hindu theosophists, Buddhist theosophists, Christian theosophists, Mohammedan theosophists, and Jewish theosophists, as well as other theosophists who belong to no religion — except to theosophy as the religion of religions. Hence it is our bounden duty to cultivate in our hearts the spirit of brotherly love towards all, however much they may differ from us in philosophical and religious or scientific opinions; but while we are thus absolutely free as members in our choice of religion and philosophy, we all hold to the primeval prerequisite of a theosophist, which is a belief in universal brotherhood and an adherence to the sublime ethics which theosophy teaches.

Making Resolutions

RESOLUTIONS ARE VALUABLE precisely because of the training that we get from them if we are sincere. A man breaks a resolution and, sensing truth in his heart, he immediately says: What use is a resolution? But another man of somewhat more experience behind him realizes that it is the constant re-resoluting, to coin a term, which makes a man over anew. Rome was not built in a day. A god never became such in one single cosmic cycle. But it is the constant effort of the will, the constant, new resolving, which changes character and turns humanity into godhood.

There is the value of resolutions. True, we are weak and do not carry them out, but if you argue like that, you have the brains of a child, because that is the way a child might reason. But the grown man who has experience, realizes that he grows strong precisely by the exercise of the powers that are within himself; and there is something magical about a resolution at the beginning of the year, no matter how often you may violate it. There is the remembrance of a hope, a hope springing from an inner intuition that one has the capacity for grand thinking, and that it is his own fault if he does not follow out that thinking; and following it out becomes easier with every new repetitive assertion of his own power to change his life.

There is the value of resolve; the repetition of the resolve which finally molds character correspondentially. It is so simple. By and by the resolve becomes a habit of mind, and a habit of mind controls your actions, and your actions control your destiny.

I think resolving is grand and very beautiful, for there is no other way to change character; and if you are satisfied with yourself as now you are, you are less than human, for there is an inextinguishable immortal hunger in the human heart for better and grander and greater things; and every normal man feels this, and the more than normal man allows himself to be guided by it. Once get that conception clear in your mind and then your resolves will not only become New Year resolutions; they will become resolves with the dawn of every month, ay, with every sunrise.

Help from the Teachers

THE TEACHERS NEVER REFUSE any earnest human soul, never. As soon as the cry for help issues from one, be it only in the silence of one's private chamber at night, when lying in bed, be it elsewhere, where the human need is greatest and the cry for help springs forth from a sincere human heart, that cry reaches its objective along those wonderful power currents that we call the ākāśa, and every such call is investigated — every one. The results depend upon whether the teachers see in the human heart even the faintest gleam of the buddhic splendor: that is, a self-forgetful yearning for greater things. But the call must be not for oneself alone: "Me and my wife, my son John and his wife, us four and no more." That is no call to the universe, that is merely personal; that call does not go out, there is no splendor there. But when there is a true call for help and light, there is a touch of the buddhic splendor, a touch of the light coming to us from the gods; and the masters watch this, foster this touch of heavenly brilliance burning in that human heart, watch it carefully and foster it and help it as best they may. They help and guide by all proper means, without affecting the man's will or choice, throwing chances in his way to come up higher; perhaps putting books in his way that will help him. He is carefully watched, watched over and helped and, if the man fails, this is his own fault and not that of the teachers.

Encouragement on the Path

No human being is without trouble of some kind, and let us remember that it is the sorrows and the troubles of life which are our true friends — friends because they strengthen our character; they give us a feeling of sympathy with those who suffer and are in pain. Also they enable us, by the strength of the moral fiber that they build into us, to carry our own burdens with a lighter and a more joyous heart so that in time, when the suffering has wrought its magical work upon us, the suffering no longer seems to us to be suffering, but we see it with quiet and luminous eyes, and a glad heart, as being the mysterious working of the very gods.

It is through suffering and yearning for light that we advance; and, when the light comes, then also come the great peace and the great wisdom, and our hearts are at rest.

So keep these thoughts in mind when your troubles come upon you, and try to cultivate beautiful, calm, sweet inner peace, and a love for your fellows; and you will discover that these bring happiness and success in all things worth while.

Remember that the karma of suffering is never eternal, and is usually short, although it may seem long at the time; and once this karma has worked itself out, exhausted itself, then it ends, and gives birth to a new and better cycle.

Now, I will try to answer your question regarding your lack of time to make a regular study of the deeper theosophical teachings. I know just what your situation is, and I know how you long to devote more time to getting a knowledge of technical theosophy. This indeed is very, very important; but, on the other hand, may I not point out to you that even greater and even nobler than having a knowledge of technical theosophy is the devoting of one's life to Masters' cause, and this is what you are doing. This latter makes a karma even nobler than the spending of one's life in study of technical theosophy. Your situation reminds me of that of some chelas whose hearts yearn to pass more time in technical study of the wisdom of the gods, but who are called upon to sacrifice their wish and to go forth into the world as messengers and envoys in order to give to others what they have already acquired. Don't you see that your case is somewhat like that of these chelas, who, in giving up their own heart's wish for more light, are growing spiritually, and actually gaining more interiorly than they would gain if they neglected a duty laid upon them by their teachers?

Therefore take comfort in this thought. You are progressing spiritually and intellectually. You are also growing morally because you are living a noble life in service to our sacred cause, giving all you can without thought of reward; and the masters ask no more than this even from their highest disciples.

Therefore, do not feel sad, and do not be discouraged. You have asked for my frank opinion, and for my advice, and I am now giving these to you; and I tell you again that you are growing spiritually and intellectually faster in what you are now doing than you would if you sat down somewhere alone in luxurious ease and devoted your life to study for yourself alone. Remember that the chela's path begins in self-sacrifice for the world, and ends in self-sacrifice for the world — if indeed there be an ending, which is not the case. It is thus that the great masters of wisdom and compassion and peace are evolved. It is thus that the buddhas are developed.

Nevertheless, technical study is very, very important, and I am so glad that you speak of this so frequently, because it shows that you have the exactly right view. But I know too that you are gaining a great deal of technical knowledge just by throwing yourself so wholeheartedly into the theosophical work. You are absorbing it without perhaps realizing it. You are imbibing it from the theosophical atmosphere; and all that I have read that you have written shows me that you are gaining a great deal of the technical *understanding*. It is an actual truth of white magic, that a man learns more by self-forgetful service in our cause than he does by thinking only of his own advancement and devoting his whole time to merely personal development. The latter, after all, and in the last analysis, is selfish, and closes the doors of both heart and mind to the entrance of the spiritual light; and therefore, although the desire for self-progress is de facto a noble one, yet when it is followed selfishly, the selfish desire actually prevents the attainment of the objective which such a man longs for.

You have nothing to fear in this respect. Your life of beautiful service in our sacred cause is placing you in a position spiritually and intellectually where you are really learning more, as I have said, perhaps without realizing it now, than you could in any other wise.   —*Extracts from a Letter*

Nature in Silent Prayer

HAS IT EVER OCCURRED TO YOU that man's religious instinct, perhaps the profoundest and most subtle and in one sense the highest of all his being, is his because he partakes of it in common with all the universe? That awe and reverence so dignify man because he loses his petty personality when he is in these states, and that even the awe and reverence which are in him when he is even a little awake are in nature? Do you get the reflections that you yourselves are bound to draw? To me even from my boyhood, these thoughts were familiar, very familiar; and I used to go out at nighttime, and look at the glorious stars. I used to climb in the mountains in the daytime, lying back on the greensward, and study the changing clouds, and I saw reverence and awe everywhere.

It seemed to me in those days, to express it in the thoughts of my boyhood, as if all nature were in silent prayer. I saw majesty, ineffable wisdom, everywhere because I felt it within me, undeveloped of course, but the germ was in me because I am a child of the gods. They are in me because they are in it. To me nature, in the highest sense of the word religious, has always been a religious structure: her orderliness, her stateliness, her sympathy, measure her ineffable power, her wisdom seen everywhere and in everything. They have always bespoken to me the presence of what in me, so small, lies as yet scarcely awake, beginning to express itself.

How reverential should we not be in our attitude towards our fellow human beings, for having these thoughts lending their great dignity to us as men, when we put our hands out and touch a fellow human being, as the poet said, we sense that we touch a god. There is something grand in that. Man's consciousness has risen above the light and petty and small and mean and imperfect, to the great fundamental measures of the universe and life.

Just think: nature, even our little solar system as one of the infinitude of entities in boundless space, is a religious entity. Its measures show reverence and awe and orderliness. Why? Because of the indwelling cosmic soul, as Emerson says, the indwelling spirit drawn from the Boundless. Child of space as you and I, we are likewise children of the Boundless.

Two Ways of Viewing Reality

THE REAL, THE REALITY, *Sat*, or more accurately, *Asat, Tat*, is that which *is* during cosmic mahā-pralaya; and all the manifested universes are dreamed forth when Brahman falls asleep during what we call manvantara.

It is to be noted that just here there is a divergence not of knowledge, but of expression, even among the occultists themselves. The more common way in ancient times was to speak — and I will now use the Hindu terms — of Brahman awaking, becoming Brahmā and the manifested universe with all in it. In other words Brahman awakes when manvantara begins, and falls asleep when pralaya comes. This is quite correct if you want to look at it from this standpoint and, I might add, was a familiar notion to Greek and Latin philosophic thought, as in the statement attributed to the Stoic philosopher Cleanthes which has been rendered into Latin, although he was a Greek, in the following words: *Quodcumque audiveris, quodcumque videris, est Juppiter*, "Whatsoever thou mayest hear, whatsoever thou mayest see, is Jupiter" — a thought very familiar in ancient Hindustan where Brahmā is said to evolve forth the universe from itself, in other words, Brahmā *is* the universe and all of it, and yet transcendent to it. Which reminds one of the statement attributed to Krishna in the *Bhagavad-Gītā:* "I establish all this universe from a portion of myself, and yet remain transcendent."

But the other manner of viewing this matter and equally correct — and I will frankly say that sometimes as I ponder the matter, perhaps more spiritual, perhaps more correct than the former, but more difficult of understanding by us humans — is to think that Brahman awakes when mahā-pralaya begins; for then Reality, so to speak, recommences its flow of lives. The phenomenal universes have been swept out of their existences until the next manvantara, and disappear like autumn leaves when the autumn ends and winter begins. Driven along, as it were, by the winds of pralaya, all manifested life is swept out of existence *as manifested life*. Everything that is real is withdrawn inwards and upwards to its parent Reality, and then divinity is in its own. This is paranirvāna. It is then awake and dreams no more until the next manvantara.

Those in ancient times who grasped this other manner of viewing, of making Reality come into its own when manifested or phenomenal things pass away into pralaya, have stated the matter after various tropes or figures of speech, the favorite one being this: all the manifested worlds are but the dreams of Brahman. Brahman sleeps and dreams karmic dreams, dreams brought about by karma. These dreams are the worlds of manifestation and all that is in them. When the dream ends and the universe vanishes, when the dreams end and the universes vanish, then Brahman awakes. It is coming into itself once more.

I think both views are correct. Yet, as I say, I have often wondered in my own mind whether the second way of viewing it be not somewhat loftier, closer to the ineffable truth than is the more popular way that is more easily understood. We have analogies in our own lives. When we awaken in the morning, we go about our daily duties and we do them and they are karmic. But it is when we fall asleep at night and the things of physical matter and the lower mental plane vanish away, that we come closer to the divinity within us. We rise upwards, closer to the god within us, towards the abstract and away from the concrete.

I think this second view, though perhaps no more true than the first way of viewing the matter, makes what they call mahā-māyā, cosmic māyā, somewhat more understandable to us.

At the end of Brahmā's life, when even the Days and Nights of Brahmā pass away into the utterly Real, the Reality at the heart of the Real, when all is swept out and away or indrawn and withdrawn upwards: I wonder if in this last thought we do not have a striking confirmation of the statement that perhaps the second way of viewing Brahmā awake and Brahmā asleep is not the more real. For at the end of Brahmā's life, when Brahmā rebecomes Brahman, not only do all manifested things pass out of existence as so much dissolving mist, but even cosmic Mahat is indrawn or vanishes. Mahā-buddhi disappears and naught remains but Brahman. For an infinity, as it would seem to us, hundreds of trillions of years, Brahmā is awake, itself no longer dreaming dreams of karmic universes but, as we are forced to express it, sunken in Reality in the inexpressible deeps of Brahman's own essence. All has vanished except Brahman; the dreams are ended. Then when the new life, when Brahmā rather, imbodies itself again, then the galaxy reawakens, but Brahman begins again to dream, dreaming the worlds, dreaming the universes into existence, dreaming the karmic dreams of destiny. Then the One becomes the many: the armies, the hosts, the multitudes, begin to issue forth from the consciousness of the Ineffable. Abstract space is once more filled with suns and solar systems and whirling worlds.

We see therefore that Brahman and Brahmā, the offspring of Brahman, may have reference not merely to a planetary chain, but to a solar system or to a galaxy, and on a still more magnificent scale to a supergalaxy including many galaxies in the womb of endless space. In other words, Brahman and its offspring Brahmā may apply to any one or to all of these different ranges on an increasing scale of grandeur. Brahman dreams karmic dreams of destiny and the universes flash into being; they appear like seeds of life or the spawn of Mother Space, and this we call manvantara or mahā-manvantara. Conversely, when Brahman's dreaming ends, the worlds are swept out of existence and Brahman awakens as Brahman's Self.

Let us also remember as a final thought, that when we speak

of frontierless infinitude, or of the beginningless and endless or boundless, we call this *Tat*, from the Sanskrit word meaning That; and that innumerable Brahmans greater and smaller, in countless numbers, are comprised within the boundless *Tat*.

Oracles of the Ancients

NEVER DIRECTLY DID THE ORACLES answer Yea or Nay. They spoke only in figures of speech. Always their language was involved in such fashion as to place upon the inquirer of the Oracle the necessity of making his own choice, thus using his own free will and intelligence. Otherwise — and you see the ethical meaning of this — man's free will in times of stress and strain, which are exactly the times when a man should choose from within, would have been interfered with. His pathway would have been made so smooth for him by showing him the way to safety and peace and success, that his karma would not have been readily worked out, the man would have been morally injured. An evil man asking a question of the Oracle: "Shall I succeed if I do so-and-so?" and the god saying "Yes" — that would have been pointing the way by the divinity to the Pit.

Example: Croesus, King of Lydia, was a powerful ruler in his day, ambitious, with an overweening hate of the foes surrounding him; and the time came when the Persians disputed some of his actions. King Croesus doubted whether he should war upon the Persians or not. So, desiring to obtain divine authority for his act, he sent his representatives to Delphi, to ask the God Apollo: "Shall King Croesus make war upon the Persians?" The Oracle's answer came: "If King Croesus makes war upon the Persians, King Croesus will destroy a mighty empire." Croesus in his folly and selfishness thought that this was a divine promise of success to his selfish ambition. He made war upon Persia — and lost his powerful kingdom! He destroyed an empire which he had built up. Do you see the ethical background?

Duty and the Moral Balance

IT IS ONLY THE KNOWLEDGE of blessed karma with its infinitely just measures of harmony which saves the man of mind and heart from being utterly discouraged. It is this key, to the man of the world when he understands it, which leads him up gentle gradations, upwards with an expanding vision, until finally he sees Reality, as much of it as his mind can contain; and he knows that, despite all his suffering in the world due to karmic necessity, fundamentally all is well.

Let no man harden his heart at this and think that he need not bestir himself to help others or to extend a helping hand or to give a draught of cooling water to the thirsty. Remember the old law that H. P. Blavatsky taught: Inaction in a deed of pity becomes an action in a sin full of fate for you.

I wonder how many of us forget our fundamental teaching of universal brotherhood. Such simple words! They seem so trite, and yet they contain the doctrine of the gods. They, these words, *Universal Brotherhood*, contain all the Law and all the Prophets. Remember that knowledge brings not only power but responsibility. What might be excused unto you when you are ignorant, will be counted against you when you know the Law. This is just one of the reasons the masters keep the higher teachings of theosophy, the occult doctrines — one of the reasons at least — so strictly secret. Much is excused of a man who does not know. Little is excused the man who knows and who remains inactive. Nothing is excused the man who knows, who has power to act, and who lacks the urge to act. He is guilty of a crime against nature; and the only thing we have to watch, as students of the ancient wisdom, is this: let us never so act that we offend a brother or injure him. It matters not

how right we may think we may be. It matters not how wrong
we are convinced our brother is. Your duty, my duty, is to
care for our own dharma. Forgetting our own dharma or duty,
and presuming to judge a brother and thereupon acting against
him, offending him, is full of danger. The duty, the dharma,
of another for you is dangerous. Therefore do not criticize.

Such simple truths, so logical, so clear, so appealing! Our
earth would be a heaven if men and women would but follow
them. And yet today they flatter themselves, and they flatter
those in high public posts, for the same evil: thinking that
struggle, punishment, hate, become a moral duty. Show me
one passage by the Saviors of the world that endorses this, one
single passage. You will not find it. The secret is to do your
own duty wherever you are and at any time. You have a duty
to yourself, to your soul. The first duty of all that a man has
is to think uprightly, to think cleanly, to live rightly, never
to hurt a brother. Then comes the duty to his family, then
the duty to his country; and to certain rare ones there comes
a duty to the gods, or demigods. This is all included, however,
in the one statement of a man's universal duty to mankind which
includes all.

Do not for a moment imagine that I have uttered contradictions, that there will ever be a struggle between your sense of
right to Y or your sense of right to X. There never will be.
Impossible! If there is a conflict in your mind, it shows that
your mind is not yet clear, that you are hanging on to something.
When your mind is crystal clear to the spiritual inspiration, you
will have no doubts. Duty will always be clear before you; and
duty never calls for injuring someone else. The difficulty for
us is sometimes in moments of distress, when we are striving
hard to know what is right, to *know* what is right. That comes
of our imperfect spiritual and intellectual growth, and all we
can do at such times is to do our best, keeping the principles
of the rules before us: never injure another; be loyal to your

word, be faithful to your pledge. Be honest, be cleanly in all things; be upright and harmless; wise as serpents, which means adepts; innocent or harmless as doves. The dove was in ancient times an emblem of the chela.

A great European once, when asked what he thought to be the most important in a conflict of duties, answered briefly: Do the duty which is first at hand; then all others will find their proper places. Thus, a man who is true to himself will be true to his family; he will be true to his country; and with the enlarging vision that this rule brings, he will be true to all mankind.

One Life — One Law

How MARVELOUSLY DOES THE ancient god-wisdom of mankind reduce all the phenomena of nature to a majestic generalization, so that all things fall within the compass of a single law understandable to human beings: for the god-wisdom shows us that just as we are born and live our little sphere of life and die, so do the worlds likewise, and the suns in those worlds, and the planets and the various kingdoms of the different suns, and the atoms which compose all things, and the electrons in the atoms. All are periodic, not only in the sense of being cyclic but in the sense of having periods: beginnings, culminations, endings and, rounding out the cycle of the worlds invisible, beginning a new beginning, a second culmination, a subsequent passing merely to vanish again into the worlds invisible, there to experience new and vastly greater adventures than those that our smaller solar system can give to us.

All things function alike because nature has one law, one fundamental law which is at its source, a divine source, all energy; and habits, courses, procedures, all are governed by the same cosmic powers and intelligence, which simply means that all things follow these fundamental laws in similar manners, all under the governance of the cosmic life, ringing all the possible changes that nature so lavishly provides for our admiration and utmost reverence. For while all things, all beings, follow the same fundamental laws and courses, every unit, precisely because it is a unit and an individual, has its own modicum of will — call it free will if you wish — and therefore can more or less change, modify, its own courses, but always within the encompassing energy of the universe.

This means that while all beings follow these general rules

or analogical procedures — analogy being therefore the master key of life — yet all beings, precisely because they are beings, by their own innate power drawn from the cosmic source, more or less modify the details of the procedures and movements. Thus the sun is born as a child is born, but the details are different. Details are not so important as the main fact. The birth, the growth, the death, the invisible worlds, the new adventures, the coming again to a new imbodiment, a new culmination on a plane somewhat higher, a new death to be succeeded by the same round on the wheel of life — but always advancing, always growing, always enlarging. Step by step all things progress.

Thus actually, as occultism, the god-wisdom, points out, if you wish to know the destiny, the birth, the origin, and the temporary ending of a sun, study a man from birth to death. And if you can, study him after death in his adventures, and you will see what the solar divinity undergoes, but of course on enlarged and higher planes in the worlds invisible. Why, this visible world of ours is but a shell, is but the body, the exterior carapace, the skin of things. The life, the individuality, the power, the will, the thought, the real entity, is not this outer shell. Whether a man, or sun, or solar system, or galaxy, or an entire universe: the reality is within; and the body more or less expresses, although feebly, what the inner powers produce on this outer plane.

Those of you who have followed the experiments undertaken in scientific ways will understand this more clearly than those who have not studied them. But all of you, if you think a moment, will know that you shed your strength from hour to hour, physical strength and mental strength. The man who produces a great thought shakes the foundations of civilization. The man who produces a majestic system of cosmic philosophy and definitely guides mankind — does not his vitality move men? These are facts. The only difference between a sun and a man is in the details, some of them majestic, admittedly majestic; but it is only in the details that the procedure differs. The main principle of fundamental law is the same for all. Every man in fact is but an embryo sun, a sun in the making for the distant future — not his body, for that is not the man. His body is but the skin of him, the clothing of skins spoken of in Genesis. A man is the power within, the spirit or the monad; and it is this energy or power which makes the man be the same from birth till death, which makes the sun retain its form and follow its functions from its birth to its death. An atom, a flower, a tree, or a beast — all are subject to the same cosmic law of similarities if not positive identities. It is but the detail that changes.

The wisest and greatest men of antiquity pointed out that Father Sun was indeed Father Sun, but likewise our elder brother; our parent and yet our brother. The beast and the plant are in a sense our children because they look up to us as we look up to the gods. They are, in a sense, our children and they follow in our footsteps towards mankind, towards the status and stature of humanity. The beasts are slowly crawling up towards us, as we look unto the gods, our parents and grandparents; and when we find our souls infilled and inspirited with their life force and a spark of their shining intelligence, then we become on this earth like god-men, because our thoughts are godlike, and our feelings are godlike, and our actions following our thoughts and feelings become godlike too.

Thus the atoms of the body, and the molecules and protons and electrons that make up the physical stuff of the body, are in a sense its children, and they feel the impact of our thought and of our feeling. They suffer for our sins in proportion, and they are raised by our virtues, so closely are all things knitted together, a web of life of which each strand is a production of spiritual magic.

We are responsible for the very atoms which compose our bodies, whether we dirty their faces or cleanse them. Some day, if we dirty the faces of the atoms composing us, they will return to us to be washed, washed clean of the sin we put upon them. And so with all the interior realms of man's constitution, the vehicles of his mind and of his feeling and of his thought.

Birth and death: what are these changes? A birth in the body is a death to the soul, for it leaves its own inner spheres, its own inner arrangements of its life there, and as it were descends or falls like a star to earth, and is born in the physical body of a helpless human babe, tasting for the time being the karmic retribution for all its past. And when we die, then are we released, then we spring forth and upwards and onwards on the wings of our soul, those strong pinions carrying us through all the planetary habitations to the very throne of Father Sun. It is rebirth to the soul, as rebirth on this earth is death to the soul. So with the sun, so with the worlds which are born and which die. The sun when it imbodies on this plane is shorn of much of its splendor. When the sun's hour shall strike and it passes from this plane, it will spring like a divine thought right into the invisible realms, taking off into grandeurs only very dimly imagined by us. The flower expressing its soul in scent and beauty but repeats the same cosmic law in its birth from the seed. Little brothers of human beings are the flowers. Some of them are to us venomous. In some way in past time we envenomed them. Now in karmic retribution they envenom us.

The birth of a man from ordinary manhood into mahatma-hood is an interior birth. The growth of the mahatma into buddhahood or bodhisattvahood or, as the Vedantists say, the becoming one with the ātman: this growth is in your hands to achieve, and in the hands of none else. You have it in your power to become god-men on this earth; or, every one of us has it in his power so to ruin and blast his life that he shall become like the fury-driven victim of Greek legendary story, driven by unspeakable remorse and haunted by the feeling: I have played my play and I have lost. Too late, it is too late! But theosophy says: never too late. If you have played your game awry, re-assemble your cards and play like a man, play with the devil for the salvation of your own soul, the devil of your own lower self, and win! If you win, divinity lies ahead of you. Over the peaks of that mystic east, the east in the heart of every human being, dawns the sun of truth which carries healing in its bosom. The truth shall make you free!

The Theosophy of China

You have heard today, from one who is a lover of the sages of China, something of the theosophy of that ancient land. You have, in fact, been listening to bits of the archaic wisdom-thought of ancient Atlantis carried down and still preserved in China; for the Chinese even today, although mixed with other bloodstreams of the human race, are the strongest and most faithful, so to speak, remnant of ancient Atlantis. The Chinese psychology is even yet typically esoteric Atlantean in character, in svabhāva, and it is set forth preeminently well in the teachings of Confucius and Lao-tse, the former teaching virtue, respect for law and order, eminently Atlantean thought at its highest; and the latter, Lao-tse, teaching that quaint seductive mysticism of the human soul which fascinates the humanity of us and leads it upwards. The teaching of sages — both. And into this dual thought of archaic China came growing the newer spirituality of our own fifth root-race, as found imbodied in the teachings of Gautama the Buddha — the essence of whose doctrine was universal love and compassion without distinction or bonds, and spiritualized intellectuality — the characteristic of us at our best. Actually, when analyzed, the teachings of Jesus called the Christ and of Gautama the Buddha called the Awakened, the Buddha, are one: different clothing in each case, different embroidery in each case. The same fundamental fifth root-race thought at its best — theosophy in both.

I am going to be bold with you, but I trust not overbold, and I am going to venture upon the paraphrasing of the meaning of the title of the only great thought of Lao-tse that has survived to our time: the *Tao Teh Ching*. *King*, or *Ching*, means "book," "work," "treasure." Learning was so revered in ancient China that even the printed or manuscript book, because it contained thought, was revered from this fact. No true Chinese — coolie, mandarin, emperor, or whatnot — of Old China would ever degrade a printed page by putting it to foul, obscene, or evil use. A Chinese seeing a book or written leaf on the ground at the mercy of the wandering breezes would pick it up reverently to give it safety. Thus it was that from ancient times in China learning was so revered for itself and for the discipline it gave to the mind that it was considered virtually the sole and most proper preparation and training for statesmanship. How, they said, could an unlearned man govern a people, an untrained mind, not knowing even his fellowmen, not knowing history, not knowing thought, not knowing the effects of thought? How could such a man, they argued, an unlearned, an unawakened man, learn to govern himself or his fellowmen? Native genius they recognized, yes; but, they said, in our land where the Child of Heaven rules, anyone may put native genius to its proper use, which is developed for the purpose of gaining learning, for the purpose of serving the State. *King*, or *Ching*, therefore, means "book" and, because imbodying wisdom, the word likewise signified "treasure." It is not a translation, it is a paraphrase.

Tao-Teh cannot be translated word for word. There would be about forty words for *Tao* and forty words for *Teh*, but the essential meaning, as I have always understood, is something like this: The Book or Treasure of the Strong and Beautiful Doing and Being of the Reality of All — Tao, that reality comprising all law and order and love and wisdom and intelligence and power. Tao is the way, and the wayfarer, and the goal: all of them. It is exactly what is found in the New Testament in words ascribed to the avatāra Jesus: I, the Christ — not the man but the Christ-spirit, the avatāra, which is in you likewise, in every one of you — I am the way, the truth, and the life. I am the wayfarer, the doer of truth, and the one who lives to do. I am the liver of the life and the life is the goal. Now that, as I understand it, is the essence of the meaning of Tao. That goal is not outside, it is within and outside, for it is everywhere. Every man is the wayfarer, and every man in himself is the way; and the way and the goal are one. That is Tao.

Responsibility of Scientists

FOR THE SAKE OF OUR common humanity which is at present passing through one of the dark periods in its history, when the wisest of men are bewildered and uncertain whither to look to find help, what is more needed than anything else is a conviction of the reality of spiritual and moral values, not only in the world of men, but in the general world of nature, of which after all men are but undetached portions or parts. Restoring to man his spiritual intuitions and his realization that nature is conscious both in the whole and in its parts, and furthermore conscious in various degrees from the spiritual down to the physical, will compensate for the tragic loss of the sense of responsibility which the materialism, the mechanism, dead and soulless, in past science has been largely responsible for, to say nothing of the materialism and dogmatism of formally organized ecclesiasticism.

It is for these general reasons that theosophists so greatly value pronouncements from eminent scientific men which, to those who look unto scientists as their guides, point the way forwards to a spiritual and intellectual rejuvenation of the human race. A heavy responsibility rests upon the shoulders of scientific men, precisely because the public believes in them as guides. The scientists of the future in my judgment will, if they remain honest and true to their sublime work, become the high priests of nature, whose temple will be the universe, whose altar will be the altar of truth, and whose ministry will be spiritual and intellectual, as well as physical, service to mankind.

Angel and Demon

THE QUESTION HAS BEEN ASKED what I think is the angel in us, what the human part of us, and what the so-called demon. Theosophists use these terms, angel and demon, not in their old Christian significance as actually implying that an angel from heaven has taken up its abode in the human constitution, or that a demon from outside of nature has taken up its abode in us. The highest part of man is a spiritual being overshadowed by divinity; and we at times speak of this as an "angel" because the term is well known in the West due to Christian thought. What we mean when we speak of the demon I myself would describe as the animal part of us, a very real entity, which the human part of us, the central part of our constitution, usually converts into a demon.

The animals occupy their place in the universe, and their lives are remarkable in many ways, fascinatingly interesting; and they have a certain amount — what can I say? — a certain development of individuality. No one would say that a dog is a cat, or that a cat is an elephant, or that a pig is a horse. These are different kinds of animals, each with its own individuality, and each kind having its own virtues; and in the ordinary course of nature it is these virtues of the animal lives which are predominant and interest us humans. It is when men spoil the unfortunate beasts that we find them departing from the innocent and natural life which nature has endowed them with. Most of the beasts have noble virtues, instinctively such, unless man betrays their unconscious trust in him and distorts their instincts. Look at the fidelity of the dog, the horse, even of the house cat! It is we who cause them to lead unnatural lives, distorted lives, lives bent or twisted out of their natural current; and it is just this that the human part of us does upon and in the animal part of ourselves.

Let me make my meaning clear. I don't believe it is a good thing to suppress the natural innocent animal in a man, but to control it. Why, he is but part human. He is only part man. Man, as we understand him, consists first of an inner god, call it an inner Buddha, an inner Christ, the source of all his being; and to this part of human nature the Greeks gave the name *nous*, the noetic part, the source of all our highest, the center of consciousness and of conscience, the center of discrimination, of compassion, of pity, of wisdom, of comprehension of other things in the universe, of intuition, of sympathy, sympathy for the souls of men and of all things. This is the highest part of us, our spiritual part.

The particularly human part of us is what we call the higher *psuche*, the psyche; and what we call the animal we can otherwise call the natural part of man, and this is not his body. That is a silly mistake that people who have not looked into and studied this question all make. They blame the body for man's faults and sins. Don't you see that if it were the body which sinned there would be signs of it? You know perfectly well if you examine yourselves that your body sins only because it is impelled or impulsed by emotions and low thinking to be the instrument to do certain things.

I think it is altogether wrong to teach — kill out the animal. On the contrary, we want to refine and lift, raise the animal, in other words ensoul it with our humanity instead of allowing it to control our human essence — and that is what so many men and women do. They allow the animal in them to run them. Yet what would a man be without his animal nature? He would be but part human. Do you think that I, G. de P., a human being, could ever want to drop the animal part of me? Not on your sweet lives! It gives me an opportunity to manifest on this plane. It is my duty, my job, to make that animal a decent animal, a human animal, to humanize it so that I, the ego, can work through it.

Sin with us humans actually does not reside in the body, nor in the animal part of us. It resides in the human parts of us, in our emotions, in our willful, selfish thoughts which stimulate the animal in us, rousing up the wrong side and impelling it to do things which carry the body with it. No, I want to be a full man, a complete man: spirit, soul, controlled and refined animal, and human body. Then if I misuse part of my being, from health I shall obtain ill health, from decency I shall become indecent, from human I shall have become animalized.

Those people who talk about killing out desire and killing out the animal to me are just plumb stupid. They lack psychological penetration. A man to do his work in this world of ours needs to be a complete septenary being. If he wants to be a god, he dies, and for the time being he is a god, or a demigod. But as long as he is on earth, it is his duty to be a full, complete man, and to act like a man, not like a degraded human run by the animal part of him; but to use the animal as a vehicle through which to work and manifest, bringing out the finest qualities of the human animal in him, the devotion such as the dog has, the affection such as the horse has, the animal instinct of remembrance such as the elephant has: to use these in order to manifest humanly through them. That is the way for a man to live and finally to die.

This animal is in his charge, it is part of his constitution which in indefinite future ages will itself be a human being. Just as the spiritual part of us today, the Christ within us, the Buddha within us, was formerly in past ages a man, but has now become bodhisattva-like, Christ-like, through evolution, which means growth from within; just so we humans today, the central part of our constitution, are striving or should strive to rise towards the bodhisattva-like part of us, the Christ-like part of us.

Do you think a man would be as lovable, as approachable, who was only part human; if he had only part of his present constitution? It is a peculiar paradox and a beautiful one in some ways in our human understanding of each other, that what we love most in each other are not the cold, exquisitely beautiful crystalline virtues, but those things which we sense as fellow feelings, the common humanity amongst us. Think over that. That does not mean that the beautiful, holy, starry, pure, crystalline virtues are not the highest part of us. They are. They are our ideal and our lodestar. We are evolving towards them; and the greatest man is precisely he who has developed them most greatly. But if they have not instruments to work through — a receptive understanding human consciousness to work through, which in turn can inspire and control the animal part of us, so that we shall become fully human all along the line — then we have a man, outwardly complete, who because of what is modernly called an inferiority complex will run off and shut himself away from the world because he dare not face it.

The theosophists' conception of the ideal man is not the washed out, pallid ascetic who abandons his duty to mankind and to the world merely in order to cultivate his own intermediate constitution. Our ideal is the full man, the complete man, a man like the Buddha, a man like the Christ, a man like the masters, a man who lives in the human animal, but controls it, and governs it, and makes it a fine instrument for himself, transmuting it into harmony and beauty. He must be a full seven-principled human being as the normal man is, but with every one of the principles at work and all working in noble harmony for the universal good. That is the ideal.

What is the use of flagellations, whipping the body, macerating its flesh, or starving or abusing its health? All these things show weakness, weakness of understanding and training, and an utterly wrong psychology. If you are afraid of yourselves, it is because your human part is as it is, weak, vacillating, untrained, unreliable, an imperfect vehicle for the light from above.

We do not, moreover, look upon as living an ideal life the man who, for the sake of inner individual salvation, trying to attain nirvana by the backstairs, or by denying himself the right to do his duty as a man in the world, macerates and flagellates the body and kills it sometimes in the totally mistaken idea that wrong and evil and sin arise in the body itself. The body is but the passing instrument of the mind. It is the mind where wrong is born, in evil thoughts. It is a wicked thing, in my judgment, to abuse the gift which nature has given to us all, the gift of a healthy body, and do our best to ruin it and make it unworthy for the duty for which nature has intended it. The Christ did not that. The Buddha did not that. The masters do not that. It is only the selfish monastics, the so-called yogins, fakirs, who follow that parade of their virtue before the world, or at best choose the hatha-yoga way, so that they may have peace from worldly responsibilities and duties. That is not the masters' way.

Don't imagine for an instant that I am preaching animalism. If you do you have not got my thought at all. My meaning is the direct opposite of that. The true human is never animalistic. He is essentially human, tender, compassionate, pitiful, intelligent, self-sacrificing, full of sympathy, with a fellow feeling for others; and because he himself has a lower part, the animal part of him, he has sympathy and compassion and understanding and forgiveness for the failings of others. But our eyes should always be turned upwards, heavenwards; because if we keep our eyes turned downwards, earthwards, then the human is lost in the animal — and we all know the degenerate results of this.

The old Greeks, in fact all the ancient peoples, understood the psychological composition of the human being very clearly — something which modern psychology is beginning to discover anew. This knowledge of man's constitution and nature is as old as thinking mankind. First in order is the divine or the spiritual within him, the source of all the highest, the source of all the rest of him, his consciousness coming down like a stream from the god within, passing through every part of him, glorifying, enlightening and illuminating until it reaches the lowest part and his brain is touched. This is the *nous*, the noetic part. Then comes the merely human, the vehicle of the former, the higher *psuche*, then the psychic, the seat of our emotions and ordinary thoughts, you and I as ordinary human beings. Then comes the animal part of us by which we perform certain functions in life, very necessary indeed, and which also helps us to understand each other to a large extent; in fact, without which we could not manifest on this earth plane. Then comes the poor unfortunate body. The body is a mere tool, an instrument which follows the feelings and thoughts we have. That is where the trouble is, in our feelings and thoughts, not in the unfortunate body. Sin is born in the mind, in thought, in feeling. If you want to eradicate sin, go to your *self*, the human part.

The point is, friends, let the angel, the higher part of us, be dominant, not recessive. Let the animal have its own; let it be innocently instinctual, but always under control. Let it be clean. Simply let the flow from above, from the human, drop like healing dew into the animal soul or animal mind and enlighten it and guide it instead of distorting it, as happens so often today. Then you will have a fine man, a gentleman in the old sense of the word, and a man who instinctively loves the right, understands self-sacrifice, and is determined to follow that law no matter at what cost to himself. That is the gentleman; and because that is our human being, when the spirit within us, the spiritual light, fills our human part and passes the radiance on down to the animal, it is beautiful. Then you have a man who in his higher part is a hero, in his human part is a true leader, a true chief of men, a guiding teacher, who in his human part is sympathetic, faithful, affectionate and true; and the body will show all these fine things.

About Healing

BEING WHOLE, AND BEING healed or well — in other words, being whole and in health, or "wholth" — mean the same thing; the two words, health and wholeness, come from the same root.

"Thy knowledge hath made thee whole." *Pistis* is usually translated "faith" — a word which has been so badly understood: it means the inner conviction of cosmic verities, knowledge of things unseen; and when a man knows, he needs no further proof. Proof is the bringing of conviction to the mind. When you have it, you look upon proof as superfluous.

When a man is whole, he is well, he is healed; and this more than anything else is the work of the Theosophical Society, spiritually, morally, and intellectually speaking: to make men whole, to make every one of the seven principles in the constitution of the normal human being active, so that there shall be a divine fire running through the man, through the spiritual and intellectual and psychical and astral and physical — and best of all for us humans, the moral, the child of the spiritual. Then we are whole, we are in health, for our whole being is in harmony.

Thus, then, the work of the Theosophical Society is so to change the hearts and minds of men that their lives shall be changed, and therefore the lives of the peoples of the earth. What is this but healing at its roots instead of healing the symptoms? The god-wisdom goes to the very root of the disease, and cuts it; and the successful theosophist is not he who can preach the most and say the most in the most fascinating way, but he who lives his theosophy. "Theosophist is who Theosophy does."

You remember — I speak of the New Testament because it is so familiar to Westerners — you remember the accounts therein given of acts of healing done by the avatāra Jesus. You will find exactly similar tales in all the different religions or philosophies of the world, ancient and modern. Even among the pagans in the temples of Aesculapius there were patients who came and slept there for a night, and were healed, healed in the morning. The common report said: "healed by the God." The actual truth was, "healed by the conversion within," not the conversion of the brain-mind thoughts but the conversion of a life: a life turned upwards instead of turned downwards. And the grateful sufferers now healed of their troubles put up *ex voto* offerings on the walls of the temples of Aesculapius, with carven or engraven images of the part or parts cured — a head, a leg, an arm, a liver, a heart, or whatnot, as mute witnesses or testimonials — "I am healed." Such things happen, have always happened, and everywhere. This is the case of those who heal themselves by becoming whole, this one thing.

When we speak of the work of healers working upon others, that is different; and that healing which is done by the transference of vitality from a healthy, clean body, from a man or woman with a healthy, clean mind, is good and right, and there is no harm in it. As the New Testament has it, the Master Jesus said: "Virtue hath gone out of me." "Virtue"— the Greek word here is *dunamis* and means strength or power — while etymologically fairly correct as giving the same sense, in its modern connotation utterly fails to convey the notion of the strength or power leaving Jesus, i.e., life force, vitality. From this Greek word *dunamis*, we have the many words in modern European tongues, like dynamic, dynamo, dynamite. "Virtue is gone out of me" — the vitality, the sympathy, passed over; and the teacher felt the loss. A healer can heal only by giving of himself; and see how wonderfully the old truth applies even here: by giving of yourself to others.

I have heard it said by those whose hearts are harder than their heads: "Lo, behold, a theosophist and ill, sick, ailing, wretched, cannot even do a full man's work in the world. His karma, let him work it out!" Of course, but you are not the person to tell any other person when the karma is worked out. Your duty is to help, and leave to nature the healing processes, and it is an awful cruelty to say of any other — theosophist or not — that because he is ill and suffering, his sin has found him out. True, but it is not for us to sit in judgment. Let us again remember the words of the Master Jesus, after healing by transferring abundant spiritual vitality: "Go thou and sin no more"— for thy sin wrought thy disease upon thee.

Because we suffer now is no proof that in *this* life we have done the sin that has brought it upon us. It may have been ages in the past, and only in this life when the man or woman needs more than ever before the vitality and the strength and the health to go forwards, his sin hath found him out, and taken this form. Learn the moral in this, for your sin will find you out in this or in some later life; and better to have the disease out at once than to dam it back to come out in some future life when you would wish then that you had suffered from, had got rid of, the poison in the former life, and had done with it.

Yes, I for one — I speak for myself — had liefer die when the disease is coming out, if it cannot be healed, than to dam it back by black magic and store it up for some future day when I shall need every ounce of my power and strength and health to achieve. It is not for us to judge another, and to say his sin hath found him out. That is no way to help him. It is not encouraging, it is not kindly, it is not generous, and for all we know from our viewpoint it may not be true. Abstractly it is.

Here is another thought. A chela does not become a chela because of his body. He becomes a chela because of the rapidly evolving inner man, the emotional, mental, and spiritual parts of him. The genius, an ordinary genius in human life, is not a genius because his body is spiritually evolved, a relatively perfect physical frame. As a matter of fact, look at the annals of history and you will find the almost astounding fact that the majority of geniuses have been born in enfeebled bodies, often sickly ones, sometimes actually decrepit, cripples. But the flaming fire of genius within — it was that which actually crippled the body, deprived it of the life forces which would have built it up, which were gathered up into the soul to feed the soul.

Sometimes gross, robust physical health is actually a deterrent to inner growth, because the physical forces of life are so strong they act as a heavy veil around the soul.

Man in a Just and Ordered Universe

THERE IS NO CHANCE ANYWHERE in infinitude. Just apply your reasoning faculty to that statement, and see how far afield it will carry you. The first deduction is this: there being no chance anywhere, therefore no fortuity, everything that happens is a link in a chain of causation — cause, effect — the effect immediately becoming a new cause producing its effect, which in turn becomes a new cause producing its effect. This is what we call karma.

Everything that happens is therefore caused by law, which is just another word for cosmic vitality plus intelligence, plus what we call the ethical instinct, order; and these things are precisely what our studies of the universe show that it exhibits to our inquiring gaze. Everywhere we see order, law, procedures acting according to causational and effectual relations. If there were chance in but one atom of infinitude, there would be chance throughout, for then infinitude were not infinitude, but an atom short of infinitude, which is an absurdity.

Now with all you know of the teaching of modern science, and all you know of the god-wisdom, carry your thought on logically a step farther: since whatever happens is causative and effectual, it is therefore justified in infinitude.

We discern, in our investigations or researches into nature two things: an all-embracing, all-encompassing orderliness, or what we call the laws of nature; and within this, embraced by this universal law, an infinitude of individuals or individualities, each one an entity, working under the mandate, as it were, of cosmic law — no entity can do otherwise. We have therefore unity, divine unity, working through virtually infinite multiplicity. Among these multiplicities are we human beings. There are also the gods, angels or dhyāni-chohans, the plants, the animals, the atoms, etc., etc. They are all individuals working in and under and subject to the mandate of this fundamental background of cosmic orderliness. You see how these thoughts are rigidly logical, carrying us step by step from point to point, until we reach not only new conclusions, but conclusions that are always in accord with everything that we know of universal nature. The point is to apply these to our lives, which means likewise to our thoughts and our feelings.

When a man realizes that there is no chance in the universe, that he is but one unit in a hierarchy and that these hierarchies are virtually infinite in number, and that so far as we human beings know they are endless, like the bodies in space, children of the infinite life as we are — when a man realizes all this, several things happen to him. When he thinks these thoughts and becomes through reflection upon them convinced of their inevitable force, first he loses all fear of death. He realizes secondly that he is responsible for what he does, which means for what he thinks and for what he feels, and that there is no escape from the result of his thinking and feeling and acting; and that just in that impossibility of escaping the retribution or the reward of cosmic law lies mankind's highest and noblest hope.

To phrase the thought popularly, in the old-fashioned language of the Christian, he can escape neither heaven nor hell. He cannot escape reward, that will come unto him somewhen, somewhere, for the good that he has done in the world. It will seek him out wherever he may be, and brighten and cheer his life and give him renewed hope and renewed courage. For the evil that he has wrought, the injustices, the crimes, the unfairnesses that he has committed, equally will these consequences in the chain of causation seek him out; and though he hide in the cleft of the mountain or the deep of the bottomless abyss, he cannot escape a just retribution, for eternal and universal nature is on his track.

There is no chance in infinitude. See the immense weight of these thoughts as moral motors upon us. We see the reason for all the ethical, all the moral teaching of the greatest sages that the human race has ever produced, and we see the reason why their teaching is the greatest hope that mankind has.

And a third reflection: we on this little earth of ours, so big to us, so small when compared with the giants of even our own solar system, should remember that each one of us, as an inseparable part of the cosmic structure, is equally weighty in importance to the cosmic law, so to speak, as is the mightiest giant of the stellar host. The New Testament alludes to this in its teaching, strange to so many: Know ye not that the hairs of your head are counted? And that no sparrow droppeth unless it be in accordance with divine law? There is the same thought: that we are not merely the children of the gods, but embryo gods ourselves, for we are the very offspring of the divine life, the divine stuff in the universe. Otherwise what are we? Can you deny it, and say, "We are not; we don't belong to the universe, we are not in it; we don't come forth from it"? That is absurd.

Our divine origin makes us kin with every thing and every being that is, for not only are all mankind kin, but all beings and things that are are our other selves. All spring from the same universal ocean which holds us forever — the Mother Eternal, the Father-Mother. It is a wonderful thought.

The next time you pluck a flower, remember you are touching a younger brother; and that perhaps in the way we look upon these buds of beauty, young embryo souls as it were, or monads in a young state on this plane, expressing their life and beauty and fragrance to us, so do the higher gods look upon us. I have often wondered how often do the gods pluck us because mayhap in their spheres we shed beauty and fragrance and they love us: Those whom the gods love die young. A whole mystery lies behind just that one thought. Death is no accident. Birth none. Yet never think for a moment that this chain of causation is the old scientific dead soulless determinism of the days of our grandfathers, when the idea was that everything moved like a soulless machine, and never stopped. Did they not forget that to have a machine there had to be a machinist to build it and run it? They just used words then and were happy. It is not of that soulless determinism that I speak, but of the structure of the universe arising in hierarchies of imbodied consciousnesses providing the cosmic variety, and the innumerable families of beings, and all enclosed in the encompassing, sheltering, protecting, guiding and guarding, vastly great hierarch, of whom we in common with all other things are the children — that hierarch, which is not different from our inner self, but we, as it were, are sparks from it, the central flame of our universe.

Where Can Truth Be Found?

I LOVE TO SEE BREADTH of vision, richness of thought, instead of narrow-minded, dogmatic, bigoted framing of thought in a framework to which human genius must conform or be considered outcast. The world sadly needs it today, believe me, when the Middle Ages seem to be flowing back upon us with intolerance and with less and less respect for human rights, and less and less conception of the larger human duties of men to men, duties even nobler than rights.

There is an old Spanish proverb which runs thus: *La verdad no se casa con nadie:* "truth is not married to any one being." You will find truth everywhere, wherever human genius has flowered, wherever human effort for the attainment of truth has succeeded in grasping at least some of the cosmic realities, not merely from outside, from the environment, but, I venture to state, more especially from within. For it is within the secret resources of the human heart, of the human spirit, that truest truth, most real reality, is to be found. And why? Because this inmost essence of us all, where truth abides in its fullness, is of the very essence and stuff of cosmic life, of cosmic intelligence, of cosmic space, for we verily are the children of Space.

Truth can be found in every one of the religions of the world. Every one of the great religions and philosophies in the past has ultimately sprung from the Theosophical movement of its age, or has been founded by an envoy coming from mahatmas sent out to do so, sent out once more to strike the keynotes of truth which live in every human heart when that heart is not asleep, to awaken human hearts, to pluck the strings of harmony that every human heart contains within itself, so that there springs within men a new hope, and a new vision comes to them. Once again they see and they have confidence because inwardly they know. The strings of the intuition or the heart have been touched.

I pray only that our Theosophical Society proves true to the work which it was given to us to do.   It is a heavy charge, and it depends upon us, and upon brothers and friends who are with us in heart, so to guide the Theosophical Society and its workers that more and more as the years pass by human souls will be attracted to us.   If we fail, it will be our own fault. Let us see that we do not.   Remember that the Theosophical Society is but one hierarchy working within an encompassing sphere, the vital life, the vital sphere of another, greater hierarchy.   We can call it the hierarchy of the Sons of Light.   It matters not much what names we use.   We may call these hierarchies of the Sons of Light as the early Christians did by the name of Angels and Archangels, Virtues and Principalities and Powers, Cherubim and Seraphim.   The thing is to get the thought behind those words.   We call them generally dhyān-chohans, a beautiful phrase when it is understood: lords of meditation in wisdom — so expressive.

No human soul, no matter where it may be, has ever had an utterly unselfish and worthy aspiration unanswered.   Never. This world is ruled by spirit, by intelligences so high that ours are like the minds of little children.   The symbol of the Buddha with the long ears is but a symbol of the master who hears the cries from whatever part of the world they may come.   Those great ears which so often cause amusement in the West, with which buddhas are picturated, symbolize that the buddha-part hears the cry from afar, no matter whence it comes, and aids it, always in silence, except when the knock is very, very strong; and then discipleship enters into the life.

One of the tragedies of the West is that men and women have lost the knowledge that the affairs of this world are regular, not chaotic, that behind all there are governing intelligences, hearts cosmic in their sympathies.   It is but the smaller ones like us that bring confusion into the picture.   With our hot tempers, our fevered desires, we bring disharmony where harmony should be. But it is comforting to remember that all nature is harmonic; and the way to attain entrance into that harmony of nature, that cosmic harmony, is to bring harmony into our own heart. That is the knock.

Win with Gentleness and Kindness

I HAVE NEVER ENJOYED breaking idols, for I believe in the divine instinct in the human heart which at some past time brought those idols into being as works of love and understanding. It is we who do not understand what they represent and mean. It is rather we who are at fault than the Great Ones who gave birth to those works of past ages which have comforted millions century after century; and I do not enjoy breaking idols and crushing ideals in human hearts. Much better is it to teach, to show, to win with gentleness and kindness: "Search this out, Brother, here is something I have found to be supremely grand and good. Try it yourself. Subject it to your own closest inspection, and if you find it good, come and help to give to others what you and I have found."

Smashing idols is easy work, and has persisted for too long in my judgment, beyond its appointed place in the history of mankind. Oh, indeed, you can say that an idol contains a precious stone, and in order to get it by all means let us smash. But there are other ways. If that idol contains a precious stone, it was put there by very wise men, and there is a way to get that precious stone out without crushing the idol which thereafter becomes useless and is discarded.

And what are some of these idols? I do not mean brass and stone or wood only. I mean generally those idols which men worship and which they carry around in their minds and in their hearts. Don't you realize that sometimes by intemperate iconoclastic action you can actually set human hearts backwards, discourage them, throw them off the path? It is easy to be an idol-smasher. It is easy to smash; it is easy to crush; it is easy to overthrow — and it is often popular. But there is grander work for true men than that.

The Hill of Discernment

ALL TRUTHS ARE LIKE DIAMONDS. When cut and polished they have facets, each one such reflecting what is before it. For truth is comprehensive, not exclusive; it is a spiritual thing, and the spirit comprehendeth all. It is only the smaller things of us humans, and of beings lower than the great cosmic spirits, which are bounded by frontiers because of the imperfection of the evolutionary vehicles through which these great entities work. We should bear this fact in mind, for it makes us reverent, and humble in the nobler sense, when we realize that others than ourselves may have a vision sublime of reality.

How great and how good and how noble a thing it is for men to dwell together in brotherhood. Each man is a revelation unto all of his fellowmen, for each one is a marvelous mystery, a child of eternity and of the infinite; and despite the imperfections of human evolutionary development, when we see the vision from the "hill of discernment," we penetrate beneath the veils of the merely seeming into wonders ineffable which the human heart contains.

In my own life it was a revelation when this great truth came back into my human consciousness of this imbodiment, and from that moment I looked upon my fellow human beings no longer just as men, but as wonder-beings from whom I could learn, learning from the least as from the greatest. And what I learned in brooding over this wonderful thought, taught me to seek truth everywhere: as much indeed, had we the eyes to see it, in the plant or in the stones or in the circling orbs of heaven, as when we look deep into the eyes of a fellow human being and see marvels there.

What is this hill of discernment? It is one of the oldest

thoughts that human genius has ever given birth to. In all the great philosophies and religions of the past, you will always find this wondrous figure of speech, this trope, this metaphor, this climbing the hill of vision; whether, as the Jews had it, the hill of Zion, or after some other way of speech, the thought is the same. The noblest expression that comes to my mind, the most graphic and the most profound, is that passage in *The Mahatma Letters to A. P. Sinnett* that A. Trevor Barker published, in which the mahatmic writer speaks of the "Tower of Infinite Thought" from which truth is seen.

What, then, is this hill of discernment? Confessedly it is a metaphor; but what is it really so far as we human beings are concerned if not that wonderful organ within man's own constitution which theosophists call the buddhi principle, the organ of understanding, of discernment, of discrimination, of cognition of reality without argumentation? This organ of understanding for a man is the man himself in his highest, his link with the divine. That is the hill of discernment within each of us.

The burden of all the teaching of the archaic wisdom is simply that: recognize yourself as an instrument of reality, as one of its vehicles; ascend out of the miasmas and the fogs and the clouds of these lower planes upwards and inwards to rejoin in consciousness the divinity within, the ātma-buddhi; and then all knowledge, all vision of reality, is yours at will. For this is the organ clothed with no vehicle dimming its power. It sees reality as it were face to face, because itself is the reality. It is, as said, our link with divinity, which is reality, which is truth, which is all wisdom and all love and all knowledge.

So this hill of discernment is within man himself; and while it is the same for all of us, for each one it is in a sense different. It is like the pathway to truth: one for all, and yet differentiated into the wayfarers on that path, who are themselves both the wayfarer and the path itself. Man has no other means of attaining reality except through his own power, through his own organ, through his own being. He can and does receive help from outside, help which is wonderful; and it is our duty to give and receive help. But the receiving is merely the outward stimulus to awaken the inner organ of the receiver. This inner organ is not the deceptive organ of physical vision. Remember the story told in Hindu philosophy: A man returning home at night sees a serpent coiled in the path and jumps aside, and in the morning he sees it was but a coil of rope. So deceptive are all our physical sense-organs! The blind man cannot see the wonders of the dawning east. But even the blind man has an organ within him which if he can reach it needs not the deceptive organs of physical vision to see reality.

This buddhi principle which is in us and which we may use, if we will, knows no deceits. It cannot be blinded; it cannot be deceived. Its vision is instant and direct; for it is on the same plane as reality, and by opening up the intermediate channels between this our highest and our mere brain-mind, we inspire, breathe in, receive inspiration, and then we become like the gods.

That is the hill of discernment, of vision, and therefore of wisdom and knowledge and love, perhaps the three most glorious attributes of human consciousness: to be lost in cosmic love, to be lost in the vision sublime which is wisdom, to be lost in the higher interpretation of the vision which is knowledge — religion, philosophy, science, three in one and one in three; and this is not a theological trinity, but unitary truth.

Three Aspects of Karma

THE GREEKS HAD A MOST interesting and indeed profound way of describing karma. They spoke of Destiny— often called by the Latins the "Fates" — sometimes as unitary, and sometimes as threefold or the three Moirai — much as we speak of karma as being unitary or as being threefold and separated over the three great time periods: past, present, and future.

So the three destinies, or the three Spinners of Destiny, said the ancient Greeks, were three in one and one in three, and were respectively named *Atropos* which means that which cannot be changed or set aside; *Klotho*, the spinner; *Lachesis*, that which happens to us out of the past.

Atropos was the future, that which is inevitably coming. It was connected with the sun; mystically it was connected with our spiritual-intellectual parts, or the treasury of destiny imbodied in the mānasaputra. In art, it was expressed as a grave maiden pointing to a sundial, signifying what is waiting in the womb of time as the flowing hours bring it closer to us.

Klotho was the Spinner, that which is taking place now, that which we are now spinning or weaving in our minds and in our feelings. Called the present, it was represented in art as a grave maiden holding a spindle, spinning the thread of present destiny to become the future. It was linked in significance with our psycho-personal nature, what we call our mind, having intimate mystical and historical connection with the moon, the shadow of the sun as it were, the reflection, the reflected light.

Lachesis was connected with the earth and represented the past which we are now working out, and was depicted in art as a grave maiden holding a staff pointing to a horoscope: that which you have built in the past is now yours.

Atropos, the future, the sun, the mānasaputric intelligence; Klotho the Spinner, the present, the moon, the active present mind; Lachesis, the past, which we are now working out, in this body, on this earth. Don't you think this Greek conception is rather a marvelous way of envisioning karma as at once unitary and triple? The more I think of the subtle Greek mind having thought this out, the three in one and the one in three, the more I admire the conception. Karma is divisible by such methods into three paths of destiny: past, present, future, one in three.

So a man predestines himself, has done so in the past; what he now is on earth is the fruit: with his mind or lunar part he is now weaving his destiny which, when he unravels it, will find lodgment as garnered knowledge in the solar part of him, in the sun, in the mānasaputric treasury of destiny, some day to become the present, and shortly thereafter the past.

How Easter Became a Christian Festival

WHAT IS EASTER, this age-old festival time? To theosophists Easter is a very holy time indeed, one of the four main holy seasons of the year. The word Easter is not only used in English but is in use in other languages. It was taken over originally from the Anglo-Saxons and was adopted by the English folk. In other countries they used a word derived through the Greek from the ancient Hebrew. The Greek was πάσχα, *pascha*, and the Hebrew פסח *pesahh*, meaning "to step over," "to jump over," and hence "to pass over"— from the ancient Jewish Biblical story that when the Lord God led the children of Israel out of bondage in Egypt, on the night before they began their journey the exterminating Angel of Jehovah passed over Egypt slaying all of the firstborn of the Egyptians, and skipping over, passing over, the houses of the Jews because they had been instructed by Jehovah to put a smear of the blood of a lamb on the door. A quaint old tale, and it was accepted, as it happens, by most Jews and Christians literally, and is calculated to induce disrespect if not contempt for what ought to be a truly beautiful and holy tale.

The Passover was adopted by the Christians from the Jews. The Christians, while adopting this Jewish festival celebrated by the Jews at a certain date, did not like to have it exactly as the Jews had it. Though borrowing a great deal from the Jews, these new Christians like to have things a little their own way, so they changed the date somewhat. They accepted, took over, the Jewish Passover festival, but gave it Christian coloring and a Christian twist. The Jews celebrated their Passover on the 14th day or the full moon day of their month *Nīsān*, originally called *'Ābīb*, when spring begins to come to fruitful earth, when the buds and the trees begin to burgeon. 'Ābīb and Nīsān meant the first month of spring, and spring meant the beginning.

Now the Jews, as I stated, celebrated their Passover on the full moon day of the month of Nīsān, that is, 14 days after the new moon. So did the Christians, but they wanted a distinction from the day the Jews had it; and perhaps from ignorance, perhaps from other reasons, and after disputes lasting for centuries — and very bitter indeed in the second, third, and fourth centuries — they finally decided upon this rule: Easter, the time of the resurrection of our Lord Jesus Christ shall hereafter fall upon the first Sunday following the full moon after the spring equinox. Note the entrance of an archaic cosmic thought there. First find the spring equinox, then find the first full moon after that, then find the first Sunday after the full moon, and that is Easter. But the original Jewish way and also pagan way was to celebrate the whole festival of Passover on the full moon day of the Spring — of 'Ābīb or Nīsān.

Easter is not a local festival, or rather a Christian festival alone. It is a festival of cosmic significance, depending upon the seasons and mainly on the date upon which the spring equinox falls. There is the key to the original holy festival. It had not anything to do whatsoever with Jesus Christ. But they chose it as the date of his so-called resurrection for an excellent reason. They knew something of what took place in the adytum of the Sanctuary. They knew something about the four sacred seasons of the year, which, as the great pagan philosopher Plato pointed out, make a cross in nature, the two solstices opposite each other, the two equinoxes opposite each other: the so-called Greek cross; and during all initiations the candidate was laid upon a cruciform couch or bed, a bed in the form of a cross, and there he passed his trance.

Now then, this lying down, this beginning of the torture, of the trial, of the test, of the struggle, was on the new moon day in every one of the four sacred seasons. The beginning was always at the new moon time; and when the new moon coincided with the equinox or solstice, it was considered, and indeed was, especially holy.

Do you know that there is a Christian fact, known by a few, ignored by most of the Christian clergy, that Passion Sunday, considered to be the beginning of the Passion or agony of their Lord Jesus, is the 14th day before Easter?

Why did Jesus as a type, this holy teacher, avatāra, become connected with the lamb, and undoubtedly with the teaching concerning the zodiac? For this reason: that the Christians in every way wanted to connect their teacher with the promised messiah of the Jews. They could succeed in doing so, with even a coloring of truth, only by adopting the old Jewish stories. The Jews celebrated their Passover by eating a meal of lamb killed and baked in an oven on the day of their Passover. They were making a ritual, a ceremonial, as all the other ancient nations did, caught by the esoteric wisdom of what were in nature herself cosmic laws and cosmic events.

Time, Duration, and the Eternal Now

THE MAIN THING TO REMEMBER about time is this: that it exists, but is not in the absolute sense. That which *is* in the absolute sense is duration. What is the distinction between time and duration? Time like all things in manifestation is relative and is divisible. Time has past, has present, has future, and these three are distinct each from the other twain. Duration has no divisibility. It has no past, it has no future, and consequently there is no distinctive time present. But there is what we in our feeble language call an eternal Now. Oh, how difficult it is to describe this, and yet it is so simple to catch the thought.

For instance, the Romans lived and suffered and joyed and died and strutted their little ways upon the stage of life in their time, as Shakespeare said. But they are now gone. That is ended. Yet in duration those Romans are just as much alive now as they were then, for all exists in an eternal Now. Similarly with us of the present; and we look to the future as something that is coming. Time in our consciousness has an effect of distance, which it has because our minds are relative. But in duration that future is here now.

For instance, if my mind, if my thought, if my consciousness, were now at the present instant functioning in duration, I would not see people, such as the Romans of the past, dead, gone forever; then ourselves here now, and something unknown to come in the future. But functioning in duration all beings and things would be present in my consciousness with me now: what we call past, what we call future, what we call present, would be with me now, and not only those things, but all the Now of infinite space, and endless, frontierless duration.

Time exists most emphatically, it is an illusion, a māyā, which merely means we find it very difficult to understand it and do not perceive it exactly as it should be understood; but that is not time's fault, that is our fault. Our understanding is too weak to grasp it as it is, as it exists. Therefore, we call it a *māyā* to us, an "illusion." But illusion does not mean something that does not exist. If it did not exist, obviously it would not be an illusion. It means something which deludes our understanding, an illusion or a delusion to us.

Newton, as they now try to point out, had an idea that time was an absolute entity, like space and matter; and that time as an absolute entity was in actual movement, flowing was the word, flowing out from the past into the present into the future. The scientific philosophers of today have rejected that idea. They say it is all very well to look upon past, present, and future, as easy, convenient ways of doing our daily tasks, of understanding the life around us; but it is an unreal thing. Time is not an absolute entity. You ask then, what is the absolute entity? They will say it is the space-time continuum in which there is a lot of truth, for they have at last welded together in one, space and what we call time; and both of these are what we call duration. For duration is space, and all its manifestations are time, in time, of time.

Many illustrations come readily to mind to show us how time is illusory to our understanding. When you are happy, time passes quickly. When you are a child, time passes very quickly, or terribly slowly, depending upon the mood of the child. As you grow older, time just flows by, or drags, depending upon your mood. Therefore what is time itself? It is the functioning of consciousness, in the present case our human consciousness, and our human consciousness is an attribute of what we call the space-time continuum of cosmic infinitude.

Now I wonder if you are much wiser after all this philosophical discussion! I can tell you this though. There is a way of becoming conscious of duration per se when the consciousness seems to be taken right out of time. It is something you cannot describe. You have to be it for the time being to understand it. Yet I wonder how many of you have not had that experience, at the instant between dreaming and waking, or just before falling asleep, or perhaps during a fainting-fit or just before or after it, when all the attributes of time suddenly have vanished and you are conscious only of utter immensity, utter reality, and timelessness, and everything has vanished that is comprehensible to the brain-mind. Very understandable, however, by the intuition, and this raised to the nth degree, i.e., into the pure unadulterate consciousness of the spirit within where all wisdom and knowledge and vision are, is what the Hindu yogins mean when they talk about sambuddhi-samādhi, or simply samādhi sometimes. When the consciousness is fixed in this state, the Buddhists call it nirvana — nirvana means "blown out." Do you know why? Because of just what I have described. All the lower attributes of the personal ego have sunken into latency, have gone, or have been surmounted. Your consciousness is for the time coextensive with the universe. Therein there is no consciousness of the movements and changes of things combined with the psychological interplay of attributes, with these together producing division or sense of time; the procession of events has passed out of the picture, for the consciousness has risen above these events of manifestation, and you are now in timeless duration.

As a mere illustration of how illusory time is — and please remember that such an illusion does not mean that it is nonexistent, for if it were nonexistent there would be no argument about it — I would recall to those of you who have had dreams, vivid or vague, how curiously time and its phenomena seem to change in these dreams. It is a well-known fact of psychology that in dreams, or even under the influence of some drug, the events of a lifetime seem to be condensed within a few moments; or contrariwise, what would in waking, feeling life take but a few moments, can in these sub- or super-normal states be so stretched out as to cover years. It is the same consciousness which experiences these extraordinary visionings, and thus "time" in any of these states or in the normal jāgrata or waking-state seems to the experiencing consciousness just as "real" as any other of its experiences in and with time.

These facts lead the reflective mind almost instantly to see that it is the experiencing consciousness which really is the time-maker, weaving time out of the stuff of timeless duration, which in a true sense is identical with the essence of consciousness itself. Many a drowning but later resuscitated man has had all the events of his lifetime pass in a rapid panoramic vision before his consciousness; the whole procession of events which originally took years to experience now flashes before the mind's eye in a few moments of clock time, and yet the experiencing consciousness is cognizant of no incongruity.

Time, therefore, when compared with duration, is something like extension when compared with space. Time is a phenomenon of duration, just as extension is a phenomenon of space, and in both cases duration and space are realities or noumena, and time and extensions are the phenomena or illusions — māyā in each case.

Remember also that there are collective māyās, such as we human beings ordinarily experience as when all human beings on earth have the same time-consciousness of day or night, or a group of men and women will have the same consciousness of an hour passed for instance in a theater, or on a picnic, or in a train, or a week at sea.

Nature's Way after Death

I BELIEVE THERE IS NO POSSIBLE written or oral communication between those who have passed on and those who are here on earth; and there are a thousand reasons why this should be so, reasons based on nature's laws of harmony. But there is one exception to this rule: it is the cases of those who are dying or have just died. At that instant an idea held in the mind of the dying person has something of a powerful magnetic intellectual force behind it, and it will cast itself through the invisible waves of the ether to the one thought of; and there will be a kind of appearance, a shining presentment of the dying one striving to do something to the one held in mind. Sometimes the thought passes over, often not. These are the only occasions where the dying man or the one just dead can communicate orally, or in writing, with those on earth.

The Spiritualists have evolved their various ideas in a period of time slightly less than 100 years, and they themselves have been trying to digest, to make a kind of philosophy out of, the various messages they thought they received from their dead friends; and the contradictions in doing so have been tremendously numerous. These contradictions prove to us that there is no revelation coming to us in the body by such means from the outside. On the other hand, the entire consensus of mankind, civilized and uncivilized, from immemorial time has been telling us, teaching us, the exact opposite of what our brothers the spiritists have themselves been trying to understand and explain with the few facts that they have. All the great men of antiquity in whatever sphere of human thought, in whatever sphere of life, have always called this intercourse between the living and those who have passed on by one word, necromancy, and have unhesitatingly condemned it while at the same time explaining it. I do not state these things harshly, but to recall to your minds certain facts of history.

Have these revelations, these communications, this intercourse, ever given to the human race one fact of nature, one scientific, religious, or philosophic truth? On the other hand, examine these communications. With the exception of a very few, they are what in sheer honesty must be called amiable drivel: "Dear father, dear wife, dear daughter, dear son, I am happy, I am in the spiritland. My guide tells me you are waiting. Please be happy. Give my love to little Janie. I must go now. More next time."

There is infinite pathos in this. We should never condemn the spiritists for believing these things. The hunger of their hearts has been to have some proof, as they call it, of survival. But our point is this: Brothers, the only thing that will persuade you of a truth of nature is reason, the preponderance of evidence, something that will sway your minds; in other words, facts, not theories.

Now it is right to accept the honest testimony of a single mind, and it is just that due weight should be given to what a single honest man has to say. I believe that in the courts of law the testimony of an honest man is accepted. The testimony of two is much stronger, of three is supposed to be almost conclusive. But when we place against this one, two, three or four, the unchanging witness of all mankind since immemorial time to the contrary, must we not give to the testimony of the greatest minds who have ever lived in the past, or who live in the present, as much weight as we give to a few enthusiasts, however honest? Enthusiasm and sincerity by no means spell truth. They spell honesty but not truth.

Furthermore, pause a brief moment in reflection and look at this thought from a different angle. Suppose that when we die we are conscious of what happens on this earth. Suppose that nature allowed what we call the dying to know what happens on earth after they pass out. What kind of merciless hell would that be for those who have passed out! Would there be peace, repose, happiness, in the dreadful vision of earth's misery and sorrows? Would any one of you be happy dying, tired and wishing for peace and rest which you are entitled to by nature's laws, as she gives you your sleep at night to rest the tired body — would any one of you be happy dying now, and seeing what will take place on earth in the next 10, 20, 50 years? Nature makes no such mistakes as these. She does not treat her children in that way. Even when she causes us to fall ill because of our own foolishnesses and weaknesses, often, perhaps always, there is a dulling of the nerves of the body and the gentle balm of oblivion steals over the suffering man. Nature is built on harmony and compassion. When we die we are just unconscious, utterly so, mercifully so; there is no suffering, there is the unconsciousness of a brief, perfect, dreamless sleep. Then for the average man — I am not now speaking of extremes, the very good and the very bad — for the average millions, the next thing the consciousness is aware of is as it were an awakening in what we call the devachan, to unspeakable happiness and bliss. It is a dream, if you will, but like a dream which rests the whole being, the tired mind, the tired heart, all resting and recuperating.

What is this devachan? It is the flowering into activity of all those beautiful and lovely things which on earth we built up into our minds and could not find expression for. And when the body dies, the free mind automatically recalls to itself, sets into motion, these lovely ideals and aspirations, everything that was most glorious and beautiful and high, and the mind dwells on these, and it experiences peace and bliss and happiness and rest. All misery and horrors of the lower plane are forgotten.

Nature cares for her children better than we do, infinitely more carefully and more lovingly than the most doting parents know how to care for their children, protecting their little ones. Do you doubt this? Let me put a question to you. Do you realize that this instant and all your lives you have been surrounded by the most virulent disease germs, which would kill you off in no time unless there were a protective apparatus working in your body? What does this? Mother Nature. You don't know it, but nature protects you and guards you against perils you wit not of; and it is only man's own insanity, evildoing, the wickedness sometimes of his heart, his own weaknesses, which make the hells upon earth which we know. It is not nature that does that; and any man who tries to shift his moral responsibility by saying it is nature, in his heart knows that he lies. It is himself. Nature protects if we will allow it, and protects us as the parent tries to protect his or her child against that child's own ignorance. Nature, governed by divine law, will even attempt to heal the bodies which we with relentless and sometimes voracious lust for evildoing constantly attempt to weaken and corrupt. Nature heals, forgives, gives us another chance and one more and one more still, and allows our bodies to live on, weakened it may be, but healed. What damage was caused, was caused by us.

Thus the heart of nature is infinite love and compassion and harmony, and we see manifestations of it around us all the time. Nature cares for her children. She protects them and helps them. The trouble with us is that we are continually fighting against our mother, the only utterly compassionate, utterly wise mother the human race will ever know. So therefore comes the doctrine: help nature and work on with her and nature will regard thee as one of her masters and make obeisance.

Wine as a Mystic Symbol

AMONG MANY PEOPLES WINE and the drinking of wine has been used as a mystical symbol. If we understand this one fact we shall understand many otherwise inexplicable situations in the alleged lives of great occultists. How about the charge of drunkenness in connection with Paracelsus? Any supposed occultist who drinks is not an occultist; and that fact has been known since the beginning of thinking man. No one has ever proved that Paracelsus ever drank, ever was an habituary of the taverns or the inns. Hasn't it ever occurred to scholars that it is wise to put ideas together when they are stating something? How about the well-known habit of mystical thinkers the world over to speak of the wine, and the spirit of the wine, of God. The very word "spirit" even today attached to alcoholic drinks shows the early idea. Not that alcoholic drinks in themselves are good, but that just as grape juice can develop alcohol in itself and give forth as vapor what medievalists called "spirit" which is inflammable and can be lighted, so from this and other ideas connected therewith grew up the idea, the thought, of the idealist philosophers that wine is a good symbol of the spirit — the wine of God, the wine of Life.

How about the Christian church with its early communion, with wine as the emblem of the very blood-stuff of their savior? This is no longer a mere theory; the idea is no longer used merely mystically; it is the very blood of their savior. The Latin phrase is *vere et realiter*. The idea is of course credal, and yet it is based on a sublime and beautiful thought — that partaking of wine in the communion of the spirit was partaking of the spirit of Christ. And this was the earliest idea of the so-called pagan Greeks in their mystical communion in the rite of Bacchus.

How about the Sufis? They are among the most mystical of folk who used the symbol of the wine cup, the flowing wine, the flowing bowl, as symbol of the fullness of the heart which has been lighted, which has been filled with the light of the spirit. When a man was in communion with the divine within him, he was said to be drunken with the god, drunken with the spirit; in other words, illuminated. See how beautiful thoughts can be degraded; and the more beautiful they are the worse can become their degradation!

The quatrains of Omar Khayyam should tell anyone when the Sufis wrote of the tavern and the inn and the flowing bowl what they meant. The Sufis were notoriously sober. The orthodox among them probably never touched alcohol in any form; and yet their poetry is couched in the vein of thought just stated, in order to hide it, to make the thing innocent-appearing when danger was abroad. It was the way by which the persecuted mystics spoke in confidence to each other.

The Four Yugas

CYCLES SHOULD INTEREST EVERY intelligent human being because they are the functioning of nature itself. They are not extraneous thereto, imposed upon the universe by some outside power, for that universe is infinite and in its evolutionary changes eternal; and, being so, it must be the true expression of the indwelling divine powers which form all the invisible sides of universal being. Precisely as in the small, man's body is but the outward and visible sign of the inward and spiritual entity, so it is with nature. Man merely copies nature in the small, for he cannot do otherwise, there being but one fundamental law, one fundamental cosmic reason, one fundamental cosmic plan. Therefore every entity, be it small or great, within the cosmic whole, must function according to that cosmic whole, not only in action but in substance and in plan.

Therefore the cycles that pertain to the cosmic bodies, the celestial bodies, be they suns or planets or comets or nebulae, are but in substance the grander cosmic laws of which indeed these smaller things, however grand and great they may be, are faithful copies. Being in subjection to the cosmic law, they follow this law, they follow those schemes of action, they follow the cosmic plan, they cannot do otherwise, because if they did otherwise they would be following a plan contrary to the cosmic plan and to the cosmic intelligence and the cosmic powers, and that is impossible.

So cycles are but repetitions in the small of the parts of the divine plan, and to ask whether cycles are causes of evolution or effects of evolution, is merely to miss the point. They are both. Cycles are merely the functioning of nature, and therefore they are at one and the same time causes and effects. You cannot break the chain of nature, you cannot break the chain of destiny. The precedaneous cause produces a child, an effect, a consequence like unto itself; and that effect is but a link in the cosmic chain of life, becoming instantly another cause producing its child, and so forth forever. These effects are nature's procedures, nature's workings. It cannot be otherwise. Therefore make the simple and inevitable deduction and logical consequences of that in your own minds. Whatever is is cyclic. So when we speak of the doctrine of cycles, we are not enunciating anything new which no human being ever thought of before. We are simply stating a fact of nature, a cosmic fact. Look at the course of fevers, diseases, epidemics, look at the constant turnings of the sun and planets, the cyclical and sequential movements of nature everywhere, day and night, summer and winter, cold and heat, wet and dry.

I would say also in a sense that cycles not only are the functioning of Mother Nature herself, but from a slightly different viewpoint are evolution, the way that strange law which we call the evolutionary progress towards an ever increasing perfection works.

A good old Hindu saying has it that every great age or root-race is composed of four cycles, four smaller ages, and that in the first of these called the *satya* — a Sanskrit word meaning "truth"— truth stands as it were on four legs; and that in the next, the second called the *tretā* yuga, meaning the "third" counting from the bottom up, truth stands on only three feet. It does not mean that the fourth foot has been lost, but the meaning is that the fourth foot has been forgotten to a certain extent, seemingly atrophied or paralyzed and temporarily useless, not wholly so but largely so. Then in the third age which is called the *dvāpara* yuga, the "second" counting from the bottom up, truth stands on two legs. Two legs have become nonfunctional to a large degree; and in the fourth age, the present age, the *kali* yuga, the Age of Iron, the "black age," truth hops along on one leg only, not meaning that the other three feet have been lost, but that to a large extent their use has been forgotten. Now the meaning of this very interesting Hindu parable is simply this: there are four main or principal qualities in nature — there are seven as a matter of fact, but in the present period of evolution only four are apparent to us, being, as we are, in what we call the fourth round. These four ages are respectively spiritual, intellectual, psychical, and physical: they are the four supports of nature, the four legs on which truth stands, as it were. The first age is marked especially by spirituality, but having the other three qualities functioning under the aegis of spirituality. In the second age, spirituality has become dim but is there, and intellectuality has become predominant, although the other three are there. In the third age, the psychical instincts in the human being and in nature are predominant, and the spiritual and the intellectual are there indeed and doing their part, but are not recognized by men as the dominant powers in their living. When we reach the fourth age, the kali yuga, the present age, when truth hops along on one leg only, this is the leg of matter, the leg of physical nature. Spirituality is still with us, intellectuality and the psychical part of us are functioning; but we dream about them now as ideals instead of their being the dominant powers in our lives, and we see only matter. Our dreams are of matter and of power and of force and of violence. Truth indeed hops along on one leg only.

When this cycle is ended, then the new cycle will begin, and for the duration of that cycle truth will have again its part to play as the dominant in our lives. Human beings will then reason and think and feel and act mainly in accordance with spiritual attraction.

How Can You Prove Reincarnation?

How CAN YOU PROVE reincarnation to be a fact? This is one of the commonest questions that we are asked, and I always wonder how such a question could be asked. Do you expect to prove after the manner of the laboratory something that does not belong there?

What is proof? The bringing of conviction that a thing is true to the thoughtful mind. That is proof— so stated in courts of law, and properly so stated. Now, if by the adduction of evidence the mind is not swayed into the belief that a thing is true, that thing has not been proved, even though it may be true. Don't you see that the only way to get proof of a thing is by thinking it through to the end? Then you are convinced; and while you may be entirely wrong, still that is the only possible way for thinking human beings to get proof. But don't mistake evidence for proof. I have a receipt which shows that a certain sum of one thousand dollars has been paid. Does that prove that the money has been paid? Any lawyer will tell you it is not proof. It is evidence tending to substantiate a possible fact that a thousand dollars has been paid by so and so to so and so; but it may be a forgery; that receipt may not be an actual receipt. But if an individual hearing detailed circumstances about a thing, sifting and analyzing the evidence laid before his thinking mind, is convinced that X has paid Z a thousand dollars, then that evidence substantiates the conviction brought to the mind, making the conviction more strong.

Now then, how can you prove reimbodiment to anyone? By bringing conviction to the impartial and thoughtful mind that it is the only possible and satisfying explanation of the existence of human beings. And how is such evidence of proof adduced? By thinking. Thus: we are here. We are not all alike. We vary as amongst ourselves more than the leaves on the trillions of trees on the surface of the earth do. Each man is a unit. How came that thinking, feeling unit on this earth? Created by God? Prove to me first that such a creating God exists.

How much simpler and more reasonable is the supposition — as it seems at first — that here we have a thinking, feeling, self-conscious entity, which we now in this one life find amongst us. We find this entity at one stage of what is evidently an incomparably long journey of evolution. That is the first thought. *We are here.* We were not created by a marvel — some extra-cosmic God of infinite injustice, making some men almost godlike and others heavily, woefully, afflicted. You can cheat the mind by saying, "These are things which belong to Divine Mercy and are beyond our power"; but that is no answer and no proof to the thinking mind. It is sidestepping the question.

What we are faced with is the fact that we exist, that we differ greatly amongst ourselves; that we show in ourselves the evidence of growth. And where can you get all this needful growth in one short life on earth? How about the poor infants who are born and die before they have a chance to grow? Haven't they another chance to come back — a chance to try again? We have to take things as they are. I never would be one to accuse this spirit, whose attributes are harmony and cosmic justice, of acting with injustice and partiality — never!

Another thought: Who are we — we human egos, with our wonderful powers and feelings? Whence our ethical instincts? A thought that obliged the German philosopher Kant to admit of there being divine justice, because these ethical instincts often act contrary, so it seems to us, to the merely selfish, personal man; as, for instance, when a man gives up his life for some grand ideal or for someone whom he loves. There is divinity in that. We show divinity in our very composition. Does not this tell us that we are essentially sons of God, as the Christian would say; sparks of the divine flame which keeps the universe in orderly progression — sparks of that divine harmony and intelligence which makes the manifold marvels around us in the heavens or on earth? We are in this universe because we are intrinsic parts of it. We cannot ever leave it. We belong to it. It is we and we are it in essence. And what does this mean, this being formed of its stuff, of its essence? As it is eternal, so are we eternal. We are coeval with the universe, and we perdure as it does. It is but we in essence.

Let us carry our thought a step farther. As there is no chance action anywhere, no fortuity, naught but ineluctable procedures of cosmic law, therefore we humans, one small hierarchy in that cosmos, are not here by chance, therefore our being here has a meaning, and that meaning is rooted in the cosmic life, in the cosmic intelligence, in the cosmic law. It would be utterly meaningless if we simply appeared on this earth for one short earth life and then vanished and no good came of it, or mayhap no retribution for our evil doings.

Why are we here on this earth? Why are we here now? Why were men living in other ages, or what about the men who will follow us in future ages? Why will they then be? These things are matters of cosmic law. Now pray follow the reasoning, because we are advancing from link to link of thought. Being here by law, and one life being utterly insufficient to produce the purposes of cosmic mind, it is obvious that our being here once is a proof of reincarnation. Otherwise what brought us here? What cosmic mind put us here instead of on some other planet in some solar system, either ours or outside of ours? We are here because we have been here before, because here we sowed seeds of destiny, and we come back on this earth to reap those seeds which we sowed. This universe, governed by cosmic law, will not allow us to sow corn or wheat in San Diego County, and three or four months afterwards travel into Arizona or Nevada and attempt to reap the corn and wheat there. Where we sowed the seeds, there shall we reap the harvest. It is obvious. Our very being here, to the man who can think clearly and logically from step to step, or thought to thought, is a proof of reincarnation. Otherwise we must say cosmic law put us here by chance. And who believes that? If fortuity governed this world we would see the stars in their courses and all the planets running helter skelter all over the cosmic spaces without law, without reason, without order, without intelligence, without system.

There you have your proof. Just think about it, reason it out, advance step by step in logical thinking. We are here on this earth because we have sown seeds of destiny, of life here, and we come back to reap them: to undo the wrongs we did in the past, to reap the rewards that we sowed in the past. And that is why we will come back to reimbodiment in the future. We are now making ourselves to be what we shall in the future become. We are now preparing our destiny for our next life on earth. I am not now speaking of the intermediate phases of life between life on earth and life on earth. That itself is a wonder-story. I am now merely pointing out that in the universal law things move lawfully, causatively and effectively, every cause produces an effect which cannot be escaped. If you distort your soul by evil thinking and feeling, you will not become by such action an angel of pity. You will become ugly and distorted within, and you will reap the reward and the retribution of what you yourself have done unto yourself.

The universe is ensouled, and that soul is to the universe what man's soul is to him. The physical universe we see around us is but the body of the universe, as man's body is but the body of his soul; and both the physical universe and the body of man express but very imperfectly the divine and spiritual and intellectual and psychic and astral and all the higher laws and powers and energies and forces and substances that *are* the invisible worlds in space.

Don't you see how from step to step, by reason, instinct, careful thinking a thing through, we are led to the belief that we are not only in our inmost essence very children, offspring of the divine fire, but that, being such sparks from the divine flame, we are in evolutionary cyclic growth constantly advancing from lower to higher things, just exactly as the child is born and from unthinking childhood grows to be a thinking, feeling man with ethical instincts?

So, pursue these ways of reasoning, and then you will never ask anyone: prove to me that reincarnation is or exists. You will have the proof of it yourself.

The Invincible Fire of Spirit

BEAUTIFUL INDEED AND WONDERFUL is it that the things of the spirit override and rise above the things of the mind and of the body. There is where we humans are invincible — in the fire of the spirit and in the flame of that fire which burns in all our hearts. No matter what a man's belief may be, no matter what his brain-mind thinking or convictions may be, within, as the inmost part of himself, there burns forever that soul-light of union with the divine, which means union with all brothers of the human race.

Remember this: behind all clouds is the golden sunlight, a sunlight which is inner as well as outer; the sunlight of vision, of conviction, of hope, and of what the early Christians called *pistis* or faith, which is the essence of things unseen but known.

A man is great in proportion to his thinking, and by naught else. Shall I add, his feeling? It may not be required, because deep thought is likewise deep feeling.

Knowledge Brings Responsibility

IT IS NEVER TRUE THAT the adept or initiate, or one who knows, is allowed to follow and practice the left-hand path. Never! That is always wrong; if we believed that, we should simply descend to the level of those who say: the end justifies the means. What is true is that the strong helps the weak, the powerful extends the helping hand, the one who knows instructs the ignorant. The followers of the left-hand path are always weaklings, always in the dark — a synonym of the left-hand path — whereas those on the right hand are strong, illuminated, and have the light with them.

Knowledge brings responsibility as well as power and obligates those who possess it to use it for all, irrespective of right-hand path or left. If the treader of the right-hand path could misuse his knowledge, his wisdom, his power, even against one of the left, he would belong not to the right, but to the left. The White Magician helps even the Brother of the Shadow — not to go down, but to come up! He uses power and wisdom for purposes of beneficence, but never by following the left-hand path, which would be not merely degradation, but retrogression, backward going. So that from the practitioner of the works of the right, from the follower of the right-hand path, more is expected than from the follower of the left, because he knows more, has more strength; and knowledge and strength clothe one with responsibility.

Do not let the idea ever insinuate itself for a single instant into your mind, that because you have knowledge and power you are entitled to misuse it, or that less is expected of you than of those who have it not; in other words, that license is permitted to you. It means that you are entitled to employ it only for good, and that does not mean sickly sentimentalism. Sometimes you have to use your strong right hand. Sometimes the policeman is just as necessary as the nurse; and we can qualify the proper use of both as belonging to the right hand. Misuse of any or either belongs to the left. Strength contains obligations of honor. Knowledge entails honorable obligation. *Noblesse oblige* — a fine old French proverb, which does not mean nobility is obliging, but nobility obligates. The mark of gentility is the willingness to sacrifice self and to carry responsibilities for others — the carrier of the load, the helper. No man even today has a right to call himself a gentleman if he puts his own interests first. That is not the mark of the gentleman.

The Adversary

IT IS VERY INTERESTING to me to see how many people are interested in what some branches of religio-philosophy have named the "Adversary," and I believe that this is largely caused by the fact that outside of dogma from which the life has fled, there abides a residuum of reality even in these exoteric teachings of the outer instead of the inner time. The human heart realizes that at the bottom of all these various theological doctrines there is a fact of deep meaning, and this accounts, I believe, for the reason that the Christian church and Christians struggled so long to overthrow the gross anthropomorphic and really ridiculous ideas that had clustered around this central core of pure reality.

What is this central core? There is in the universe opposition — there is the keynote of the meaning of the Hebrew word *śātān*, "adversary," "opponent"; or of the Greek and Latin word *diabolos*, from which we have the German *Teufel*, the French *diable*, the Italian *diavolo*, and the English *devil*. These variations of spelling and pronunciation on the original term were the products of different peoples, the original term from which they all derived, as stated, having been the Greek word *diabolos*, meaning the "accuser," and hence the "adversary." How grossly this wonderful philosophic and religious idea of an adversary has been distorted to become a mere anthropomorphic or human-like personification of opposition in nature — opposition which in truth may be and indeed is most beneficial and helpful, or opposition, on the other hand, which may be malign and evil.

That is the keynote of the doctrine; and hence, using words to explain a great cosmic reality, the Hebrew said the "opponent," the "adversary," and the nimble-minded Greek spoke of the "accuser." Why? This is explained in the theosophical teaching that there is no such actual cosmic individual acting as an opponent or adversary of men or of the gods; for the accuser, adversary, or opponent is in actual fact, so far as humans are concerned, our own weaknesses, evildoings, evil thoughts, evil emotions which some day sooner or later karmically spring up in our path to face us, and facing us, accuse us, as it were, point us out as the evildoer. They, our own former selves, have now become the adversaries and accusers of the present self. In nature and in human nature, the early Christians personified this and spoke of the *diabolos* or Satan, for to them it was a very real thing.

But mark how amazingly and marvelously every truth becomes capable of teaching us wondrous things, for the adversary, as should appear clearly enough from the foregoing remarks, becomes in reality a most valuable teacher; we learn by the faults of the past, not only to avoid them in the future, but to become stronger than they in the future. The karmic adversary therefore becomes the instructor; the faults learned and overcome and surmounted thus prove themselves to be our guides and teachers — former stumbling blocks when surmounted become stepping stones to higher things.

Following this idea in one more but parallel significant meaning, it was always stated by the ancient mystics and occultists, by theosophists of ancient lore, that the name of the teacher, of the guru, of the instructor, of the savior, is the adversary. He will not allow the neophyte to pass upwards until that neophyte has proved his worth, until he has learned the key words, the passwords which mean primarily, self-conquest, and future safety. See how wondrously this thought, this key doctrine, shifts from one explanation to a parallel one, and yet seems so difficult. Thus were the ancient teachers always called *nāgas*, "serpents" of wisdom. Thus was likewise the opposing power in nature, whether divine or malign, spoken of as a nāga, a serpent in the Garden of Eden or a serpent of wisdom.

A Christian teaching in the New Testament, coming from supposedly inspired intelligences, tells us to worship the serpent. Look how graphic is the injunction: "Be ye therefore wise as serpents, and harmless as doves." For such are all the grand adepts, all the Buddhas and Christs, the pitiful, sorrowing ones, sorrowing for mankind's ignorance.

We learn from our weaknesses to mount to higher things. Our weaknesses themselves become our teachers; and once we have learned their lessons, it is no longer needful to turn to them for instruction. So we say then that they become evil instructors, for we have already learned much and mounted higher through their help. We are not only wasting time, but we are doing wrong to be affected by the thoughts and feelings and counter-emotions of the past. It is our duty to pass to higher things, to challenge the new opponents, the new accusers. "Behold, I stand at the door and knock." Do you catch the thought? The door opens. The adversary, the opponent for the nonce says, "Who are you?" If you give the right answer you pass; the wrong answer, the door is closed against you, because it is so in reality. You cannot take a step onwards and upwards until you know the passwords which are parts of yourself, in other words until you have the will and the intelligence to do right. You yourself then, in such instance, become the adversary, the so-called Satan. You must conquer yourself, this part of yourself, in order to go higher. Therefore we learn on the stepping-stones of our former selves to become new selves. Our best selves are an ideal before us, to mount upon and to build with. Our present selves in their turn some day will pass and we shall meet the spirit, the divine self of the future, and it too will ask us: "Who art thou? Give the password." And the password is knowledge, is wisdom, is altruism, the great treasury of long past spiritual experience. Be ye wise as the serpent, but innocent and harmless as the dove. This is a most beautiful and profound allegory. No wonder it has been adopted by race after race of humankind in different parts of the world. Climb on our dead selves to higher things.

One aspect of the adversary is our present self, marvelous thought. Shall we overcome the present self, the adversary which prevents our going higher because it is not higher, it is simply a self? If we do, then we have given the password and we ascend, we pass the portals of wisdom. The adversary is no longer a tyrant. No longer is the initiator examining our spiritual and intellectual and moral credentials, our own self, our own inspiration. The adversary becomes the divine friend, the savior of all men, the serpent of wisdom.

It is a beautiful allegory pregnant with meaning. Even the poets of relatively modern times have caught the idea; they caught it from recollections of previous lives on earth when they were taught it. Milton, the English poet, for instance, describes the fall of Satan or Lucifer, according to Christian theory one of the highest of the angels who "fell." The same idea with a new angle of vision to it, a new twist of thought. The angel climbs upward within the celestial spheres, self-redeemed. The self, the main adversary, whether it be of god or of man or one of the innumerable hierarchies of living beings in human nature, for each one there is an adversary, itself or himself. And yet, marvelous wonder, so compassionately is nature constructed, that out of our faults we learn better things. From ugliness we learn beauty. From weakness surmounted is born our new strength. From the unholy do we advance to holiness. What was once the opposition, the opposer, the adversary, when we challenge it with courage and take the kingdom of heaven with strength, becomes the savior, the initiator.

So with our own selves. Have you ever thought that a fault overcome becomes a new strength in your character; that a temptation surmounted has given you more power, for you have done it through exercise of your will? Your will has become stronger. The pity for others within you has become keener.

Your vision becomes more luminous, a far-seeing clairvoyance. It is experience which makes us think. It is experience which gives us growth. It is this experience which is the adversary, the accuser.

All peoples have taught of opposition in the universe, and they taught beautifully of it. But as far as I know it is only the very savage tribes and later Christianity which have ever personified or humanized this cosmic principle into an angelic entity, in Christianity of demoniac type. The essential idea is the same over the earth. So when we look upon this opposer, under whatever multitude of guises we meet it, whether of divine character or of malign, the principle behind all is the same. To us humans it becomes demoniac and malign if we weakly succumb. We have forgotten the challenge of our own soul. On the other hand, when we use our will to achieve and take our selves in hand for training, we become strong because we become more universal. Our vision is no longer restricted to ourselves, and therefore raises itself proportionately towards the divine. That is why the divine is always spoken of as being divine, and the immensely restricted and constricted and therefore selfish as always being evil, because the small thinks but for itself and opposes the world to gain a tiny kingdom of the lower self, setting its power against the universe and thereby becoming so much evil, like the seeds of a disease in the human body. When that seed of disturbance is cast out, as happily it may be, health, universal peace, in the body, returns. There is the idea. The more we become universal, the higher we are. Phrase it otherwise: the closer we approach the divine which is universal, the higher we are. To quote again a Christian thought of great depth and to me of wondrous beauty: "Know ye not that ye are the temple of God, and that the Spirit of God dwelleth in you?" There you have the companionship of the divine, if you will take it by your inner strength, for here within us is its tabernacle, its temple, in the human heart.

There in just these simple thoughts is a whole cosmic philosophy, in the study of which you will find illumination which is life, comfort, immense intellectual activity of the highest type, and last but not least, peace, that inner peace which passeth all understanding, but which can be known.

The Christmas Tree

THE CHRISTMAS TREE, dotted with lights and bright with tinsel that reflects those lights and multiplies them manifold, is an old pre-Christian symbol used by the peoples of northern Europe at the time of the winter solstice; and here is the inner significance of it:

Have you never heard of the World Tree with its roots in the realms of spirit and whose branches are the great suns and systems of suns? This World Tree began in the beginning of this cosmic age to bring forth all the stellar hosts. Now the winter solstice is the beginning of the cosmic New Year, and so these northern peoples, knowing some of the ancient truths, celebrated this cosmic event with the Christmas tree. It symbolizes the World Tree, and the lights are the suns that bestrew the deeps of space, hinting to us the message from the divinities who constantly give us the light of love, the light of mind, the light of hope eternal. But so far have we fallen from the wisdom of our forefathers that now the Christmas tree has become merely a sign of festivity, except for the few who preserve its significance in their hearts.

The giving of gifts on the Christmas tree was emblematic of the self-dedication of the gods so that the worlds might come into being. "Here is my gift. It is born from myself."

The Living Buddhas in Tibet

REGARDING THE SO-CALLED living Buddhas in Tibet, I think that the Occidental world is too apt to build frameworks of thought constructed in the Occident around Oriental doctrines and teachings which we in the West only vaguely understand. The Occidental idea that the Tibetans believe that these living Buddhas are the imbodiment of Gautama the Buddha is radically wrong. The idea is this: that there is a cosmic Buddha, just as now some thoughtful Christians are beginning to intuit that there is a cosmic Christ of whom Christlike men, who have lived or who may live now or in the future on earth, are exemplars, rays, imbodied representations. Jesus so called was one such. That likewise is the ancient Tibetan teaching regarding the living Buddhas of Tibet: that there is this cosmic Buddha identical with what these few forward-thinking Christians call the cosmic Christ, the Christ immanent in the universe and therefore immanent in man's consciousness. The Tibetans call this in their beautiful teaching the Celestial Buddha of whom all human beings are rays; in other words, every human being has a ray from this cosmic Buddha which is his inmost being, his inmost self; and that when a man raises his consciousness to become at one with this flame of divinity burning in his heart, a ray from the Celestial Buddha, that ray coming as from the sun into this man's heart and firing him with inspiration and wisdom and love, makes of that man a living human Buddha. Gautama the Buddha was one such, but an outstanding and remarkable example.

It is a marvelous teaching, for mark you the endless hope in it, the undying inspiration in it, that each one of us, all of us, has as his inmost self this celestial fire; and that we as human beings can become at one with it if we will, and if we live the life and pursue the course of study so that it will become manifest in our lives, imagine ourselves in it, vision it. Make your vision filled with grandeur and beauty, and your human life will begin to manifest it likewise, for you are imbodying a cosmic Buddha in which you think and feel and therefore are.

That is the very essence of the Tibetan doctrine of the living Buddha, for when this cosmic glory takes up its residence in human hearts and minds, then such men become what the Tibetans call living Buddhas, Christs on earth. It may be in small degree — it depends upon the response of those themselves who feel the inrushing of the divine fire. But in so far as we increase it, or rather open ourselves to the influx from within-above, our Buddha-stage or Christ-state is by so much the more increased, made so much the greater.

Thoughts on Karma

HERE IS A QUESTION that I have often been asked: Does karma imply exact reaction in detail? That is, if I injure someone, does that individual have to injure me in the identical manner in which I injured him? We do not teach a scientific determinism; we teach the exact opposite, although it is true that the god-wisdom teaches a universe of ineluctable law. That is the main foundation stone of all the structure of hope, of religion and philosophy and science that theosophy is. But here is the point: If I, for instance, cheat a friend and break his heart, is that friend going in some future life to cheat me and break my heart in identically the same way with all the same details reproduced? The answer is No, not in all the details. But my friend whom I cheated, despite his own will, driven by destiny, and myself attracting the retribution to me which is my due, will so act in some future life closely along the lines of the way I cheated him, but not in identical details. He too perhaps against his will may break my heart.

If I kill a human being deliberately, if I murder him will that same human being murder me in some future life? Personally I am inclined to say Yes. The details are not the same, but the general foundation of the structure of destiny will bring it about. Mark you this, the teaching of all the titan seers and sages of all the ages: *That which ye sow, that shall ye reap, not something else.* This is a Christian saying and a grand one.

Now notice the immense moral effect this teaching, once sincerely believed, has on a man, not only for his own protection in the future, but because of the revolution in feeling and in thought it works upon his character. He will watch very carefully lest he ever injure a fellow human being. Think what this one doctrine alone would mean for the safety and happiness of mankind if it were commonly accepted as once upon a time it was all over the world. If I sow good, I strengthen and beautify my own character, the thinking of good makes my own character symmetrical. The feeling that I am doing good strengthens me to greater goodness in doing. This is simply karma. If I think evil and feel evil, and wreak evil upon my fellows, outside of the wrong that I am doing to them, running up a retribution for my own future lives, see what I am doing to my own mind and my own feelings. I am distorting, I am making them ugly, twisted, gross. This too is karma. You cannot think these thoughts without feeling the repercussions of your own thinking apparatus. Evil is ugly. Thinking ugly things will make that apparatus ugly. Feeling ugliness will make you feel uglier the next day.

Now what is reincarnation but a carrying out of this same law of destiny? We have lived on this earth almost innumerable times in the past. We are here today because we are attracted back here. Familiar scenes attract us, just as the traveler traveling away from home looks forward to the time when he will return. The familiar scenes, the happy home, the fireside, the gentle, beautiful, even perhaps lovely remembrances of that home all call him back. And that is what reimbodiment is anywhere; reincarnation, coming back to familiar scenes on this earth. And we have familiar scenes on other planets also — but that is another story.

We humans are pilgrims of destiny, children of the divine wandering purposefully, and purposefully driven by karma, driven by destiny. We are children of the divine, therefore having a spark of the divine intelligence and of the will of the divine. Therefore we ourselves can face the universe and all its impacting horror, for within us, unconquerable and deathless, is this divine spark. By following its mandates we have free will, the free will of the universe, that all the power of the universe coming upon us at once cannot ever overthrow, for we are children of the divine and that universe is we ourselves and we are it. Its heart and our hearts are one and call to each other. Abyss of destiny calls to abyss of destiny, and we understand each other.

Every man having a modicum of free will, despite the irrevocable past, can at any moment, once the idea comes to him, change his destiny for the future. Eradicate the past we cannot ever, for that is destiny and must be worked out. It is built into ourselves. But we can change, modify, make ourselves more shapely for the future by exercising our divine prerogative of thought and free will in the present, taking destiny in our own hands and making it more shapely for the future. In this as in other things we humans are akin to the gods, our parents.

How wonderful is the vision that the sensitive heart and quick mind have the power to see, bringing light everywhere, therefore a sense of perfect security, a sense of perfect justice, a sense of perfect peace. Sometimes we feel that our own past destiny is too hard for us to bear and we cry out in our anguish: O God, may this cup pass from me: yet not my will but thine be done! But if I must drink I will drink. Instead of this let me remember that I am a child of the divine and, drinking that cup of destiny which I myself have brewed by my own acts in the past for good or for evil, I now begin to build for the future. Within that future, now that the revelation has come, I see beauty unspeakable, holiness ineffable, peace ever-increasing, an expanding love with its richness of life, and understanding without bounds which makes me loving to others.

The Ancient Doctrine of
Vicarious Atonement

THE VICARIOUS ATONEMENT DOCTRINE, as it is today understood by Christians, has indeed stood in the way of their acceptance of the doctrine of reimbodiment. But it was not so in the beginning: the earliest Christians accepted reincarnation. What took place then? We find evidences that the doctrine of the Vicarious Atonement prevailed in the very origins of Christianity, but there took place a slow changing of the understanding of this doctrine to one of words instead of spiritual occult meaning. So that when it became a mere theological dogma, it was a great stumbling block, a closed door rather, preventing the true follower of the Christ, today and in past centuries, from accepting this doctrine of hope, of great hope — human reincarnation.

In the earliest days of Christianity, the primitive Christians — being the Theosophical Society of that time *for that portion of the earth* — knew, were taught, that every man born into this life is a son of the divine in his highest part — not as a physical man — his spirit, his soul, was a spark of the cosmic All, a breathing, living flame of fire from the heart of Being. He called this the Christos spirit, even as some Christians have intuitively grasped this holy teaching of the immanent Christ in man. That was the primitive Christian thought, and it is taught today in theosophy as it has always been taught by theosophy in the different ages.

So it is the spiritual part of us, this flame from the divine, which is the deathless essence of our being. It is the anchor of our life, and of our growth, and of our progress, from imbodiment to imbodiment, carrying from each life on earth all the spiritual aroma of the good deeds, beautiful thoughts, noble ideals, fostered in the heart and mind, carrying these over from life to life. We call this inner spiritual part the monad. It is the inner Buddha in us, the inner Christ in us.

Thus it is that this monad is enchained by us, by our weaknesses and feeblenesses and mistakes — aye, and by our good thoughts and deeds, to carry us from life to life as a spiritual "plank of salvation," as H. P. Blavatsky says, meaning the inner Christ chained to the cross of matter, our light, our hope, our origin, our destiny. And because it suffers for us enchained in these spheres, according to the ancient doctrine, and carries our burden for us — our own being, mind you, our own inmost spiritual essence, the Christ within us — we can say, not in the theological sense but in the theosophical sense, it atones for us and endures through all, *just because it is* our spiritual self. The process is vicarious only in the sense that the divine part of us carries the weight, the burden, of what we, the lower parts, have thought and felt and done: dealing us perfect justice in life after life, making us what we are and what we shall become. In this manner was the doctrine of Vicarious Atonement first understood: that the mere man of flesh is naught, but that the lower, unevolved, imperfect side of man had this plank of salvation in his own spark of divinity, in his own immanent Buddha, his immanent Christ, the god within him.

This ancient doctrine likewise tells us that as a man grows and evolves from age to age and learns in life after life, more and more does this truly spiritual part of his being come to manifestation and express itself through the mind, the lower mind, the ordinary human being. When this is done with relative perfection we have one of the great seers and sages, one of the imbodied divinities, one of the imbodied Buddhas or Christs, one who expresses through himself as a human being the godhead, the godhood, *which is his own link of selfhood with the divine,* an imbodied Christ, an imbodied Buddha.

Nevertheless, it is perfectly true that when this *inner* meaning of the immanent Christ was lost sight of in Christianity, the words of the teaching took the place of its occult meaning; men lost the teaching that they themselves were the Christs within, sons of the divine, and that by thinking and feeling and living in the Christlike way it was their most glorious privilege and duty from life to life to express this inner godhood ever more and more, growing from humanity to mahatmahood, to masterhood, until finally the goal is achieved, and we can cry: "O god of me, how thou dost glorify me!"— the true rendering of the Hebrew words alleged to have been uttered by Jesus on the Cross: *'Ēlī, 'ēlī, lāmāh shabahhtānī.* As the words stand translated in the gospels they are wrong, for "to forsake," or "to abandon," is in Hebrew *'āzab;* and "to glorify" or "to make perfect" is *shābahh;* and the word in the gospels is *shabahhtānī,* "thou dost glorify me," "thou dost make me perfect."

The Christ within the man spoke; nor is this an exterior Christ except in the sense that the Christ within the man is a spark of the cosmic Christ. The Buddha within the man is the representative in him as an individual spark or ray of the cosmic Buddha, the Ādi-buddha — use what terms you will.

Thus it came about that one of the most beautiful, helpful, and consoling doctrines of primitive Christianity became an illogical theological dogma — a shell of words from which the spirit of their meaning had fled.

The Golden Chain of Platonic Succession

IT WAS HOMER WHO FIRST in Greek thought spoke of the Golden Chain between Father Zeus and men, his children, and that it was this Golden Chain of sympathy and feeling linking the gods with men by which we humans could climb to the divine stars where Zeus the father of gods and men is. But it was Plato who popularized this magnificent Homeric idea so much that from his day scholars often spoke of it as the Platonic Chain.

Now what does this mean really, the idea of this wondrous Greek conception of hope, filled as it is with the majesty of the divine? It means that there is a way for human beings to walk to reach divinity, that this chain in reality is but a pathway which we may tread if we will. It is called golden because it leads to the golden heart of Father Sun and thence onwards, to the very heart of divine Being where the gods are; and that all along this ladder between gods and men, there are posted gods, teachers, showing us, the wayfarers, the farers on the upward climb, where we should look, which turn we should take, how to go upwards and onwards forever. On each such link of this wondrous golden chain there stands a teacher whose whole and sole duty is to help those below to stand where he is. In other words, there is a hierarchy of teachers between us men, learners alike, and the divinities towards whom we aspire, and this hierarchy exists to help all those below.

There is a way, as the teachers have reminded us, steep and thorny, but it is still a way, and it leads upwards and inwards, to the very heart of divine Being. We are treading that way, we are farers on that path even now, although most of us, alas, know it not, and we stumble alone; but the way is there, and along this way, could we but see it, could we but realize it, are

companions ahead of us, marching steadily upwards and forwards through the ages of the past and into the ages of the
future; and we humans are amongst this marvelous army of
farers on the way. Some of us are not happy to be stumblers
always, nor to be laggards on the path, but desire to move more
quickly forwards and upwards, to train ourselves, teach ourselves, take ourselves in hand, and let the inner and higher part
of us rule our lives. That is advancing in quicker time.

There I think is the inner meaning of this wonderful Greek
teaching of the Golden Chain between men and the gods, a
marvelous doctrine!

Lost Continents and Our Atlantean Heritage

THE ACTUAL EVIDENCE FOR the existence in prehistoric and former geologic times of now sunken continental land massifs is simply enormous. Items of proof have been brought together by clever researchers and writers, not theosophists alone, but eminent scientists and other investigators; and all in an attempt to solve the mystery: How on earth did the flora and fauna of the land massifs, as they now exist, ever pass from one to the other over hundreds, maybe thousands of leagues of rolling, stormy oceans?

An attempt was made during long years to explain the presence of similar and identic flora by means of migrating birds. Birds eat seeds and drop them, and perchance by the time the birds drop the seeds another land is reached, and the seeds take root. Or perhaps things float on the waves of the ocean, and after weeks and months, it may be years, are thrown up on some sandy coast and there take root! But common sense prevailed after a while. It was soon seen that these labored efforts at explaining the similarity if not identity of the vegetation and animals in widely separated continents, required something firmer and more concrete than speculative evidence of that type.

So it was the scientists themselves who, long preceding theosophists, began to ponder the existence or the possibility of formerly existing lands where now the oceans roll their stormy waves in the Atlantic and in the Pacific and elsewhere. Certain scientists collected data to prove that something like that must have existed during some former period in geologic history, in order to account for these things. And when geology and its discoveries brought further proofs of the existence in these widely separated continents of flora and fauna in the Old World similar to if not identic with types in the New World, and discovered these in the Eocene, the Miocene, and Pliocene deposits, they said to themselves: surely there must have been land connections between the Old World and the New, somewhen, somewhere. Those facts remain still unexplained.

Scientists themselves for decades now have granted the existence in former geologic times of a great continental land massif in the Pacific Ocean. Sclater called it Lemuria, from a little monkey-like animal called Lemur. Later a similar continental land massif was imagined and called by some scientists Gondwanaland to explain puzzles in distribution of flora and fauna in the Pacific and elsewhere that without these supposed land connections could not be explained. And they have not yet been explained.

The reluctance of the scientists to accept the evidence of their own eyes is remarkable. They themselves brought the question forward, brought the proper answer forward, and in the case of the Atlantic continental land massif, it is still, as they say, possible, even probable, but not proved. I don't know why. They have accepted it for the case of the vast Pacific Ocean lying to the west of us here, but not for the other ocean as yet; and yet the proofs are there.

Now then, I think one of the reasons for the reluctance of so many thousands to accept what must be the case arises in an erroneous idea of what these former geologic land massifs were. They seem to have got the idea that Atlantis, an immense stretch of land, exactly similar in type to our own present system of ocean and land, all sank in a night; and out of the then existing oceans came the new land, which is now ours. This is an absurdity. It is one of the commonest facts known to all even today, that land is slowly sinking, or rapidly sinking, all over the world; and that other lands not only are with slowness, but with equal regularity, rising. This process of submergence and emergence through long and short geologic periods is just what took place first in Lemuria and ages and ages later in Atlantis. It took hundreds of thousands of years for the main portions of the great Atlantis-system of continents, big islands, small islands, and seas, even notably to change places — the land sinking, the oceans overwhelming the lands which sank, and other new lands rising to take their places. This has continued through all geologic time, is continuing now, and will continue into the future. Yet there have been cases where islands even fairly large have sunken or risen rapidly, even in our short human view — cataclysms, as in the case of Plato's Poseidonis, an actual event of European prehistory as we now know history, which sank in a day and a night, some eleven or twelve thousand years ago, after fearful earthquakes and tidal waves. Poseidonis was an island the size of Ireland or less, which lay a good distance in the ocean off what is now the Straits of Gibraltar. But that was one of the last island remnants of the great Atlantic continent, just a headland, as it were, which remained until it finally also sank.

Similarly so with Lemuria, the home, as theosophists say, of the third root-race. It was not just one big land. It was a system of continents, great islands, small islands, oceans and seas, just as we have them now. As a matter of fact, there are some remnants of Lemuria still remaining above the waters of the ocean, and also of Atlantis. Talk about scientific proof! Why, the call for such land connection is so tremendous that it is not for proof of such existence we should ask, but for proof that it has not existed. That is a perfectly justifiable and even a strong argument. I repeat it: even today, and during the Eocene and Miocene and Pliocene ages, the flora and the fauna were and are still so similar in so many respects in widely separated localities or lands, that some land connection at some time as among these separated lands is imperatively called for. The only alternate thing to say is that in those now far past geologic ages there must have existed an immensely civilized, powerful body of races of men, who, with mechanical devices equal to or greater and finer than ours, could transplant the vegetable life and the animal life from continent to continent in proportion with their own migrations and colonizations, and that comes to the same thing.

When we know that land is sinking and land is rising, and has been throughout geologic time, as proven by the geologic record, and that it is going on secularly, progressively, through the millennia, actually through millions of years, what is the answer? Prove to me that Atlantis did not exist. Why, one could talk for a day and a night simply about the almost innumerable data that have been collected by scholars of all kinds along this line. Books, scores of them, have been written on just these themes.

Now then, my other thought is this: the Atlanteans were a great body of races, just as we are today, a great body of races with different colored skins, different kind of hair, different past histories from ours, but all human or semihuman. Some of them were good. But most of them, when judged by abstract standards of right and wrong, were evil — even more so than we are. And we cannot throw stones! Heaven knows, we are bad enough. But we are an improvement upon our Atlantean progenitors. For there, although there were millions, throughout the millions of years that Atlantis endured, who worshiped the divine and the spirit in preference to matter and selfish power, the majority in those days were worshipers of brute power, of strength, of matter, of influence for the self. Selfishness was the dominant keynote in the Atlantean race, just as it is even yet in ours; but in ours we have reached the point where we no longer glorify it, but recognize it and are ashamed of it. It shows that spirituality is entering, although slowly, into our consciousness; and even among crooks, honor and right and reason and justice are the key words with which to charm the hearts and minds.

With the Atlanteans it was power and strength, stuff, substance, wealth. But not so with all. There were millions and millions who in their hearts worshiped the divine and right and justice, and these were the elect, and from these elect were formed the Mystery Schools which have endured to this day, out of which schools have come all the great religions and philosophies and sciences of human history, for the saving of men from worse things, for the helping, the raising, the softening and refining of men and women, and therefore of civilization.

Just as the Theosophical Society today came therefrom, so in past ages came the theosophical societies of other times, our own lineage. There they originated in far distant Atlantis: those who loved right and honor and justice and truth and reason and pity more than strength and power and selfish privilege. They were what we call the sons of the divine, the sons of God; and they gathered together, collected together, and formed the first Mystery Schools in which the spirit of truth was worshiped, revered, and taught, instead of the spirit of power and dark self-interest. Just think how these thoughts sway human minds. Look even at our world today, and see how a thought of selfish profit or advantage, an egoism, can lead men astray. We have the old Atlantean spirit back amongst us, even yet, and this was what H. P. Blavatsky meant by saying that the karma of Atlantis still weighs heavily on us, on our souls, on our minds. We are still under its influence, but we are struggling out of it, out of its embrace.

In this connection a final word: there are certain groups today who in speaking of theosophy, say, "That is very fine, but that is the Eastern tradition. We follow the Western tradition." To speak of the Theosophical Society as the tradition of the East is nonsense, for it is the parent of them all. It is neither Eastern nor Western, Northern nor Southern, it includes them all, for from it they all have come forth. Theosophy is the source of them. It recognizes its children in these various guises.

Therefore it is the great reconciler, the great harmonizer, the comforter, the spiritual parent.

How true it is that we even today yearn for truth with all our hearts and souls, and that the mark of a great man, or a great thinker, is service and learning. Do you know that the proudest thing that one can say is that he is a learner, a student of the god-wisdom, learning from others in good fellowship, charitable to others, seeing good in what another has to present, looking only for candor, honesty, purity, decency of mind and heart. This is the open sesame to human hearts. Let the Atlantean spirit die. Let it molder into the dead bones of the past. Hatred, dislike, enmity, unreason, injustice, are all its products. Smallness and pettiness of mind are its children.

Three Stages of Visioning Truth

THE PSYCHOLOGICAL OPENING OF the human being to truth, to the ingress of the god-wisdom — in other words the training that every true theosophist undergoes — begins once he is touched and his heart is opened, begins even though he knows it not. This opening of the heart may be divided into three stages. We are familiar with these in that form of Buddhism which originated in China coming from India. In Sanskrit it is called the Dhyāni form, and in Japan it is known as the Zen form of Buddhist thought. It is expressed somewhat as follows, and it applies equally well to theosophy because the Zen or the Dhyāni form of Buddhism is but a branch of theosophic thought.

The student in entering the pronaos of the temple of wisdom, and later in entering the temple itself, goes through three phases of inner opening — that is the word they use. Thus, in the first phase, the mountains and the waters of the earth are mountains and waters, and they are recognized as worthy of study and of research, and their wonder is seen and sensed; but they are only mountains and only waters.

But by study and aspiration after truth, finally comes the second psychological opening of his character, of his understanding, of his being. He realizes that the mountains and the waters, however beautiful they may be and wondrous for study, are after all but aspects, appearances, phenomena of noumena behind, the effects of invisible and secret causes; and he realizes in this second phase of the opening of his being that if he wants truth he must go deeper and study the science of the mountains and of the waters of the earth. He must investigate the causes which bring them into being, the inner causes and energies

which produced the mountains and the waters. He realizes
that the mountains and the waters, because they are effects,
phenomena, appearances, however relatively real they may be,
are but illusion, māyā, because the real truth is within and
behind them. His whole being is enwrapped in the thought of
this wonder.

Then gradually he begins to sense the profound wisdom of
the old saying that the entire universe is a phenomenon and
therefore illusory, but illusory only because we do not understand it aright. It does not mean that the universe does not exist.
That is absurd and a wrong construction. He realizes that we
do not understand it aright, that we must see behind and within.
The visible should portray the invisible, the effect should teach
us the underlying causes. In this phase he begins to sense his
oneness — and this is the finest part of the second phase of the
psychological unveiling of this system of training which the
theosophist undergoes and loves so well — he begins to sense
his true oneness with all that is, for he realizes that, as physical
man, he is but a phenomenon, an effect; that he is in fact the
product of secret and invisible causes; that behind the phenomenon of the physical man is the human spiritual noumenon. He
grows very reverent and a great sense of sympathetic beauty
enters into his heart because he realizes that he is but one of all
beings and entities and creatures which infill the universe. He
begins to sense from this moment that ethics are no mere human
convention; morals are rooted in the very fabric and stuff of
universal nature herself. He feels immensely his oneness with
all that is: "I and my Father are One."

This leads to the third step of psychological opening, and
in this third step he realizes the wonderful paradox of all that
he knew before in the two earlier states. In this third step he
learns that inwards and upwards, expansively upwards, yet ever
inwards, the mountains after all are the real, and the waters are
after all real in a certain wondrous sense, for illusory though

they may be to our relatively imperfectly evolved human understanding, nevertheless it is fundamental reality which has produced them, just as we as phenomena are brought forth.

So then we see at one and the same time that the only reality is the divine, and yet that this divine, because it is the utterly real, makes real in a certain sense even the illusory appearance of cosmic phenomena. Applying this to ourselves, we sense that the only real part of man is the divine within him; and yet precisely because this divine is reality, that very physical phenomenon which we call the physical man is in a certain marvelous sense real also. We have come back, the circle has reentered itself. We come back to the point of starting. First, there were just mountains and waters which were the only real things; and then the mountains and waters were seen to be but the garments, the clothing of secret, invisible, realities; and then the next step brought us to the realization that precisely because these are real things they could not produce essential unrealities; so that the very mountains and waters, strange paradox, are both real and unreal. Happy the man who can understand this third step.

The key to this understanding is another thought which I will again take from Dhyāni-Buddhism, because it is fairly well known in the West mainly through the Zen Buddhist writings of Professor Suzuki of Japan (from whom, by the way, I did not take this extract). This is the Zen thought. Hearken carefully, please, because the significance is so slippery. "In the wind of the mountains and the sun of the lowlands, in the fall of night and the mists of dawn, it is cried aloud: That alone was, is, abides."

The whole universe is That, and all its phenomena are the productions of divine noumena, or divine thought; so that all are essentially unified in a divine oneness. In a rather pragmatical way we can bring down this thought and say that all men are brothers, that every one is his brother's keeper. You see the path of conduct? Any violation of this path means setting yourself in opposition to all universal nature herself.

There is a way to peace and happiness and wisdom and power. For once a man realizes that he is one with nature, and nature is one with him, his consciousness becomes, vibratorily speaking, corhythmic with the pulsings of the cosmic heart. That is why the great sages and seers can work marvels in the world: heal and raise; retain consciousness after death; transport the thinking ego to distant fields and be there in self-conscious thought and see all that passes around them; and many things more. For the universe and we are one. There is but one life and this life is also cosmic thought.

Aham Asmi Parabrahma

Brilliance like the almighty wings of love knows no barriers, and can and does penetrate everywhere; and this thought was born in my mind this afternoon as I hearkened to our speaker giving us excerpts of great beauty, of great depth, from the archaic wisdom-teachings of mankind, teachings which belong to no race, to no age, and which, since they are essential truth, must be taught in spheres not earthly but divine, as they are taught here on earth to us men. For it struck me that the burden of his brilliant address was this: that we human beings, as indeed all other things and entities everywhere, are but parts of one vast cosmic whole, intimately united together, despite our failings and our stumblings, in the working out of our common destiny. And therefore in proportion to our own individual understandings, we respond to that cosmic source which the Christian calls God, and which I prefer to call the divine, from which we came, inseparable from which we are and always shall be, and into which again we are returning on our ages-long pilgrimage. Oh, just that one thought, if we could keep it alive in our hearts and allow it to stimulate our minds from day to day, how it would soften the asperities of human life, how it would teach us to treat our brothers like brothers instead of bitter foes!

Don't you see that this teaching is brilliant because it is a teaching of genius? It contains everything within it, all the Law and all the Prophets. And what is this teaching? Succinctly phrased it is simply this: that the cosmic life is a cosmic drama in which each entity, be it supergod, god or demigod, or man or beast, or monad or atom, plays his or its proportionate part; and that all these dramatic presentations are welded together, leading up to one vast cosmic climax — to which, by the way, there is no anticlimax. So that with every human day we are coming closer to that time in the immensely distant future when we all shall, once more reunited, enter into the deep womb of utter cosmic Being — call it God, divinity, spirit, call it what you wish. The drama then will have ended. The curtain will fall and pralaya will begin, the rest period. But just as in human affairs, when night is over there comes the day, so when the night of pralaya ends, the manvantara, the cosmic day, dawns again. The curtain on the cosmic stage once more rises. Each entity, each being, then begins its cosmic play, its role, exactly at the metaphysical and mathematical point where it stopped when the bells of pralaya rang down that cosmic curtain on the manvantara or world period just ended. Everything begins anew precisely like a clock or watch which, when it has stopped and is rewound, begins to run again at the exact point at which the hands themselves stopped.

Why, this single conception of human identity with the cosmos, together with all the religious and philosophical and scientific and moral implications which it imbodies, is older than thinking man. We are one and yet we know it not, we recognize it not; so that in the drama of life we commit all the follies on the stage, and tragedy becomes comedy and comedy, alas, through our own fault becomes tragedy.

I want to quote to you something that I love and have loved from boyhood. I learned it when I was a child and found it again once more in *The Secret Doctrine* of H.P.B., when in after life as a young man I joined the T.S. It is this: the picture is that of the Hindu guru or teacher. A pupil stands or sits before him, and he is testing the knowledge of this pupil regarding the teaching that this pupil has received, and he says: "Chela, Child, dost thou discern in the lives of those around thee anything different from the life that runs in thy veins?" "There is no difference, O Gurudeva. Their life is the same as my life." "O Child, raise thy head and look at the violet dome of night. Consider those wonderful stars, those beings radiating, irradiating, from the cosmic splendor above our heads. Seest thou that cosmic fire which burns in all things, and shines supremely bright in this and that and that and that yonder brilliant orb? Child, dost thou discern any difference in that cosmic light, in that cosmic life, from that which shines forth from our own daystar, or from that which burns in thine own heart both day and night?" And the child says, "O Gurudeva, I see no difference between life and life, and light and light, and power and power, and mind and mind, except in degrees. The light that burns in my heart is the same as the light that burns in the hearts of all others." "Thou seest well, Child. Now listen to the heart of all this teaching: AHAM ASMI PARABRAHMA." And the child, who has been taught Sanskrit, the Vedic Sanskrit, understands and bows his head, *"prāñjali."* The meaning is: "I am the Boundless, I myself am Parabrahma, for the life that pulses in me and gives me existence is the life of the divinest of the divine." No wonder the child has understood. Am I a child of God? Essentially it is the only thing I am and, if I fail to realize it, it is not the Divine's fault but mine.

You will find this teaching of divinity in every one of the great systems to which the genius of mankind has given birth. Religion *is* it; philosophy was born from it; science is now aspiring towards it, and is beginning to get adumbrations of what it means. Think even in our own small human affairs — small when compared with the vast cosmic majesty which holds us in its sheltering care — think, if every man and woman on earth were thoroughly convinced of the utter reality of this cosmic truth! Never again would the hand of man be raised against man. Always it would be the extended hands of succor and brotherhood. For I am my brother— in our inmost *we are one.* And if we are separate it is because of the smallnesses that make us each one an atom as it were, instead of the spiritual monad which for each one of us is our source. That monad is of the very stuff of divinity. As Jesus the avatāra phrased it in his wonderful saying, "I and my Father are one"— the Father and the divine spark, the spark of divinity which is identic with the cosmic life, with the universal ocean of life, to use another metaphor. This idea of the cosmic ocean of life, of which we are all droplets in our inmost and in our highest, was in the mind of Gautama the Lord Buddha when he spoke of that ultimate end of all beings and things; for, as he said, all beings and things are in their essence Buddha, and some day shall become Buddha themselves, when, as phrased so beautifully by Edwin Arnold, the dewdrop slips into the shining sea. CONSUMMATUM EST.

Glossary

Adept   Relatively perfected human being.

Ādi-buddha   (*Skt*)   Cosmic buddha; highest of four classes of buddhas.

Adwaita-Vedānta   (*Skt*)   Nondualistic school of Vedānta. *See also* Vedānta.

Ākāśa   (*Skt*)   "Brilliant, shining"; ethereal-spiritual substance; fifth cosmic element; aether of the Stoics. *See also* Astral Light.

Akousmatikoi   (*Gk*)   "Hearers, listeners"; probationers in the school of Pythagoras.

Ariadne's Thread   In Greek mythology the thread Ariadne gave Theseus to guide him out of the maze; symbol of the power of truth to lead to wisdom.

Arūpa worlds   (*Skt*)   "Formless"; spiritual-ethereal worlds beyond human perception.

Asat   (*Skt*)   "Not being, not essence"; the unreal, illusory, in contrast to Sat, the Real. Also "beyond Sat" — Parabrahman.

Astral Light   Invisible substance surrounding the earth.

Ātma-buddhi   (*Skt*)   Ātma "self" + buddhi "spiritual understanding"; the highest aspects of man's constitution.

Avatāra   (*Skt*)   A class of saviors such as Jesus and Krishna: a temporary combination of divinity, a highly evolved soul, and a pure physical body.

Avernus *(L)* "Without birds"; the infernal regions; the Underworld.

Avīchi *(Skt)* "Wavelessness"; the most material spheres and states of consciousness where the utterly evil soul gravitates; the opposite of nirvana.

Bardo *(Tib)* "Between"; the period between death and rebirth.

Bhöns *(Tib)* Tibetan monks of pre-Buddhist religion.

Bodhisattva *(Skt)* "One whose essence (sattva) is wisdom (bodhi)"; one stage before buddhahood; also one who renounces nirvana to live to benefit humanity.

Brahmā *(Skt)* Creator, evolver; individualized manifestation of Brahman, the Unmanifest.

Brahma(n) *(Skt)* Universal spirit; first or unmanifest Logos.

Brahma-vidyā *(Skt)* "Divine knowledge."

Brother of the Shadow (Black Magician). Follower of the lefthand path. One who uses knowledge for evil purposes; a sorcerer. *See also* White Magician.

Buddha *(Skt)* "Enlightened"; one who is spiritually awakened.

Buddhi *(Skt)* "Enlightened"; the spiritual self; source of intuition and discernment.

Buddhi-manas *(Skt)* Buddhi "wisdom" + manas "mind"; higher understanding and reason working together; the reincarnating ego. *See also* Nous.

Chela (cheta) *(Skt)* "Servant"; one who serves a guru; a disciple.

Chitkāra *(Skt)* "Thought-worker"; spiritual self; guardian angel.

Christ "Anointed"; early Gnostic term for an initiate.

Christos spirit The inner god; the Father within.

Devachan (*Tib*) Blissful dream state of the soul between earth lives.

Dhyāni-chohans (*Skt-Tib*) "Lords of meditation"; cosmic intelligences of varying grades.

Druids Pre-Christian initiate priests of Celtic Europe.

Dvija (*Skt*) "Twice-born"; an initiate.

Gāyatrī (Sāvitrī) (*Skt*) Rig-Vedic hymn to the divine sun.

Gilgūlīm (*Heb*) "Circlings"; Qabbalistic term for the peregrinations of souls.

Gnostics (*Gk*) Seekers of the ancient gnosis, "knowledge"; philosophers, including some early Christians.

Golden Chain (Living Chain) of Hermes. Succession of spiritual teachers.

Hierarchy of Compassion Brotherhood of mahatmas and adepts, custodians of truth, guardians and protectors of mankind.

Jāgrat (*Skt*) The "waking" state; first of the four states of human consciousness.

Kāma-loka (*Skt*) "Desire-world" surrounding our earth; astral dwelling of kāma-rūpas; the Greek Hades.

Kāma-manas (*Skt*) "Desire-mind"; the personal self.

Kāma-rūpa (*Skt*) "Desire-body"; astral vehicle of man's mental/psychic energies; after death the "shade" or "ghost."

Karma *(Skt)* "Action"; law of action and reaction, cause and effect.

Kismet *(Ar)* "Portion, lot"; Islamic fate or destiny.

Lipikas *(Skt)* "Scribes"; celestial recorders; agents of karma.

Mahā-buddhi *(Skt)* "Great wisdom"; cosmic buddhi, mahat.

Mahā-manvantara *(Skt)* "Great + between manus" or period of manifestation. *See also* Manvantara.

Mahā-māyā *(Skt)* "Great + illusion"; the universal illusion of manifested existence.

Mahā-pralaya *(Skt)* "Great + dissolution"; period of cosmic rest. *See also* paranirvāna.

Mahat *(Skt)* "Great"; universal mind, corresponds to manas in man. *See also* Mahā-buddhi.

Mahātma(s) *(Skt)* "Great soul or self." *See also* Master(s).

Mahāyāna Buddhism *(Skt)* "Great vehicle or path"; Northern school of Buddhism.

Mānasaputra(s) *(Skt)* "Sons of mind"; solar divinities who awakened mind in the human race.

Manvantara *(Skt)* "Between manus"; a period of manifestation and activity of a universe.

Master(s) Relatively perfected human beings; teachers and guardians of the human race.

Messianic cycle A period of 2,160 years during which a particular spiritual and zodiacal influence is manifest.

Moirai *(Gk)* "Lots, portions"; the three Fates, Spinners of Destiny in Greek mythology.

Moksha or Mukti *(Skt)* "Set free"; nirvana.

Monad "One, unit"; indivisible unit of consciousness; spiritual individuality.

Monas Monadum (*L*) "Monad of monads"; the cosmic monad.

Mystery Schools Centers of spiritual instruction, discipline, and initiation instituted in remotest times.

Nāga (*Skt*) "Serpent" of wisdom, initiate; also a serpent-demon.

Nirvāna (*Skt*) "Blown out"; the bliss of absorption in pure cosmic Being, all personal limitations having been "blown out."

Nous (*Gk*) "Mind"; the higher intelligence.

Parabrahma(n) (*Skt*) "Beyond Brahman"; the Infinite; the Boundless.

Paranirvāna (*Skt*) "Beyond + nirvāna"; period of dormancy of a cosmos. *See also* Mahā-pralaya.

Piśāchas (*Skt*) "Flesh-eating demon-elementals"; the lowest aspect of the kāma-rūpa.

Pistis (*Gk*) "Faith"; trust.

Pralaya (*Skt*) "Dissolution"; state of rest between two life-cycles.

Psuche (*Gk*) "Breath"; daughter of Nous; the personal human soul.

Qabbālāh (Kabbala) (*Heb*) "Tradition"; the secret doctrine or theosophy of the Jews.

Root-race One of seven stock-races through which the human life-wave evolves on earth during any one "round"; our present root-race is the fifth. *See also* Round.

Round   A technical term for the passage of monads through seven root-races; applicable also to greater cycles.

Samādhi   *(Skt)*   "Uniting together"; self-conscious union with the Divine.

Sambuddhi-samādhi   *(Skt)*   "Perfect enlightenment + samādhi"; omniscience; union with the All.

Sat   *(Skt)*   "Being, essence"; truth, reality. *See also* Asat.

Sushupti   *(Skt)*   "Deep sleep"; the third state of human consciousness.

Svabhāva   *(Skt)*   "Self-becoming"; true individuality.

Svapna   *(Skt)*   "Sleeping-dreaming"; the second state of human consciousness.

Tat   *(Skt)*   "That"; the Boundless. *See also* Parabrahman.

Turīya   *(Skt)*   "Fourth"; the highest state of human consciousness. *See also* Samādhi.

Vedānta   *(Skt)*   One of the six Indian schools of philosophy.

Vedas   *(Skt)*   "Knowledge"; ancient Hindu religious texts compiled by Veda-Vyāsa, the oldest being the Rig-Veda.

White Magician   Advanced human being, follower of the righthand path, who works impersonally for the benefit of all.

Yoga   *(Skt)*   "Union"; a method of training; discipline.

Yuga   *(Skt)*   "Age"; a period of time. In every root-race there are four yugas; our present age, the fourth, is Kali yuga, the "black" or Iron age which began 3102 B.C. with the death of Krishna.

Chronology

Contents listed by year as far as possible

Index

Cross (cont.)
 cry on the 290-92
Cycle(s) 226-8, 269-71, 276
 of manifestation 219-22

Darwinism, negative effects of 125-6
Death 77-80, 95-101, 175-7, 245
 an evolutionary habit 69-74
 bardo and 166-7
 birth and 229, 246-7
 grandest adventure 139-40
 stages after 31-6, 263-6
 unmerited suffering 205-6
Demon, in man 188, 234-9. *See also*
 Adversary
Destiny 8, 95-101, 287-9. *See also* Chain
 of Causation, Karma
 free will and 30, 87, 204, 207
 karma inescapable 172, 207, 254-5
 our future 19
 seeds of 274-5
Devachan 31-6, 98, 166, 206, 265. *See
 also* Death
Dhammapada 127
Dhyāni-Buddhism and Zen 301, 303
Dhyān(i)-chohan(s) 194, 205, 245
 guardian angel and 84
 lipikas 117-18
 lords of meditation 249
 masters taught by 181
Disaster(s) 160-61, 179, 184
Discipline 109-12, 189
Disease 240-43. *See also* Health
 causes of 27, 30, 69-70, 197
 none in 7th round 72
 protection against 171, 265-6
 seeds of 74, 283
Divine(ity) 101, 209, 283, 290-92,
 305-6
 aspiring toward 54-7
 don't refuse a 92
 harmony 185
 "I and my Father . . ." 112-13, 302,

308
 our, origin 226-30, 288-9
 pathway to 122-3
Divine Ideation 202-4
 avatāras and 207
Dogma(tism) 194, 211, 233, 290, 292
Doubt(s) 105, 137, 224
Dove 225, 281
Druids 84
Duration 259-62
Duty(ies), Dharma 150, 223-5, 242,
 281
 smaller and greater 19-20, 169,
 182-3, 248
 to fellowmen 25-6, 110, 235-8
 to teachers 215
Dvāpara yuga (Third Age) 270-71
Dvija 130

Earth 254-5, 273-6, 288
 continents 295-8
 our schoolroom 160
 spiritual presence in 183
Easter 256-8
Egoism 3, 104, 113, 168, 179, 184, 299
Egyptians, weighing of heart 95-101,
 114, 188
Emotion(s) 115
Ensouled being(s) 90-91, 100-101, 102-
 105, 107-8
Esoteric tradition 49-51
Eternal Now 203, 259-62
Ethics(al) 8, 28, 30, 34, 126-8, 147, 187,
 211, 246, 302
 basis of H. P. Blavatsky's teachings
 139
 instinct 63, 92, 244, 273, 276
 shift consciousness to 18-26
Evil 10, 170-73, 194-5, 245, 266, 274
 choice of 186-9, 222
 corrupts 197-8
 energy generated by 160-61
 karmic results 31-5, 127, 288

Silent Watcher 17, 207
Sin(s) 96, 235, 238-9, 242
  inaction in deed of mercy 206-7,
    223-4
  Jesus's atonement 39
Sleep 3, 175-7
  closer in, to god within 220
  death and 32-35, 72
Socrates 84
Solar system 160
Sorrow(s) 77-80, 214, 265
  altruism and 37
  from human blindness 4
  pain and 11
  we create 8
  wisest friend 78
Soul 91-2
  awakening 41, 128
  choices 187
  experience of, after death 95-101
  loss of 102, 126, 186-9
Soulless being(s), ensouled v. 67-8, 101,
  102-5
Spanish proverb 248
Spinners of Destiny 254-5
Spirit 57, 65, 84-6, 148, 248, 267-8,
  283
  highest yoga 111-13
  invincible 276
Spiritualists 263-5
Stoic philosophers 110, 113, 219
Strength 87, 123, 171, 277-8, 282-3
Suffering 93-4, 149, 223, 241
  awakens sympathy 40, 77-9
  cause of 5, 31, 33
  causing 39
  unmerited 205
  vicarious atonement 290-92
  working of the gods 214
Sufis 268
Suicide 186-7
Sun 254-5
  hymns to 111-12, 131-3
  our link with 228-30, 293

spiritual, within 122, 210-11
Sushupti 175-7
Suzuki, D. T. 303
Svabhāva 203, 231
Svapna 175-7
Sympathy 16, 40, 78-9, 90-91, 166,
  206-7, 238

Tao Teh Ching 231-2
  Tao 232-3
Tat 192, 219
Teacher(s) 13-17, 49-51, 106, 137-8,
  209, 213, 280-81, 293
Temptation 104
  how to conquer 151-2
  in Lord's prayer 199-201
That, Tat 219, 303
  infinity 192, 222
Theosophical movement 50-51, 63,
  124, 248
  god-wisdom 162
  mysteries 181
Theosophical Society 47-8, 162, 182,
  290, 299
  founded by masters 13
  no dogmas 211
  part of its work 47-8, 67, 162, 240,
  249
Theosophist(s) 20, 25-6, 47, 52, 240
  Christian theology and 126, 192-3
  ideal of 237
  nature 138
  obligation of 182-3
  prayer and 178-80
Theosophy 78-80, 120-23, 161, 290,
  299
  awakener 3-6
  heart-life plus intellect 169
  religion, science, philosophy 163, 287
  technical, v. duty 214-16
  works magic 168
Thought(s) 44-8, 96, 120-22, 164, 192,
  263